Footprints on the mountains...
the news from the Pyrenees

Steve Cracknell

for my parents,
who twice taught me how to walk

First published in 2016
All rights reserved
First edition © 2016 Steve Cracknell

Designed and produced by the author

ISBN-13: 978-1530523450
ISBN-10: 1530523451

Websites: laSenda.net and PyreneanWay.com
Facebook: Steve Cracknell in the Pyrenees
Twitter: @enmarchant

Cover: artwork by Marie Broll; photos: griffon vulture, on the Senda near Respomuso, *sarrio*, Pineta valley

Contents

Map	vi
Note	viii
Prologue	x
Sol y sombra	1
Paths crossing	32
Water, snow, ice	57
A walk in the Park	79
The heart of the matter	118
Under the yoke	133
Return to the heights	152
A whole country for shopping	172
The remembered past	191
Into the fire	226
Acknowledgements	247
Annotated bibliography	248

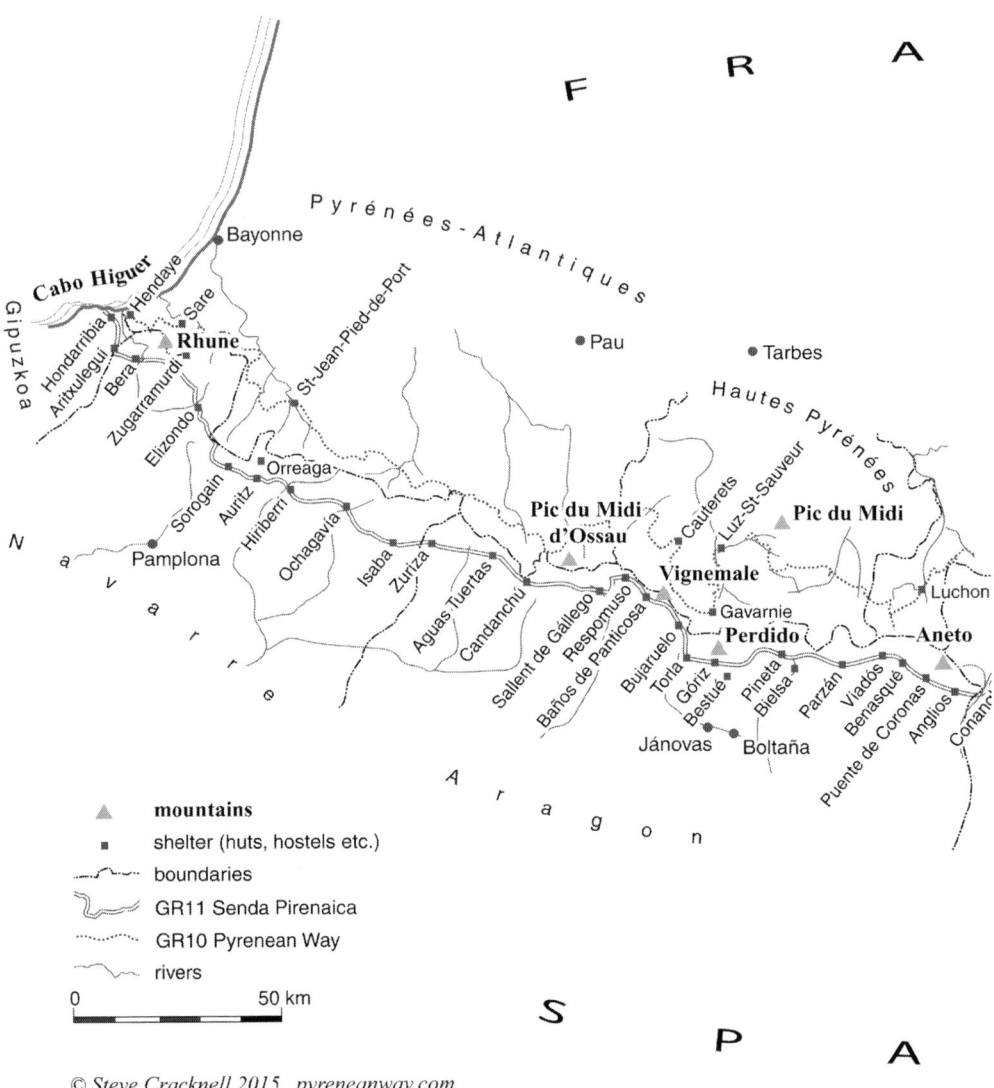

Note

In the Pyrenees, places may be known by several different names. Forced to choose, I have used the English version in the few instances where there is one. Otherwise I have followed the spellings on my Spanish map, sometimes adding a second variant when this is commonly used locally.

I am losing precious days. I am degenerating into a machine for making money. I am learning nothing in this trivial world of men. I must break away and get out into the mountains to learn the news.

John Muir, 1883

Prologue

I am hanging out almost horizontally, looking up at the clouds skimming across the sky. For the moment the cable seems to be holding and my harness is securely hooked into it but the wind is increasingly blustery. I have to bend my knees and transfer my weight from one foot to the other to stay balanced. I am exploding with anxiety but held together by the exhilaration of the moment. I know what is going to happen but dismiss it. Maybe it won't come to that. And then I slip and go crashing down.

Afterwards, when I describe what happened to Veronica she says: "The bit you enjoyed most was falling off, wasn't it?"

That was much later. For the moment I am still planning my trip.

In the weeks before I set out, I said to myself that I would take the Senda Pirenaica in my stride. I had already hiked the length of the Pyrenees once on the French side. This time I'm heading for Spain. The same direction but roughly 20km further south.

Are the two sides of the Pyrenees simple reflections of each other, I wondered? What about the fauna? The last time I walked from the Atlantic to the Mediterranean, rewilding was highly controversial. And now? As for the human population, there are changes in the wind.

But as far as the practicalities are concerned I am confident. So I don't study the route in detail until two days before setting off, only to discover that the first two stages are way beyond my capabilities. I need to plan to sleep in huts.

Then I check my train ticket and hotel booking. The train ticket is fine, but I have booked the hotel for the following week.

Veronica says: "But you usually prepare your walks for months in advance."

"I want to be surprised. I don't want a walk full of *déjà vu*."

Prologue

"And why *are* you going at the end of July? You always say it's the worst time to walk. Too hot and too crowded."

Idling away the last evening at home I make a calculation. One and a half million. A few months ago on a walk, tired and dragging my feet, I started to count my steps to reassure myself that I was making progress. One hundred, two hundred. Well before reaching three hundred I lost track. One and a half million. I know I've done it before, but that was years ago.

The next day I take the train to Hendaye on the French Atlantic coast. At Toulouse a teenage girl gets on. Bent over, dressed in black, she walks with two sticks, like a 90-year-old Spanish widow. The aisle is full of baggage and she has hardly staggered five steps before she trips over. Someone helps her to a seat. The woman sitting opposite me – a great-grandmother, she has already told me proudly – comments: "You can't criticise her for wanting to be fashionable but she needs flatter soles." The girl is wearing platform heels.

In the process of getting off at Lourdes she falls over again. We help her up. Clearly, she can't straighten her legs at all. "My mother is waiting for me on the platform," she reassures us. Luckily, she reaches the motorised wheelchair without further problems.

As the train sets off again the great-grandmother tells me about *her* legs.

"Until recently I couldn't walk four metres without falling either, my cartilages were *that* bad," she says lifting up her dress to show me her knees. "But I've been having a special treatment."

"Injections? In your knees?" I ask.

"No, suppositories. I had to go to Switzerland for them. You can't get them on the health service here and they cost 200 euros a month. But now I can walk three kilometres a day. In fact I have to."

"How long have you been taking them?"

"A year and a half. After two years I must go back again for a check-up, but they really are effective. I haven't fallen over for six months."

As for me, I haven't been falling over, but I have had a bad attack of vertigo.

It was like being inside a spin dryer but it wasn't me spinning. It was the world outside. So *that's* it. I used to think I knew something about vertigo. You stand on the edge of a precipice. Of course you're afraid! Of course you feel dizzy! But I was wrong. Fear of falling isn't vertigo.

Footprints on the mountains

This is the real thing. Horribly different. I don't just feel queasy; I feel sick. I need to get to the bathroom but I can't move at all. Then the alarm goes off. I turn my head to look at the time and the world starts whirring all over again. I don't even contemplate getting out of bed.

My doctor gives me some tablets, and tells me to use my eyes to correct my sense of balance. "You'll have to learn to walk again," he explains. A neighbour tells me that her husband had the same problem intermittently for over twenty years. It only stopped when he fell off the roof.

So what's walking the Senda going to be like? On the trickier paths I used to be able to persuade myself that my feet were glued to the ground by immense gravitational forces. I'm not sure the strategy will work anymore.

Mustn't exaggerate. I haven't had any more attacks. I don't need to go to Lourdes for a miracle, nor to Switzerland for a wonder drug.

Sol y sombra

Hondarribia

When I arrive in Hendaye, it is still only early afternoon, so I catch a ferryboat across the estuary to Hondarribia in Spain and head out to the Cabo Higuer.

The path turns uphill; a young couple sitting in their garden watches me climbing laboriously. When I reach their level they say *¡Hola!*

I point to their fig tree: "It must be ancient. How old is it?"

"I don't know," says the woman, "We've only been here since last autumn."

"Are there any others here?" I've been looking out for *higuers* but this is the first I have seen.

"One or two," she replies.

It seems unlikely that there were ever many here; they belong to the shores of the Mediterranean.

She invites me to join them and sends her husband to fetch another tumbler. He pours me some cider, quickly raising the bottle high above the table so the liquid cascades in a long bubbly golden stream. They tell me about their time in America.

Once the glass is empty, I lift the latch on the gate and continue. Walking is a different world; intersecting with other people's stories.

The next story is rather ambiguous: at the top of the hill an orchard contains a sapling for each of the 179 babies born in 2003. Egoitz born on 1 January, the latest addition to the Silanes family tree, finds himself in a row named Ogallurretako erreko after a local stream. But that's as far as the poetry goes. Egoitz's contemporaries are arranged in brutish rows, 21st-century industrial style, in strict order of birth rank just as they fell off the assembly line. No room for jealousy, individualism, or sin in this world of little boxes.

Footprints on the mountains

My approach has taken me to the Cabo Higuer without treading on the Senda, officially known as the Spanish *gran recorrido* 11. I want to begin properly, at the lighthouse which marks the start. As I arrive, the siren sounds: a test, given the colour of the sky. A sturdy young man is coming along the path.

"¡Hola! ¿De donde vienes?" I ask.

"I don't understand," he replies, in English. He seems a bit dazed.

"Where have you come from?"

"The Mediterranean. Two months ago."

I shake his hand and invite him to a celebratory drink in the bar on the nearby campsite.

"Thanks but I have to get on."

"But this is the end, you've arrived... Where are you going?"

"I'm not sure. To San Sebastian at least, maybe further. Then I'm going walking in the Andes," he says with conviction. "Bye."

The Senda dips its feet in the Atlantic before setting off eastwards so I clamber down from the campsite towards the water's edge. At the very end of the peninsula, sitting on a ledge of black rock, a young woman is sunbathing topless, gazing out to sea, wet skin glistening. As I approach, a sound, a warning, comes from somewhere way out on the waves. She slithers into the water and with a flip of her tail is gone. I slip-slide across the moss, crabs scuttling sideways. It smells of seaweed. In the time it takes me to reach the rock she has joined the voice. They dive under the water and disappear. I fill a shampoo sample bottle with Atlantic, as the tradition dictates, and stow it away in my rucksack.

The Senda runs along the north coast of the promontory through suitably antediluvian rock formations, ferns, and greenery back to the town. Officially there is only one Hondarribia, but really there are two.

Hondarribia-on-the-hill is full of ancient buildings – stone on the ground floor, half-timbered jetties above – and contemporary quarrels. The numerous flags hanging out of the windows demand: "*Euskal preso ta iheslariak etxera* – Bring the Basque prisoners back home".

In one square excited youngsters are twirling exuberantly on the cobbled streets in preparation for a folk dancing competition. But their enjoyment doesn't last. Once they are on the stage in front of the judges, their smiles become fixed. The audience concentrates. Hondarribia-on-the-hill takes its

Sol y sombra

Hondarribia-on-the-hill

culture seriously. And its past. On the town gates, the coat of arms shows the castle; a ship sails across the ocean in search of whales; mermaids with mirrors take selfies; a dozen *banderas* (flags) celebrate victories. Throw in Saint Peter (the humble fisherman) with the key to Paradise and the date 1694 and there you have it, as the tour guide explains, a potted history of the town.

A little later, a child fills in the gaps. I have just returned to the central square when I hear her exclaim "*¡Mira, Carlos Quinto!* – look Charles V!" The object of her attention is a Scotsman in full regalia, including tartan kilt, heading for a wedding in the nearby church. With all this history around, a Scotsman could be king again, at least in the imagination of a five-year old.

I head downhill to my rebooked hotel in Hondarribia-on-sea. There, the decks are awash with strollers, as the *paseo* gets into swing. A human statue, painted gold, is pouring a never-ending stream of water from a bottle into a never-overflowing cup. The kids are fascinated, paying more attention to

Footprints on the mountains

Hondarribia-on-sea

the water than the man. The adults are more interested in the flow of cider, beer, and wine, to be consumed along with *pintxos* in the endless row of cafe-bars lashed onto what were once fishermen's cottages. The drinkers swashbuckle from one bar to another, finally washing up in the restaurants. The smell of whitebait frying is everywhere. Unlike Hondarribia-on-the-hill, Hondarribia-on-sea lives very much in the present.

A squawking seagull sitting on a television aerial draws attention to itself: the aerials are as tall again as the houses, more like masts, as if an imaginative planning authority had insisted on retaining a symbolic link with the fishermen's past.

Somewhere down the road a brass band launches into a jubilant tune and the crowd parts like the Red Sea. The Hondarribia rowers have just added the Pasaia *bandera* to their growing collection.

The obvious place to eat is just next door to the rowers' headquarters: La Hermandad de Pescadores (fishermen's guild). Walking through the door into the steam I notice two distinct groups of clients: old men wearing black berets standing drinking at the bar, and Japanese tourists eating at the tables.

Sol y sombra

Neither of these groups was conspicuous in the streets outside, so what is it about the Hermandad de Pescadores which attracts them? I ask one of the Japanese tourists, guessing that he will speak English: fish soup is his answer. He saw it in an in-flight magazine. I don't speak Basque so can't ask the old men, but I suspect the answer would be the same, albeit with a nuance: 750 years of fish soup. The guild was founded in 1361.

I later read a curious sentence on the Hermandad's website: *"En este restaurante es normal que coincidan comensales de diferentes partes del mundo* – Naturally you will meet diners from different parts of the world in this restaurant". Here, in the last vestige of the old Hondarribia-on-sea, the staff are regretfully rearranging the deckchairs.

After the arrival of my bottle of cider and a demonstration of how to pour it without spilling onto the tablecloth, the first course is brought out: seafood parcels with soy sauce.

Hondarribia to Collado de Aritxulegui

Next morning, Monday, I take a winding country road to Irun, passing in front of an edible house – its façade decorated with sweetcorn. Irun has not yet surfaced from the weekend and the suburban shopping centres are as compelling as retail therapy with a hangover. Even the town centre is deserted, but more oddly it is empty of buildings as well. Much of the town was burned to the ground in the Civil War; the buildings have never been replaced. After those few days in the limelight, today's Irun seems remarkably workaday; rather like that generation of Europeans who lived through the Second World War and who had seen and done so many horrible things by the age of 25 that all they craved was a simple life. The height of ambition was a dishwasher. Irun just wants to be left in peace.

Once I'm out of town the Senda magically reappears, in the form of a route map: a large panel with an aerial photograph. On it, the path looks like the work of some domestic goddess sewing together the mountains and the foothills with red and white cotton.

I follow the thread up a steep hill paved with wide steps to emerge from the woods at the San Marcial Hermitage. The chapel there affords a fine view over Irun and, in the opposite direction, the less enticing prospect of a field bestrewn with the remains of the weekend's picnics. A woman is cleaning the toilets.

"Is it always like this?" I ask her.

"After the San Marciales it's worse," she replies cheerfully. "But it keeps me in a job."

I ask about the San Marciales and she tells me about a different Irun, one which has never forgotten its military past. On 30 June each year, literally ten thousand men march up to the top of the hill and then back down again, following the path I have just taken. I fill in the picture when I get home. Wearing white (shoes, trousers, shirts), red (ties, neckerchiefs, berets), and black (jackets) they are not dressed for war.

But still a war *is* going on. For the last few years there have been two rival *alardes*. In the traditional *alarde* all the soldiers are men. The new mixed *alarde* also includes women. Such is the animosity that riot police have been called out.

The far end of the picnic area is bounded by a second plantation of family trees, like the one near the Cabo Higuer, in this case oaks, in curved rows. It is a sapling *alarde*: a Birnam Wood for children with Basque roots.

I'm walking quickly on the flat when a huge naïve statue of a Basque peasant pops his head over a hedge and toasts my health with a glass of wine. Nearby, shaggy stacks of bracken are pinned to the ground by massive stakes, like giant *pintxos*. In the sweet chestnut woods on the way up the next hill a walker tells me that the hut where I'm hoping to sleep has a roof and drinking water but nothing else.

The next walker is a different story. He is standing at a crossroads.

The first thing he says is: "Do you speak English? Do you know where the path goes?"

"That depends a good deal on where you want to get to," I reply.

"Bera, on the GR11."

"It's that way," I say pointing up the hill. "Have you got a map? I'll show you where we are."

"I got a map from the tourist office yesterday, but it's not much help."

He refuses to take it out of his rucksack, so I show him mine and explain the waymarks.

"There's one just before each junction showing the direction you should take and there's one about ten metres beyond it to confirm. If you go in the wrong direction you'll see a cross."

Stuart is half Australian but lives in Denmark where his mother was born. The last traces of acne are disappearing from his chin at the same time as the first traces of hairs begin to show.

His green tee-shirt and black shorts cover an emaciated body. But what fascinates me is his shoes.

"Every morning you dip your feet into a pot of thick blue and white paint and then leave them to dry," I suggest.

"Come on!" he says. "They're Vibram five fingers."

They are not shoes, but foot gloves. They match his feet exactly, with each toe detailed individually. He lets me examine the soles.

"Four millimetres," he says.

I look at mine: 35mm more or less.

"I don't feel the stones too much," he tells me.

Although he is following the Senda at present, he is thinking of hopping over to the Way of Saint James instead. He asks my opinion.

"The paint would wear through before the end of the day," I say. "Too much tarmac."

"Yes, that's what I've read. But I don't have much experience of mountains. You know what the highest hill in Denmark is called? Himmelbjerget. It means 'sky mountain'. It's 147 metres above sea level."

The next thing he tells me is that he is hoping to find himself. It isn't just a matter of knowing where the path is going. It is also a question of what he wants to do with his life. He thought he wanted to be a chef but a six-month course persuaded him otherwise. He doesn't want to be tied down. I tell him about my chequered career – engineering, archaeology, web design. He hints at some kind of traumatic event, but doesn't elaborate. I think about my life at his age, about despair, dark days, but don't say anything either.

He doesn't have a sleeping bag or a tent, and his rucksack is really only a day sack. It isn't even full. He can't afford to stay in hostels. He's doing everything wrong, almost aiming to fail, but what can I say? He has a kind of insouciant courage. We walk along together through the woods, chatting and then I decide to have a rest and he decides to continue. I will never see him again.

The track follows the valley past piles of freshly cut logs, to a second Senda noticeboard. Big red stencilled lettering runs diagonally across it: '*Sendero descataloguado* – path declassified'. As if this weren't enough discouragement, the sign has been slashed violently with a knife and the letters 'ETA' sprayed on top. It seems that I have been heading in the wrong direction… but have nevertheless arrived at the Endara dam.

I turn my back on the Senda again, this time deliberately, walking west instead of east, towards the hut I have read about. Half way up the slope towards the pass the empty restaurant looks rather sinister but the day has been hot so I sit down at a table on the terrace. And wait, and wait, and then go inside and call out "*¿Hay alguien?* – Is anybody there?" A woman materializes from the darkness behind the bar and plonks a beer in front of me.

A mare, her foal, and other horses try to block my way as I climb further up. From the pass I can see the Aritxulegui Borda hut set in a natural amphitheatre. Made of breezeblocks and partly dug into the ground, it may once have been a military installation; but the outside has been repainted in a friendly green and dotted with random pieces of stone making it look rather like an infants' climbing wall. I can relax, sleep with a roof over my head.

The metal door scrapes against its frame. Inside, the walls are a Spartan white. Concrete floor, concrete benches, concrete tables, concrete hearth. No other furnishings. A brush and a notice inciting its use. Graffiti is noticeably absent, except for a recently painted '*¡Gora Euskadi ta Askatasuna!* – Viva ETA!'

Outside the hut, there were once five tables but they have been decapitated so that only the uprights remain. The picnickers and the *paella* have long gone. The hut and the mutilated tables are discouraging, but it is sunny and all is well.

I wash my socks and a tee-shirt in the spring and cut bracken for my bed. A couple of men come walking up the hill – they must be shepherds given the crooks they are carrying – and pass in front of me. I say "*buenos días*". No reply. I say it again, but they conspicuously ignore me. I don't know enough Basque to dare "*kaixo*". Perhaps I should have said "good afternoon", as Francis Chevillon once advised me at the other end of the Pyrenees.

"I was in the *estive* [summer pasture in the mountains] when I saw a couple of shepherds on the other side of the frontier in Catalonia," he told me. "It was in the 1970s I suppose. You don't get much chance to talk up there so I went and said a few words to them in my schoolboy

Spanish. They turned their backs on me and whenever they saw me later they deliberately walked away. It took me some time to realise what I had done wrong. I don't know any Catalan but if I had begun in French or even English, even though they wouldn't have understood a word, there wouldn't have been a problem. It was just that for them Spanish was the language of the Fascist oppressors."

Perhaps the same applies in the Basque country even now. Then again perhaps the shepherds simply didn't want to talk.

Continuing to cut bracken, I almost catch my hand on a barbed wire fence. Looking more carefully I see that it is protecting a minuscule garden containing *pieris japonica*, hydrangeas, a beech sapling, and a carved stone: a young man's face picked out in low-relief silhouette along with a poem:

> *Senid etan senide*
> *lagunetan lagun*
> *adiorik ez quen*
> *betiko maitasun*
> *Aitor Txiki*

With my pocket dictionary I manage to decipher some of the words: brother, comrade, adieu, love. And then I work out who the man is: Txiki, a member of ETA, killed by firing squad in 1975, in the last days of Franco, after a show trial which caused shockwaves well beyond the boundaries of Spain. But what is Txiki doing here?

Some cyclists hurtle by on their mountain bikes. They don't say hello either, but then again, perhaps they never saw me, their attention concentrated on staying in the saddle.

I eat outside, watching the horizon. In the low light of dusk, the sea rises from the land, red, framed by the rolling hills. It is peaceful here. The only extraneous noise is an occasional neighing.

Thinking about the horses, before I slip into my sleeping bag, I take the precaution of tying up the door with my washing line. It takes me a long while to fall asleep but sometime in the middle of the night I am deep in a dream.

And then I am awake. Instantly. It is completely black. I can hear a wild, powerful howling very close to me in the hut, and at the same time the scraping of metal on concrete. Something, someone is trying to force the door open. The noises last for perhaps two seconds. It is only when the guttural wail stops that I realise that it was coming from my throat.

My heart is bursting through my eardrums. My dream has burst into consciousness.

"*¿Hay alguien?*" It is a man's voice.

Without thinking I reply: "*Sí. Espere. Voy a abrir* – Yes, hang on. I'll open up."

I scramble for my head torch and switch it on. I don't know what to expect, but I can hardly pretend I'm not here. What does he want? I look at my watch. Two-thirty. Who would arrive at this time of night? Could he be a lost walker?

I pull on a few clothes feeling strangely calm, realising that it is my own howling, the howling which frightened me so much, which has succeeded in reassuring me. I think of digging my knife out of my rucksack but reject the idea.

Opening the door, I stumble on bare feet towards the 4x4 parked outside. The driver switches on the lights and blinds me, but then switches them off again. Inside I can just make out three, perhaps four people. Two men, one woman and a shadow. Thirtysomethings.

"*¿Hemos despertado?* – Did we wake you up?" I blink and start to open my lips but quickly clasp them shut. 'Is there anybody there?' 'Did we wake you up?' In other circumstances I would laugh out loud. I reject some kind of sarcastic reply.

"*Podéis entrar si queréis* – You can come in if you want."

"*No. Vamos a un otro sitio. Somos del pueblo* – No. We'll go somewhere else. We're from the village."

They drive off. They weren't aggressive and didn't appear to be drunk or drugged, but they didn't apologise for waking me up either. So why did they come here on a Monday night? It's too late to *start* partying, surely. But that isn't the question going round in my head. What I don't understand is the howl. I've never heard a sound like it before and have certainly never made it. But I recognise it. There was something primitive about it, powerfully animal. And then the answer comes to me. I haven't heard it before, but my mother has, and she has described it to me in detail. Some years ago she woke my father up to tell him that their daughter – my sister – had died suddenly. She told me that on hearing the news he howled, a sound she had never heard before, a sound he had never made before.

I go back to sleep, more-or-less, only waking with the first glimmer of dawn. For some days subsequently I try to work out why anybody might drive to such an isolated spot in the middle of the night, without coming to any conclusion. And why did the man say "*¿Hay alguien?*" in Spanish and not its Basque equivalent, if they really were locals?

When finally I arrive home I enquire further. Aritxulegui Borda, with its natural amphitheatre, was the site of a festival in 2006. The tone was set by an immense Basque flag tied to the nearby electricity pylon. The artistic programme mainly consisted of traditional Basque culture. An *aizkolari* chops his way through a log. Two *txalapartariak* musicians drum out galloping rhythms with wooden sticks on a table. Macho men – *joaldunak* – parade up and down, bells attached, bouncing and clanking with every step. (I've seen them in Ituren – I'll be there in a few days.)

But the event which most marked the audience was the spontaneous appearance of three masked gunmen firing into the air and reading a declaration from ETA. Afterwards they hid the guns in a nearby cache.

It was the *Gudari Eguna* – Day of the soldiers, dedicated to ETA terrorists. Specifically, it commemorates the deaths of Txiki and his comrades in arms. Incidentally, Txiki was a keen hill walker.

I still don't know why I was woken up in the middle of the night, nor who the visitors really were, but I don't think it was quite by chance.

Collado de Aritxulegui to Zugarramurdi

I walk past the sinister restaurant again, down to the dam to re-join the Senda and follow it through woods, bracken, and pastures to the hamlet of Tellegui where a notice advertises accommodation for walkers. If only.

Further along, visible through gaps in the woods is La Rhune, comparable in height with Skiddaw in the English Lake District. Here it is considered a suitable site for television masts. Down below, the sheds of Bera de Bidasoa are crushed into the valley; matchboxes opening and shutting with metallic scraping and crashing sounds.

The official entrance to the town is indicated by a roadside panel. Like almost every town in the area Bera has a double-barrelled name, the two halves sometimes differing by a single letter. Or less. Bera-Vera. Irun-Irún. The Spanish father's name is still there but, anticipating the impending divorce, this post-Franco generation has revived the earth-mother's Basque version. It is only retaining the patronym out of politeness.

On the outskirts of the town I am studying a map when a van labelled *arrainketari* happens to pull up in front of me. A man leaps out and goes around to the back, emerging holding a big fish with a piece of greaseproof paper wrapped around its midriff. He says something in Basque. I must look hesitant because he then tries again: "*El GR11 está por aquí* – the GR11 is this way," pointing the fish down the road. I look at the fish, he looks at the fish, and we both laugh out loud.

In the town centre, I head for a café and ask if they have anything to eat. The only thing on offer at this time of day is a dish from the other end of the Pyrenees: *patatas bravas*. The potatoes come with a splodge of mayonnaise smothered over them and a portcullis of tomato ketchup drawn across the top. It looks like kitsch 1950s food photography, but tastes divine.

A steep climb out of town through bracken takes me to a small hummock and a military bunker. On top is a much more enigmatic structure: three metallic triangles pointing to the sky. Stuck to one of them are three kaleidoscopes backlit by the sun, each filled with broken glass: green, crystal clear, and red – the colours of the Basque flag. A work of art for those in the know.

I have hardly walked twenty paces away from the bunker when I hear a bang and feel a sharp pain in my back. I fall one way and my rucksack falls the other. Lying injured on the ground, taking stock, the first thing that I notice is that my rucksack has exploded. It is still attached to my waist but the shoulder straps are broken. Once I have undone the belt and disengaged the carbon fibre strut from my back I can see what has happened. One of the connectors on the frame has broken. My rucksack is the lightest in the world, but perhaps Joe has sacrificed a little too much in the way of robustness.

Further along, in a pine forest, the air smells fresh from the resin seeping from injured trees, then dusty from sawdust, then, in a prairie, of newly mown hay. By the time I arrive at the Venta Lizaieta the restaurant is closed, but this is nothing new. It has long been replaced by rusty cans of vegetables, porcelain souvenirs, sad chairs, and listless tables. I ask the woman behind the bar squeezed into one corner if, despite appearances, she has anything to eat and she points to a sandwich in a plastic display case. It looks several days old but I nod. She turns round and pulls a fresh baguette out of a sack and cuts some ham for me.

Four retired Frenchmen arrive, in celebratory mood with only two days left before reaching their goal. They have all walked from the Mediterranean, though they didn't set out together. They give me recommendations and tell me that the route has been changed radically in Navarre. But, anyway I'm going to leave the Senda for a couple of days to look into a mystery which has been nagging me, so I call a taxi.

The taxi driver is a fount of local knowledge, wants to talk, and can't get away from me. I ask him about the triangles on the bunker. They are a memorial, he explains. The kaleidoscopes are men, shining lights of a local mountaineering club. One day in January 2007 they were clinging to a triangle called the Taillon, near Gavarnie. The broken glass is ice. One of the kaleidoscopes slipped down the side of the triangle and the others followed, roped to the same destiny.

I am going to Zugarramurdi, one of the few places in the Pyrenees where events have had an impact beyond the edge of the mountains. (Another is Hendaye: Franco met Hitler in the railway station in 1940 and decided to stay on his branch-line.) Zugarramurdi represents genocide throughout Europe, reaching its apogee right here in 1610.

I have been here before but came away dissatisfied. On that occasion I went to a lecture where the speaker, Beñat Zintzo Garmendia, said that the *akelarres* never took place, they were a figment of the imagination. But in the cave at midnight I watched as a local amateur theatrical group reconstructed an *akelarre* – whimsical folk dancing by women in long dresses and tall hats – followed by a rather more raunchy version by professionals wearing little more than body-paint.

The word *akelarre* (witches' Sabbath) was probably invented for Zugarramurdi. In Spain, the village is synonymous with witches, like Salem in the United States, so if I'm going to understand what really happened, it will be here. I also have a more pressing problem: nappy rash. The friction means that every step is painful. Unfortunately there isn't even an apothecary in Zugarramurdi so tomorrow I will have to go to the nearest pharmacy.

Footprints on the mountains

Once I have established myself in Graxiana Sorginen Aterpea (the witch Graxiana's shelter) I go for a shuffle around the village. The houses, in traditional Basque style, are immense and designed to last. Outside one of them, two women are shelling peas. They are hiding from the heat under a plane tree, but they are not hiding from tourists: the house is on the street leading to the Museo de las brujas (Witch museum) and they have positioned themselves right next to it. I recognise my part in the script and ask if they would mind me taking a photo of the house. Of course not.

The house is typical of the village: pink stone, white rendering, green shutters, and pots overflowing with geraniums. But the detail which stands out is the broomstick above the door and the wrought iron lettering announcing its name: Barrenetxea.

One of the women tells me: "*Graxiana, la reina del Akelarre vivió aquí ¿sabes?* – Graxiana, the queen of the Sabbath lived here, you know."

I pretend not to, and ask: "What happened to her?"

"She died in prison."

"Do you think they were really witches?" I ask.

"Yes and no ..." says the older woman, adding confusingly, "... but they were innocent."

"They're going to make a film," says the other. "Carmen Maura is playing Graxiana!"

In the blinding sunlight this all seems quite absurd. As indeed does the film when it comes out a year later: a trashy comedy with more clichés than you can wave a wand at, it is anything but spellbinding. Nevertheless, it wins a galaxy of awards for its stars.

But the museum just down the road is no laughs at all. By the time I have gone round it and emerged into the daylight again, I am feeling sick. The human psyche is opened up; its bowels are dragged out and ripped apart and the shit exhibited. The list of persecutions includes not only Zugarramurdi's witches but also early Christians, Cathars, Muslims, Jews, Protestants, Communists, homosexuals, and gypsies. The whole terrifying – and ludicrous – history of witch hunting is dissected.

The museum is whispering to me: babies cry. Then men shout, church bells toll, the sentences are read out, burning wood hisses and crackles. I can smell the smoke.

In 1609 the Inquisition arrives in Zugarramurdi after a young woman claims to have been part of a coven, denouncing neighbours. Some confess in the hope of light sentences; they are encouraged to implicate others. Most of the accused are women but there are a few men. The descriptions given by those who participated together at the Sabbaths are inconsistent but that is put down to a clever strategy on the part of the Devil. One woman claims that she rubbed herself with unguent in order to fly and that she could shrink and pass through a minuscule hole in the wall. Cider, long part of local tradition – *made from that fateful fruit* – was a clear sign of endemic corruption. The pointed hats worn by the women at that time were considered phallic; a remarkable stretch of the imagination given their post-coital droop.

It is 1610 and the action has moved to the Inquisition's headquarters in Logroño. A huge stage has been built. It will be a show trial: it is said that 30,000 people have swarmed into the town, which normally houses 6,000. There will be a solemn ceremony, the *auto de fe*. The Christian faith and Spanish unity will be upheld.

One thing which strikes me about the events is the Orwellian language. The show trial is called an *auto de fe*, a communal act of faith. The informers are called *familiares*, relatives. *Relajada* might be expected to mean relaxed, happy, you can go home now. For the Inquisition it means released into the hands of the secular authorities (the Church doesn't want to get its hands dirty). It means you are to be burned alive.

There is also the sheer vindictiveness of the persecution. By the time of the trial thirteen of the accused had died in prison, most as a result of an epidemic. But even for them, there was no escape. They too were tried, represented by life-size papier-mâché statues. Five of the papier-mâché statues were found guilty and condemned to be burned at the stake. The bones of the dead had been carefully conserved and they too were added to the pyre.

Stepping out into the sun after two hours supping with demons, I feel tense and anxious, washed out. This is what humanity is capable of. We have no excuses. This is a part of us, all of us, you and me. *We are capable of this.*

Walking in the nearby fields, dazed, I think how strange it is. Zugarramurdi – the village – is incredibly perfect. Compact with perhaps fifty houses, much as it has been for centuries, unspoilt by modern development, it is surrounded by undulating pasture with the Pyrenees as a setting. It should look like Auschwitz, historically speaking. *Sol y sombra* – light and darkness.

Are there any carline thistles here? Their huge yellow flowers radiate summer, their withering remains, nailed to doors, traditionally keep witches at bay. I only find one lonely specimen.

Tomorrow I need to find a pharmacy and a map for the new route, but more importantly I want to visit the caves again.

Zugarramurdi

In the morning the air is thick with the smell of silage in the making. I start walking to Dantxarinea but before long stick out my thumb. Two black cars pass by and then a third one stops. The driver is sassy, fortyish, and blonde. She's also going to the pharmacy and insists on accompanying me. This is not what I had hoped for. Thank heavens it is nothing more delicate.

Margari runs a bar. She was born in Zugarramurdi. I ask her if the village has changed much.

"My grandparents wouldn't believe it if they saw it now. In their day everybody had cows or sheep. Now there is only one farm with milk cows."

"What happened?"

"Cows are too demanding. You have to be there all the time. The only accommodation was the *posada*. Now everybody lives off tourism. We have ten bed-and-breakfasts and the hostel."

She follows me into the pharmacy so I play for time by buying some Compeed. Then I do a lot of pointing and miming. Consultations between Margari and the woman behind the counter result in the production of a cream which looks plausible.

"You got up in a hurry this morning, didn't you?" says Margari, indicating my socks.

"No. They're always like that, even at home," I explain.

There are no maps to be had in Dantxarinea.

On the way back I ask Margari about the pasture. What happens to the hay?

"It is eaten by the *caballitos* – little horses."

She takes me on a tour of the outskirts of the village, trying to find some,

Sol y sombra

Zugarramurdi

without success. Finally she drops me off in the village square and I kiss her goodbye.

"*Adiós.*"

At the witches' cave, in between dishing out tickets, the manager tells me what she knows.

"Horses the size of big dogs? I haven't seen any. Horses yes, but normal ones."

On the other hand she does confirm that tourism is new to Zugarramurdi.

"It all started about 25 years ago, when we started to promote the caves."

"Why?"

"So that people would know that they were innocent."

This isn't the answer I had expected. It sounds rehearsed, an excuse for making money out of torture.

"But I thought Zugarramurdi had always been known for its witches. Why didn't you say they were innocent before?"

"Because it was all suppressed."

"Franco suppressing anything that was Basque? The taxi driver told me there was a big police station near here, to keep an eye on what was happening."

"Yes but mainly the Church. It was very powerful and didn't want the witches' story to be told. So when Franco died we wanted to set the record straight."

Paying for my ticket, I open the gate. By the side of the path a panel reads: "Several centuries ago, Sabbaths and other festive ceremonies took place here and in the environs". It also mentions smugglers, geology, and a lime kiln, but says nothing about innocence.

The path descends to a burbling stream – the Infernuko Erreka (Hell's river) – which sploshes joyously over the rocks. Nearby, a herd of skewbald horses and foals is hiding from the sun under the trees. The main cave, a little upstream, is open at both ends and big enough to fit a house into. It is here, some say, that villagers met for their Sabbaths. The field next to it is known as Akelarre (field of the goat in Basque). But the only emotion the experience provokes in me is one of relief: the cave is deliciously cool. I walk through it and out the other side, disappointed. There's no point in *looking* for witches. They are only visible when there is nothing to be seen. By the way, nothing, absolutely nothing, in the extensive documents of the Inquisition links the caves with Sabbaths. It is only local imagination which places them here.

Back in 1610, the *auto de fe* didn't put an end to witches; quite the opposite, it started an epidemic. The Inquisition didn't know which way to turn. Finally Alonso de Salazar y Frías was sent to enquire. Salazar had only recently joined the Inquisition and hadn't been involved in the original interrogations. He returned with 5,000 names – an even more astonishing figure when you remember this was in a rural area – and a conviction that the whole process of investigation was flawed.

> I have not found one single proof nor even the slightest indication from which to infer that one act of witchcraft has actually taken place… the testimony of accomplices alone without further support from external

facts substantiated by persons who are not witches is insufficient to warrant even one arrest.

The claims of witchcraft, he wrote, 'go beyond all human reason and many even pass the limits permitted to the Devil.' If the Devil was involved, how could he allow his machinations to be exposed so easily by children of eight years and under?

He concluded that there were no witches before people started talking about them. Therefore the solution was simple: ban talking about them. It worked. The epidemic disappeared, as if by magic.

The Inquisition had always been more sceptical than the secular authorities and went on to reinforce the rules of evidence. The Zugarramurdi trial marked a turning point. Witches in Spain were no longer to be burned at the stake (though the last trial took place as late as 1791).

Back in my room, all my possessions have gone. As this includes wet socks and dirty laundry, I go searching for the cleaner and find her in the bar, broomstick in hand. It appears that she has stashed everything in a black plastic bag.

In the evening I go to Margari's bar, the Marixan Ostatua. Glued to the counter, three blokes are mumbling lethargically in Basque, mostly looking into their drinks. From time to time one of them looks in my direction and says a few words in French interspersed with "Manchester United" and "David Beckham". Apart from that I have no idea what they are saying, except when one of them says to his neighbour "*souriez* – smile". The neighbour continues to look glum. Margari, in contrast, has twinkling brown eyes. She tells me that she has been running the bar for thirteen years. Before that it used to be a chicken shed and she used to work at the caves. Now she is behind the counter from midday to ten at night, but she closes for a month every year. At this juncture one of the men pipes up, in Spanish so that I can understand: "She's rich. She has too many holidays."

I tell her I've been to the mid-summer festival before. She hesitates for an instant before she asks me when it was.

"2010."

"It's fine now." she tells me, relieved. "For families. But before 2006 we had 8,000 people for San Juan. There were fights and drugs, and drunks being sick all over. The roads into the village were completely blocked with parked cars, and most people just came to party. They didn't even go into the caves."

The man who never smiles waves his glass at her so she says: "Another then?" in Spanish.

He replies in Basque. When she has finished pouring his (French) Pastis she turns to me.

"I sometimes forget to speak Basque. When I was young it was forbidden in public so my generation doesn't use it much. Today's kids don't even learn Spanish until they are eight years old, and only at school, so they speak Basque as well as their grandparents."

"*Agur*", says one of the customers as he walks out of the door. Others come in and order *kalimotxos*, grape juice, port, red wine, Cacolac, and *pintxos*.

I say that I am astonished that Franco's witch hunts were not mentioned in the exhibition.

"That's because the Navarre government wants to forget certain things and they financed the project."

It seems that the 2007 Historical Memory Law has yet to have an impact in Zugarramurdi. Remembering the crimes of the dictatorship is still difficult for some.

"Which party is in charge in Navarre?"

"The Partido Popular, the right."

"And here?"

"They're independent. They call themselves the Agrupación Akelarre," she says with a smile.

We talk about the referendum on Scottish independence: 'It couldn't happen here.' Little horses: 'Maybe they were just foals.' The French Inquisition's persecution of the Cathars in the Ariège: 'Write down the name of the book for me, please.'

"*Agur*," I say when it is time to go.

"*Agur*," she replies.

My search for witches has been inconclusive. I still don't know if they were merely practitioners of herbal remedies, silly women play-acting, or just figments of the imagination. But then why should anything to do with sorcery be rational and clear cut? What I do know is that Zugarramurdi has an ambiguous attitude to its past. Witches didn't exist until people started talking about them; witch tourism didn't either.

Sol y sombra

Zugarramurdi to Elizondo

The taxi arrives on time and whisks me through a segment of France and back to the Venta Lizaieta. Border checks having been banned by the EU, the two *guardia civiles* who stop us must be a figment of my imagination. The driver tells them what I am doing; they don't even bother to check me out.

The *venta* is not open but the lights are on. So I sit on a stone on the pass, with one foot in France, the other in Spain, looking down on the foothills. Finally, the barmaid opens the door. I help her to empty the room of the plastic chairs and tables which spend their days outside. I have the impression that they are the only things that move from one day to the next – apart, perhaps for the dust settling on the cans of vegetables. The same ham sandwich that was there two days ago is still in the same corner of the same plastic display case. I point to it.

Once the sandwich has been prepared, I head along the ridge, passing in front of a disused customs post. Beyond it a wooden pier sticks out from the forest into the sky, looking for all the world like a docking station for some medieval spacecraft. I ignore the 'No entry' sign and walk along the gangway. Above, the mackerel clouds are shoaling together. Leaning over the barrier at the end, looking at the sea-sky, I can hear old voices talking about these *palomeras*.

The first voice wafting in over the air waves comes from 1378: "The Etxalar *palomeras* are to provide twenty-four live wood pigeons at New Year" for the parish priest. By the 17th century one of his successors was so desperate to get to the *palomeras* for the crack of dawn that he was saying mass at two in the morning, or so the parishioners complained. (Surely a dangerous practice in the wake of the witchhunts.) Shortly afterwards he was caught hunting on somebody else's property. By 1793 the 'blue fever' was so widespread on both sides of the frontier that the Brave New World Revolutionaries looking for a new name for nearby Sare settled for the obvious choice: Palombière.

Strange to say, one of the voices on the air waves belongs to an American: Orson Welles. It is 1955. He is wearing a suit, a starched white shirt and a bow tie, and making a charming ethnographical documentary about the Basque country. The TV film will be the first in a series billed as 'Around the World with Orson Welles'. He has come here to witness 'birds netted out of the sky, like fish'. The hunters are waiting with a Heath Robinson collection of equipment: sheets, trumpets, table tennis bats painted white, and nets. The sheets, sails billowing in the wind, are used to guide the pigeons in the right direction. The trumpets warn of the birds' arrival. This is the signal for the bats to be launched into the air from the piers. Pigeons are easily frightened and just as easily convinced that a white bat is really a hawk. Since they know that the hawk's strategy is to sweep in and grab them from below they respond by diving so low that the hawk crashes into the ground. They are so busy laughing at the trick and telling themselves how clever they are that they don't notice the nets spread out along the watershed.

The technique has changed little since Orson Welles' day but the numbers actually caught have been decreasing for over a century. In 2010 over 1.6 million birds passed over the western Pyrenees but only 4900 were caught in the ten nets.

Leaving the *palombières* behind I head towards Elizondo. For the moment it is good walking weather but the cows, sheep, and horses have also read the sky and are looking for shelter, their bells providing rural background music. Apart from the animals I am alone, wading through the bracken and gorse, across pastures, through beech woods.

The ridge I am following has long been occupied. The Bronze Age is represented by tumuli. The 20th century too: tiny concrete dug outs, hardly big enough for two gunners. For the moment these modern tumuli are covered with turf but the concrete is beginning to show, like new teeth starting to poke through soft gums. Along with the bunkers I have already seen, these are part of Franco's '*Línea P*' defence against possible Axis or Allied attack after the end of the Civil War. Some 8,000 were constructed: I will see them at regular intervals.

At the end of the long hot descent I dive into a hollow way, a dark tunnel under trees, and follow it. Fluffy catkins fallen from the sweet chestnut trees wriggle nervously in the breeze, cushioning my footfalls, flying into the air as I kick my way through. At the end of the tunnel is the town of Elizondo.

The main square is alive with the sound of fife and drum and the sight of dancing. A leaflet explains that this is the *Mutil Dantza*. The participants – a score of men and women – dance solemnly in an open circle, processing anti-clockwise. Music is provided by *txistularis* (the fife and drum players). It all seems rather dull. It is only the next morning, on reading the *Diario de*

Navarra newspaper, that I grasp that I have entirely missed the point: *mutil* means young man. The dance was originally a nuptial parade where the local beaux showed off their dancing skills. Recently boys have been admitted, but women! The mayoress Garbiñe Elizegi has brought the issue into the open by participating. It's like the mixed *alarde* in Irun, but without the riot police.

I install myself in a hotel and then go for a wander. I know Elizondo from having briefly lived in the area. It is the main centre of the Baztan, a commune which laps over the Pyrenean watershed and encircles the commune of Zugarramurdi, making it into an island.

Today, at one end of the main street a fun-fair is in full swing. The six-year-olds, constrained by the presence of their parents, have opted for the rather tame Disney-themed merry-go-round, but the eight-year-olds, left to their own devices, have chosen the sex-themed tagada ride. Their choice, the *olla meneito* (wiggling cooking pot) has been airbrushed with urban iconography: fast cars, faster women and a scene from a pole dancing show. Meanwhile, their parents are drinking fresh organic milk from a nearby street-corner vending machine.

Next to the milk machine a poster features three bovine faces, impeccably groomed, with lyre-shaped horns, and decorative collars. It is headed "Feria SOS". We are invited to contribute to the cost of running a competition to promote the *raza bovina Pirenaica*.

The streets of Elizondo are lined with market stalls. I eat a bright yellow *talo* (corn pancake) and a *txistorra* sausage from one of them and then go into a bar for a beer. I have got as far as sitting down before I notice a teenage couple snogging ostentatiously nearby, so I go outside again and sit at the only free table, next to a recently vandalised telephone box: shards of Perspex are distributed over a wide area. Small boys are taking fireworks apart, combining the contents into bigger bangs. The acrid smell of gunpowder yellows the pavement. Elizondo is half-way through its six-day fiesta.

For the moment the streets are fairly empty but people are arriving all the time. Family groups, identifiable by the heart-shaped silver-and-red balloons floating above their heads, are heading towards the *xocolatada* for their daily dose of chocolate. The insignia of the local lads is a plastic goblet, empty, swinging from a red ribbon looped around their necks, or full in their right hand, in the process of being emptied. They are weaving from one bar to the next. As for the local girls, they are wearing large blue-and-white checked tea towels overprinted with a *lauburu* (Basque cross) motif tied around their waists. They are heading down the street, accompanied by a man also wearing a tea towel, in his case emblazoned with the legend '*beti zurrutak* – always drinking'. I follow them to a small plaza where a band is tuning up.

The girls are here to perform more traditional dances. Sometimes they make a big circle and dance in formation but mostly they just twirl around, arms in the air. When they twirl, the tea towels fly up like a washing line on a windy day. Gathered skirts, like those worn by the dancers in Hondarribia, would be much more appropriate but maybe I can see the logic. Apart from the tea towels, the girls are all wearing everyday clothes: shorts, leggings, jeans, tee-shirts. Pierced lips and noses. They wouldn't be seen dead wearing gathered skirts. Apparently a tea towel is sufficiently iconoclastic to make traditional dancing acceptable.

I go to another bar to escape the first raindrops and order a drink in the same subversive spirit: a *kalimotxo* – Coca-Cola and red wine – accompanied by *una docenita de churros* – a 'little' dozen *churros*.

Elizondo is just waiting for the rain to stop so that it can launch itself into an extravagant cocktail: of *xocolatadas* and fairground rides, beer and empty stomachs, wine and an indecent quantity of food. Tomorrow morning it will wake up feeling sick but for now it is having a great time. But I'm not part of it. I'm in a crowd, but lonely.

Outside in the rain even the streets are melancholy. I go into a shop and pick up an umbrella from the stand by the door.

"Do you want me to bring it back?"

"If you want, or leave it in another shop," says the assistant.

I head back to the hotel past a dripping banner on the bridge: *Euskal preso ta iheslariak etxera.*

In reception a young couple is just checking in. They have boots on their feet and tired looks on their faces.

"Are you walking the Senda?" I ask.

"Yes."

"Where have you come from today?"

"Bera. Twelve hours…" His voice trails away.

Back in my room, I ring Georgina who lives in nearby Ameztia.

"Come round for lunch tomorrow," she says.

Sol y sombra

Around Elizondo

In the morning the street is full of monstrous dwarves putting on their make-up milling around a glass table laden with bottles and cakes. All head, supported on tiny human legs and arms, they have difficulty in walking in a straight line. Their faces permanently contorted into an ugly grimace, they are frequently invited to Pyrenean carnivals.

Towering over them, a quartet of elegant giants dressed in medieval costume is practising swirling dance steps, skirts flying wide showing frilly underwear. The *cabazuelos* and *gigantes* are papier-mâché cartoon characters.

The last time I was here there were only two giants: Queen Isabella and King Ferdinand of Aragon, the *reyes católicos*. I ask a man supervising the operation who the other two are.

"Enrique II and Margarita de Orleans, the king and queen of Navarre. They're new."

Today, the giants will execute poetic square- and line-dances in the streets, punctuating the end of each sentence with a grammatical bow. But when they are alone in their storeroom, when nobody can see them, they bicker. About how exactly 600 years ago this year Navarre became Aragon and Aragon became Spain. "Off with his head," say the Queens in unison, and another *cabazuelo* is born.

"It must be a lot of work," I continue.

"We're a team," he explains. "*Mis ayudantes son la leche* – My helpers are milk."

He says it with great gusto. I search for a translation: crème de la crème?

I walk further down the street and stick out my thumb. After a few minutes a bunch of kids comes running past, as if the gates of hell have just opened, fleeing marauding dwarves. They are followed by the giants waltzing in a stately fashion, and I have to move progressively further down the street until they all turn into a housing estate and leave the main road free to traffic.

I'm picked up by a man in a minivan.

"Did you know that Mexico City is Baztan's second biggest village?" he says with a Latin-American accent and a hint of pride.

"Look," he adds, taking one hand off the wheel to reach for the newspaper on the dashboard and the other to point out the relevant paragraph. "Almost every family has some relative in Mexico."

What did he think of Miguel Ángel y el Mariachi la Cantina who performed a couple of nights ago?

"Great, but I couldn't stay long. I have to get up for work."

He is a builder. He followed his cousin to Europe and has been in Elizondo for twelve years. The firm he works for usually builds cowsheds but they have recently knocked together a hotel in St-Jean-de-Luz in France. "There isn't much work in Spain," he complains.

We soon arrive at his supermarket but he insists on driving me twice the distance to take me to the next town, Doneztebe-Santesteban, dropping me in a street full of ancient buildings: Jauregia (the palace, 1547), Garronea (1556); Domingonea (1567), Olajaunenea (1591)...

I am standing at a roundabout when somebody comes out of a shop: Sagrario, one of Georgina's neighbours. We say hello and I am in the process of telling her what I am doing when I notice her shopping trolley.

"Why are you buying milk when you've twenty-six cows at home?" I ask, shocked.

"The calves drink all the milk."

"But they must be able to spare a couple of litres."

"Actually," she admits, "I don't like the taste of fresh milk."

She still likes to make cheese for the family, she confirms. Unfortunately she is not going up to Ameztia straight away.

A few minutes later another minivan stops. The driver, a waif of a girl, says that she knows me, and after a second's hesitation I recognise her: Maika. Georgina originally introduced us, saying that she was Maika's axe holder in *aizkolari* competitions, and adding that Maika also gathers corn cobs. They are both quintessential Basque sports. She often wins, said Georgina. Maika protested that it was only because there were not many women competing.

She is the undisputed local titleholder in corn cob gathering, which probably makes her the world champion as well. Participants have to pick up corn cobs placed in a line and put them in a basket.

If this sounds a bit sissy, *aizkolari* competitions are anything but. Participants stand on beech logs and chop them in two, splitting them between their feet. The most delicate part is the last blow, when the log is about to fall apart. A doctor is often needed, not to tidy up the results of unexpected amputations, but to check the health of competitors. It is a strenuous activity and can take hours. The winner in top-level competitions can expect to collect thousands of euros. The rivals chop their way through four logs 54 inches in circumference, four of 60 inches and two of 72 inches. Despite her size, Maika excels at this as well.

I ask her about her day job.

"How are the sheep?"

"So-so. I lost twenty in a thunderstorm. They were sheltering under a tree. That's what sheep are like…"

She's in a bit of a hurry, and not going to Ameztia either, but she takes me part way up the hill, dropping me at the recycling bins, the only new thing in what seems to be a timeless landscape.

But there are changes to be noted. Along the side of the road, an unintentional outdoor museum is displaying the Three Ages of the haystack. The first exhibit is a shaggy-topped stack of bracken taller than I am, impaled by a long wooden pole, like the ones near Irun, secured against the weather and changing times, immutable. The Stone Age. Then come the rectangular bales of hay neatly stacked on the back of a trailer. These will need more care, a roof over their heads, and metal tools to shape and transport them. The Iron Age. Finally giant rolls of hay enveloped in black polythene, which can stay outside all year long. The Plastic Age.

Despite the plastic, Ameztia would be most at home in the Iron Age; it could have been a hillfort. Easy to defend, a raised plateau with valleys on all sides and views of the mountains beyond, all it lacks are the ramparts. The roads and paths are hollow ways, each century digging them deeper. On humid days it floats on the sea of cloud which fills the valleys, but today it is basking in the sun. The scattered houses are all working farms, each with its neat stack of firewood against one wall and a well-tended vegetable plot. But mostly Ameztia is pasture, and fields for haymaking. The farms are still worked on a family basis. Georgina is the only outsider in this stronghold of Basque identity.

La profesora inglesa has been here for ten years. When she arrived, a single woman in a community where women just do not live on their own, nobody quite knew what to make of her, she says. They still don't really believe that she works, because all she ever does is talk.

Georgina welcomes me with open arms; her partner Iñaki with a warm handshake. We eat with their Spanish language students on the terrace. The valley below is rounded and soft, water-coloured in green, baby blue, and terracotta with trees sketched in like goose down, and a village on a small hummock on the opposite side of the valley, just where an artist would imagine it. It is a view I know well from having lived in a neighbouring cottage with Veronica.

When we have finished digesting, Iñaki gives me a lift back down as far as Ituren, gently correcting errors in my Spanish as we go. Meanwhile Georgina goes to help the neighbours with the haymaking. Although they make hay every dry day in the summer months, they only ask Georgina a couple of times so it isn't a burden. In an area where farm work is still so valued that it is the basis of sporting competitions, participation is a sign of belonging. They are honouring Georgina by inviting her.

In Ituren I am picked up by yet another minivan. The driver will only take me to the by-pass because he doesn't want to get stuck in the fiesta. He is going to Zugarramurdi. Does he know Margari, I ask. Yes, she's his aunt. When we arrive at the by-pass he just keeps on going and drops me in the town centre. I'm no longer feeling lonely.

In the heat of the late afternoon I go in search of some Paracetamol. The first pharmacy has an electronic thermometer outside: the reading is an alarming 40 degrees. It is closed; gone to bed until it gets better. Down the street the thermometer on another pharmacy indicates a more believable 35 degrees. Considering the two thermometer readings, I'm glad I don't need anything more crucial. Pharmacists are supposed to be scientists, capable of accurately measuring milligrams, millimetres and, at least in principle, degrees centigrade. Should we trust our health to a profession that can't distinguish between a dangerously high fever and incipient hypothermia?

On one side of the main square, a poster stretching the whole height of the wall advertises the first showing of *'Baztan'*, a film which has been shot here. The valley is starting to interest film-makers and not only because of the 'witches'. In this case the focus of the film is the *agotes*. Who were they? Nobody seems to quite know. Descendants of Goths, lepers, Moorish soldiers; renowned for their beauty or misshapen cretins? Whoever they were, they were up to no good. They were obliged to marry each other and – because like witches they were so difficult to identify – registers kept track of them. Bozate, just up the road, was an *agote* ghetto. A popular saying was: "*Al agote, garrotazo en el cogote* – An *agote*? Club him on the neck". The discrimination continued until well into the 20th century.

Sol y sombra

'Baztan' is the second feature film to be shot in the valley; the first was Julio Medem's '*Vacas* – Cows'. And soon there will be another one, adding the legendary Basque figures *mari*, *basajaun*, and *tarttalo*, ritual murders and serial killers to the magic potion of witches and *agotes*.

Zugarramurdi, Elizondo, Ituren, and Ameztia: extraordinarily pretty settlements in remarkable countryside dangerously balanced on a knife edge between tradition and modernity.

Like the *joaldunak*...

Joaldunak

Today Ituren was empty when I hitched through, but go there at the end of January...

The man holding the chainsaw is swinging it around his head in a complicated pattern which owes something to his dexterity but more to the amount of alcohol he has consumed. The whoosh-whirr Doppler Effect adds to my anxiety. Will he cut off his leg first, or my head?

He is wearing a balaclava and bright blue overalls from which the arms and legs have been cut; with the chainsaw, to judge by the edges. The overalls are unzipped at the front down to his waist and beyond but his modesty is saved by a sheepskin miniskirt. When he turns round I see that he has another sheepskin on his back. The fleece looks as though it has been pulled through a hedge backwards. The effect is everything but cuddly. After a while, he turns the chainsaw off, slings it over his shoulder, and goes to watch the *joaldunak*. He jigs up and down in time to the sound of their bells.

For the moment, the *joaldunak*, dressed in lacy white petticoats, are waddling down the street like Hottentot ducks, wiggling their backsides. On their heads they wear pointed hats bedecked with brightly coloured ribbons. Strapped to each buttock is a bronze cow bell which clangs sombrely with every step: *pulunpa* is the Basque onomatopoeia for the sound. Smaller sheep bells on their shoulders tinkle pathetically. But the main attraction at present is the opening of the talos stand. We're hungry too, having followed the procession from the start in the neighbouring hamlet of Auritz.

Now the *joaldunak* are bouncing down the street in military formation, yes bouncing – as if they have a space hopper between their legs – accompanied a drummer, a foghorn, and a rather forlorn txistu flute. On top of their frilly petticoats, they too are wearing sheepskins but theirs have been combed into a soft duvet. One of them adjusts the red neckerchief on his shoulders. He is grimacing with the effort of keeping his head steady whilst wiggling his backside. He makes a grab for his hat before it falls off, almost dropping the ponytail switch he is waving. The *joaldunak* are accompanied by a man disguised as a bear, also in sheep's clothing. Curiously he sports a pair of cow's horns. With him is a bear-tamer. Frequently the bears and tamers play the lead roles in Pyrenean carnivals but here they only have bit parts.

We are standing in Ituren's village square on a grey afternoon, drinking cider under the stone arches of the Heriko Ostatua (the people's inn). The building is shared with the town hall: on one of the walls a poster demands the legalisation of Batasuna, the Basque socialist revolutionary independence party. To our left, at the top of the fronton wall, as if presiding over the ceremonies, is that flag: *Euskal preso eta iheslariak etxera*.

The two components of the Ituren–Zubieta carnival have just arrived. The folklore version represented by the *joaldunak*, which all the tourists and camera crews are photographing. And the *mozorruak* carnival, the 'off', represented by the man with the chainsaw.

The *joaldunak* take a break but *mozorruak* carnival continues. A man leans out from the balcony of one of the colossal stone houses that border the square and sprays water on the crowd below. More carnival floats come down the road. One is a jeep improbably disguised as a fir tree. It is followed by another with an African theme, complete with bamboo, a man with a blacked-up face and lipstick, and a lion. A donkey pulls in with a cart full of wooden stakes and fencing. The man walking besides it is wearing a gorilla mask and carrying a coil of barbed wire. Why? I ask myself. One of the most spectacular contraptions is a tandem bicycle which is so tall that the riders are at the same level as the first floor windows.

Another marauder wielding a chainsaw charges into the square, this one clad only in his underwear. His face is hidden by a mask, though I suspect many will recognise him from the size of his beer belly. He climbs onto a corrugated metal roof and bangs on it. This wakes up the cockerel which starts squawking and flapping its blue- and green-painted plumage. A goat butts Veronica. The men start smashing up pallets and other assorted bits of wood.

What does it all mean? I know where to find out. My informant has lived in Ituren all his life; a former *joaldunak*, he is now too old to participate. He interprets the festivities partly as a fertility rite, with male and female elements, which is why the *joaldunak* men wear frilly petticoats; the ribbons were supposedly once babies' swaddling ribbons. And partly as a means of scaring off bears, wolves, and evil spirits. The *mozorruak* are an unruly branch sprouting from the apple tree in the Garden of Eden. They are chased away by the *joaldunak*. And his word is as good as anybody's because there were no serious studies of the carnival before the 1960s.

But although the *joaldunak* look like something immemorial I've been looking at the archives. In recent years they have become more organised, more mainstream. Before the Civil War they wore masks, but when Franco banned 'immoral' carnivals and masks, they took them off in a compromise which ensured the survival of the event. The carnival date is now fixed, whereas it was previously left up to the committee to decide. And pretty, coordinated neckerchiefs have arrived.

On the other hand, in the 1970s zombies and witches were still a major element of the *mozorruak* carnival. One of the floats was a hut labelled 'Sorgin etxea – the witch's house'. These 'traditional' elements have almost disappeared.

The *mozorruak* and the *joaldunak* seem to be diverging. The *mozorruak* represent the true carnival spirit, edging towards anarchy, petrifying tourists. But more alarmingly, the *joaldunak* seem to be heading symbolically for Venice: they are becoming a petrified tourist attraction.

Paths crossing

Elizondo to Sorogain

It is still dark when I leave the hotel. Dull yellow light and jarring notes sneak out from under the doors of the bars to join the sleeping drunks on the pavement. Meanwhile, much of the youth of Elizondo is still standing, still drinking, and still debating the meaning of cows. I stride purposefully through the streets, hands on hips.

Reaching the safety of the hills, I pack my guns back in their holsters, put on my head torch, and follow a rabbit up a dark tunnel through overhanging branches just like the ones on the other side.

The day doesn't dawn. Black just merges into grey. Forest into rough grass. In the distance isolated farmsteads stand perkily on gentle hills. I climb upwards, towards the grey mist. It becomes so thick that I can smell it, then touch it, then taste it, sticky on the tongue.

I haven't been paying much attention, so the sudden appearance of border stone no. 127 trips me up. I have been walking south for two days from the Venta Lizaieta, but here is France again. I look carefully at my map. Logically, the border should follow the watershed round the head of the valley. Instead it slices off a part of it.

It is too cold to stand around staring at a map so I turn right to follow the barbed wire. 128, 129, 130. At this point the border plunges down into the valley but the Senda continues straight on. Through the mist I can hear the muffled sound of bells. Soon I smell the horse manure and see them: beautiful bays.

Checking the waymarks, I take care to follow the path closely. It enters an area of rock on the slopes of Argintzo, falters, and then stops. I go back to the last comforting red-and-white stitching and try again but don't find any convincing alternative possibilities. Even a well-used path wouldn't leave any

Paths crossing

traces here on the naked pinkish-grey blocks, or in the leg-breaking fissures. Worse, it is raining now and everything is slippery. The drops soak through my cape, making me shiver, tense with cold.

I cut myself on a barbed wire fence, then find a stile but fail to find a path beyond it. By now, I know I am lost. Finally I arrive at a signpost, showing clearly that the Senda passes on the other side of the hill.

A hasty lunch in a corrugated iron shooting butt which hardly provides any protection from the wind is followed by a walk along the broad-backed ridge, a watershed. To the west the rivers flow into the Atlantic. To the east they flow into the Mediterranean. The equivalent watershed on the north side of the massif is at Portella de la Grava, more than 40 days' walking east of here: the Pyrenees are geologically very skewed.

The clouds lift, revealing a string of increasingly disreputable shooting butts. They could equally be sentry posts: sheep and bay horses to the north keeping the pasture well-grazed and tidy; cows to the south less successful in tackling the bracken undergrowth in the forest.

Onwards I go, down the slope to the Col de Urkiaga (birch tree pass), designated as the end of the day's walking. The only possible shelter is in one of the many *nidos* as the Spanish military call them. *Nidos* may well mean nests, but the underground concrete bunkers of the Línea P are not feather-bedded.

So I continue up the winding track on the other side of the pass, meeting the first walkers seen all day, out for a stroll with their dog. Then I swim into the mist again, down a slippery track and alongside a meandering river to the Albergue de Sorogain.

At the hostel everything is new. Ana is welcoming and provides me with a herb tea before showing me the dormitory. She asks if I mind having some cyclists in with me; I abandon the idea of lying down.

I enquire about the border. In the amputated head of the valley, I learn, the soil is Spanish but the grass is French. The inhabitants are French, and pay French income tax. But they live permanently in Spain and pay land tax to Spain.

What do you expect in a valley ransomed by accountants? Back in 1237, there were no inhabitants so the king of Navarre sent his bureaucrats to tax the pigs. The inhabitants of the Baztan to the north, Erro to the south, and Baïgorry to the east picked up the tab. When the valley found itself split between the two emerging nations, the fate of the pigs became a matter of foreign policy. Eventually it was divided arbitrarily, by a line on a map. Normally, borders are born from the coupling of geography and history, even if the midwives are politicians and soldiers. Here, the parents are ill-matched; nature has had no influence.

Further along the Pyrenees, the Valle de Arán suffered a similar fate, along with the enclave of Llivia, but the biggest anomaly of all is Andorra, a whole independent country created to avoid matrimonial disputes.

Sorogain to Auritz-Burguete

In general, as I progress eastwards, I speed up irrationally: the Senda has its own imperatives, so that by the end I am hurtling towards the Mediterranean. But today I have a genuine reason to hurry. I follow the waymarks, up into the clouds and down again, through pasture and woods – oak, beech, and birch – mushroom country. I arrive in Auritz-Burguete early.

Auritz is where the youthful Senda meets the venerable Way of St James. Body meets soul. Walking has come far: when the Way was created the only long-distance hikers in the Pyrenees were pilgrims, a few pedlars, and shepherds taking their flocks up to the estives. Most of the trajectory is very recent: the first way-marked long-distance paths in Spain date to the 1970s.

I can't waste any time. Auritz marks the start of the major deviation I was told about and I still need to buy a map. The shops in Elizondo were closed for the fiesta. And here it is Sunday and everything is shut. So I need to get to Orreaga before lunch.

Walking to Orreaga on the *camino francés*, part of the Way of St James, I think about maps. Do I *really* need to consult one when I get up? The sun also rises every morning: wouldn't there be more discoveries to be made just walking in the general direction of the Mediterranean, fixing my sights on the new day? I'm equipped to sleep outside *in extremis*. So why am I so concerned? The answer is education: a *walker* plans a route, schedules a shelter, and always carries a map, a compass, and a watch.

For most of the time I am happily chained to the Senda, not seeing the map that is the wallpaper of my cell; not even feeling the weight of my electronic tracking bracelet. Certainly, I am constrained by the red line on the paper and the warning beeps of technology, but they make me feel at home. Not quite imprisoned, but above all not lost.

Maps have been a part of me for the last half century. Mr Jenkins was an inspired teacher. We were each given a large-scale sketch map of Yarm and a sheet of thick cardboard. Having coloured the roads red, the river blue, and the railway line black we were instructed to cut the cardboard into shapes based on the contour lines. Gluing the pieces on top of each other we built up the relief. The coloured map was then stuck on top. The railway viaduct was the trickiest element. For the next lesson we were taken on a walk around the town and shown the flood mark on the town hall. For me, everything fitted into place. It wasn't so much that the rivers were a watery blue or the railway line a sooty black but that the third, cardboard dimension corresponded to the ground under my feet. And it wasn't just the physical correspondence; the patterns were already there in my head. I didn't formalise it at the time, but I had just discovered the part of my brain where abstract symbols take on meaning.

Which is why I hate getting lost. It could be the first sign of something very wrong.

I still need to reach Orreaga before lunch and have been walking fast, but an interpretative panel pulls me up short.

According to the Navarre tourist board this path is part of the '*Ruta de la Brujería* – Witchcraft route':

> The Sorginaritzagako forest, whose meaning is 'oak wood of the witches', was where some of the best-known witches' covens of the 16th century were held. It led to a resounding repression and finished with nine people from the area being burned at the stake.

Where is the message of Zugarramurdi?

In the woods I meet three old women coming in the other direction, each holding a leaflet on the *Ruta de la Brujería*. I ask if I am heading in the right direction.

"*Si, vaya con Dios* – Yes, may God be with you."

The first thing that strikes me on arriving in Orreaga is quite how down to earth the building complex looks. It resembles a huge factory, albeit one built with the welfare of the workers in mind. The immense white-painted façade is complemented by an extensive lawn. A Basque Saltaire. The second thing is the emptiness. This morning's pilgrims must have already left and this afternoon's 300 have not yet arrived. And today Orreaga is only just below the clouds, so there are few tourists.

But there are some around and a woman asks me to take a photo of them in front of the road sign. They cheerfully admit that they are not going to walk the 790km to Santiago. They are going to drive there, *"si Dios quiere* – God willing".

I almost ask them to take a picture of me standing in front of the road sign. I'm not seriously considering changing direction, just wondering about asking for a *credential* in the Pilgrim Office. This is the passport to a bed in the dormitory here, reserved for pilgrims only.

I won't be the first to cheat. According to Pablo Arribas' *Coquins, gueux, catins… sur le Chemin de Saint-Jacques – Rascals, beggars, strumpets on the Way of St James* the Way attracted all kinds of marginals. When hunger was endemic, as it was for a large sector of the population, the Way provided interesting possibilities. The 'pilgrim' could expect charity simply because he was a pilgrim. Far away from the rigid strictures of home, he could misbehave more or less with impunity, as long as he moved quickly enough.

As the *Codex Calixtinus*, put it: 'Poor or rich, all have the right to hospitality and a respectful welcome'. Indeed, even for genuine pilgrims, in the near-subsistence economy of the Middle Ages the existence of charity was the *sine qua non* for undertaking a pilgrimage. On the other hand, unscrupulous hostel keepers could exploit clients who would never be seen again.

The *Codex Calixtinus* was compiled in France, probably in the 1130s. A beautiful illuminated manuscript, it was greatly read in the Benedictine monastery of Cluny. Much of it is a forgery.

It starts with a preface supposedly penned by Pope Calixtus II (he was dead), then explains how St James came to be buried in Spain, though he was martyred at the other end of the Mediterranean. It bravely attempts to connect Charlemagne with the 'discovery' of the tomb of Saint James *c* 820–35 even though Charlemagne was dead by then. It contains sermons, hagiography, pseudo-history with a hidden political agenda, musical scores, and a guidebook. Medieval multi-media, it was a great success.

The guidebook even contains a pocket Latin–Basque phrasebook with all the words the 12th-century pilgrim needs: *Vircia* (God), *Andrea Maria*

Paths crossing

(Mother of God), *ogia* (bread), *jadum* (wine), *aragui* (meat)... The one phrase it doesn't contain is 'I love you'. Describing the Basques, the author says:

> Watching them eat, one might be seeing dogs or pigs stuffing themselves. Listening to them speak, one would believe one was hearing a dog barking... [they are] vicious, dark skinned, hideous to look at, depraved, perverse, treacherous, disloyal and corrupt, libidinous, alcoholic, skilled in all kinds of violence, ferocious and wild, dishonest and false, rebellious and coarse, cruel and quarrelsome.

Just in case the future pilgrim hadn't quite got the message, someone has later added 'and above all anti-French'.

But the section which most intrigues me is a little homily:

> For the righteous, the pilgrim route is the renunciation of vices, the mortification of the body, the encouragement of virtues... It eliminates rich food, it makes gluttonous fat vanish, it overpowers desires, it restrains the appetites of the flesh which militate against the soul, cleanses the spirit, incites contemplation, humbles the haughty, raises up the lowly, and loves poverty. It hates the possessions accumulated by avarice but loves those who give to the poor, rewards those who live simply and do good works. On the other hand it does not free sinners and misers from themselves.

The path rewards and chastises the pilgrim. The path is a guide, a doctor, a psychologist, and a diet plan. He (I can't imagine the Way being female) has a strong personality. He is self-righteous, arrogant, and manipulative. In short: a monster. And the Senda: will he be a diet plan, a bully or both?

This must be the point for a libation, so I search for somewhere symbolic and find a plaque commemorating the battle which took place near here in AD778, the *raison d'être* of the epic poem *La Chanson de Roland*. This will do. I open my phial and pour a few drops of Atlantic onto it.

In the Tourist Information office they give me a map which would be too embarrassing to show fellow walkers, but in the souvenir shop they have a more suitable one. Afterwards I go back to the factory.

By now the first of today's batch of pilgrims have started to arrive.

Although I have decided to stay in Auritz, I follow them across a cloister, through a courtyard and under a stone archway into the freshly renovated reception area of the Albergue de Peregrinos. I poke around nosily, my heathen presence unchallenged.

Just behind the reception desk a small room with a row of telephones and six computers looks like a share traders' office, albeit situated somewhere in the Third World. One pilgrim is checking his email on the Web.

Orreaga has long been a hub. Eight hundred years ago the multiple pilgrim routes were like a fibre-optic network transmitting and receiving information from all over Europe. Santiago was at its heart.

> Everything which was said, preached, sung, recounted, sculpted or painted on the Way affected more people and a larger area.

But the Way wasn't only a medium for passing messages, it was the message itself: the Christians are coming! The Spanish war cry became '¡*Dios ayuda y Santiago!* – God helps, and St James' and the saint in question gained the sobriquet '*Matamoros* – the Moor slayer'.

I sneak upstairs to look at the dormitories. There are three altogether, each with room for 72 sardines. Official statistics show 59,023 pilgrims passing through Orreaga in 2011. Add to that all the pilgrims who took a different route and you have 183,502 pilgrims arriving in Santiago – with the *credencial* it is easy to keep track. It's impressive, particularly when compared with 1978 when a mere 13 stepped through the cathedral doors. But the modern figures are nothing in comparison with the Way's medieval heyday (AD1100–1250) when, according to the Centro Europeo de estudios compostelanos, it attracted an unbelievable 250,000 to 500,000 per year, in a Europe with roughly one-tenth of today's population.

One important difference between then and now is that the medieval pilgrim also had to walk back. Traditionally he took a scallop shell from Santiago home. Now the scallop shell makes a round trip, the outward journey on foot, the return in the comfort of a train. Another change is in the nature of the pilgrimage. I once asked a volunteer in a reception centre what he thought.

"I would say that a majority of walkers have some kind of spiritual motive, though not necessarily a Christian one." He attributed the recent popularity to the designation of the path as a World Heritage Site and the growing number of hostels, making days shorter.

I walk back to Auritz, stopping on the edge of the village at the pharmacy. Not by obligation; just to study the impressive selection of drugs, bandages, and medical trusses in the window: for legs, feet, and incidentally stomachs. It reminds me of one of those reliquaries in cathedrals where the afflicted come to worship a saint and hopefully touch the bone which corresponds to their infirmity.

I have already earmarked the Hostal Burguete for tonight on the basis of the outside. The door, crowned by a desiccated carline thistle, has barley sugar window-lights patterned with criss-cross ribs. Opening it reveals a hallway smelling of beeswax, lined with dark panelling and rows of matching benches. An aspidistra in a copper pan sits precariously on a three-legged stool. I check in. The stairs creak, as does the bedstead when I flop down on it. It doesn't take me long to decide to supplement the existing mattress with a second one of wine.

But where does the Senda leave town? Stepping lightly over the gutters which delimit the high street, flowing with twin streams, I walk in what seems the right direction. Standing in front of a notice board, a young couple is huddled in discussion, looking alternately at their guide and the board.

"We've already met, haven't we?" I say. "In Elizondo."

"Yes... Do you know where the Senda really goes? Nothing corresponds."

They are Catalans, they tell me, a physiotherapist and a bookshop owner. They have climbed most of the peaks and now want to join up the dots.

We go to *El Fronton* where we can spread my new map and some beer out on a table. While their fingers are poring over the red line of the Senda trying to absorb the information, I notice another couple sitting at a table outside, also studying a guidebook.

When we have finished cursing the sluggishness of publishers, I go back into the Hostal Burguete. There is an upright piano in the far corner of the room and pictures on the wall. A picture of rabbits, dead, one of pheasants, also dead, and one of Ernest Hemingway, signed.

I say to the manager: "Hemingway went to Pamplona, didn't he?"

"And here, for the trout fishing." He gives me a leaflet as proof.

"There was a look-alike contest for the 50th anniversary of his last visit. We had three of them," he adds going back into the kitchen.

Footprints on the mountains

Reading the leaflet I learn that Hemingway gave two things to Navarre: international tourism at the bacchanal of San Fermin (in bold capitals) and a few lonely walkers to the wildness of Auritz (lower case).

Auritz to Hiriberri-Villanueva de Aezkoa

I have decided to have a lie in. Saint James, on the other hand, has risen with the sun and when I open the shutters is already passing by in quantity.

Finally, I get going but the Senda spends the morning in bed, in a duvet rumpled into soft folds, covered in grass and ferns, birch and beech forest, and perfumed with honeysuckle. At each summit a new vista unfolds, closely resembling the last one. It is easy walking, well stitched together, except in the thick forest where an emaciated ragamuffin of a track, heading in the opposite direction to all the waymarks, turns out to be the correct one.

In the hamlet of Orbara I am standing outside the closed door of a bar when a young man spontaneously offers to drive me to Hiriberri where the door will be open. But I want to walk, so I go down to the river, across a bridge and up the other side in a mid-day sweat. On the ridge above, the Senda has eroded the sparse earth through to the limestone. It passes for a kilometre or so between two widely spaced hedges. Scrub and broom are invading from the margins leaving only a narrow band of rough grass and wild flowers and the path in the centre.

Soñé que tú me llevabas	I dreamt that you took me
por una blanca vereda,	on a white path
en medio del campo verde,	in the middle of a green field
hacia el azul de las sierras,	to the blue of the hills
hacia los montes azules,	to the blue mountains
una mañana serena.	one quiet morning.

Antonio Machado

This path must have once been a *vereda* like Machado's. But whereas Machado was lamenting the loss of his wife on the day after their third wedding anniversary, Spain is not lamenting the loss of its *veredas*, once a web of routes spidering across Spain, connecting livestock farms with their markets and summer pastures. These paths (and related *cañadas* and *vías pecuarias*) if joined together would stretch three times round the earth; they once accounted for perhaps 1% of the land area, passing across some of the most beautiful countryside, as well as through urban Madrid. They were effectively a linear pasture, designed to allow the animals to eat and walk at the same time. In 21st-century English: to graze.

On the other side of the Pyrenees, the equivalent routes have all but vanished, though as late as 1878 Modestine could still stop to nibble on her way across the Cevennes, much to the annoyance of Robert Louis Stevenson. Spain is following the same path: vegetation and illegal building are rapidly encroaching.

Veredas could function as wildlife corridors, particularly important in changing circumstances where the choice is migrate or die. Like the emergency exit of a cinema: it is only when the newspaper headlines deplore the piled-up bodies that anyone notices the exit has been blocked for decades.

The *vereda* threads its way across a plateau. Hiriberri-Villanueva de Aezkoa appears over the horizon, in a pastoral hollow dotted with cows, wreathed in forest-dark hills. Both names mean 'new town' although it dates to the 14th century. Unlike Auritz and Elizondo, strung out along the roads which gave them purpose, it is compact, with the houses stuck to the church. I examine one of them. The door lintel dates to 1649. The coat of arms is an oak tree with a wild boar. The most remarkable buildings are the *hórreos*: Wendy houses built on big stone mushrooms used for storing crops and hams.

I knock on the door of Maritxu's bed-and-breakfast. The woman in question invites me in. The floor is parquet, immaculately polished – so clean you could eat off it – but she insists I keep my boots on. The house is a museum piece, not just the walls, but everything. It can be dated by the near total absence of plastics – with the exception of the television, just there to remind you which century you are in – giving it a best before date of c 1950.

In the residents' lounge a copy of *Euskal Herria Magazine* from January 2009 has an article about the Senda. It explains that the new route passing through Hiriberri has just been inaugurated. That was over three years ago.

Maritxu pokes her head round the door to ask if I would like a beer. After drinking it I ask how much it was. She throws her hands up in the air; when

I ask to phone abroad she refuses to take anything for that either. In the evening, she points me to a bar-restaurant but I can't find it and she has to lead me to a building which has absolutely nothing to distinguish it from its neighbours.

A family, also wearing walking boots, is also waiting for the bar to open. Maritxu has told me about them.

I say: "We're staying at the same *casa rural*. I'm doing the Senda too."

'I'm Carlos,' says the man. 'María, and our daughter Nuria,' he adds, pointing. 'She's only seventeen, but she walks well. The other two don't come any more.'

Nuria tries hard not to grimace too much.

"Would you like to eat with us?"

We sit down together and have a drink. They live in Madrid.

"We are teachers – history and geography," Carlos tells me. "Nuria is studying French and English."

Nuria nods.

They have done the Way of St James, the GR7 across the Alpujarras, and more.

"Do you go walking every summer?" I ask.

"Not always," María replies. "Last year Nuria and I went to lie on the beach in Valencia while Carlos walked from home. It took him twenty days."

Nuria smiles.

When the barmaid comes to take our order she finds a means of touching all of us, in a companionable way, and when Carlos asks for soup "to rehydrate us" she finds a means of making it though it isn't on the menu. The Bar-with-no-name is a good place to eat and it is good to eat in company.

Hiriberri to Ochagavía-Otsagabia

In the night, the pain starts in my feet but quickly finds a weak tendon to gnaw at. An old friend. So I get up even earlier than intended. A magnificent spread is waiting for me on the table.

I leave the house with my head torch blazing. Above the village a wall of limestone, the Sierra de Abodi, arches across the sky. The Senda tackles it obliquely through the forest and then follows it a few paces behind the cliff edge, occasionally peeking over the precipice. Lilac crocuses in the clearings, black pines in the forest.

Later, I sweep along the green shoulder of the mountain, on one side the extensive Iraty beech forest, on the other the sweet valleys of northern Navarre with the path to Ochagavía clearly visible. The noise of far-away chainsaws drifts up from below, so faint as to be almost agreeable, like the humming of bees. At the Paso de las Alforjas (Saddlebag Pass) a posse of 'Burguetana' horses grazes peacefully: rustic, free, and (ultimately) edible.

A little way down the hill I poke my head into a shepherd's hut. Although it looks reasonable from a distance, the door has been torn off and the floor is covered in rubble. The graffiti on one wall gloomily predicts:

EL FUTURO ES NUESTRO – the future is ours.

Further down, the entrance to the Muskilda hermitage is blessed with picnic tables, barbecues, large cars, and even larger families. The kids laugh as I put my head under the tap and let the water run through my hair and down my tee-shirt.

The hermitage church is all Romanesque arches with a tower capped by a roof of wooden shingles. As the tower is square and the conical roof overlaps on all four sides, it looks most odd, as though the roof were a leftover from some completely different, more imposing architectural project. But that is the only thing which is incongruous.

Ochagavía, reached an hour later, is a postcard. It has arranged itself decorously on the banks of a river, a river spanned by a hump-back stone bridge, the bridge high and wide enough to cope with the flotsam and jetsam of a flash flood. The houses, stone naturally, all seem the same vintage, and many must be, the town having been burnt to the ground by the French in 1794. One building sports the town's heraldic arms: a wolf devouring a lamb. Not a reference to the French.

I visit one of the numerous cafes, the fake cider brewery, and the tourist office which tries its best but fails to find out about hostels in Aragon, as if it were a foreign country, but does rather better on flora and fauna. In a bar I go to order just as the previous customer departs, drinks in hand, for the terrace. The barmaid puts his money in the till and then puts 16€ change on

Ochagavía

the bar in front of me without looking. I say *"Gracias"*; she looks up, already laughing. It only takes one word to recognise I'm not Spanish.

The family pass by and we exchange a few words about the day. I look around. After a long hot walk, beer in hand on the terrace by the river, Ochagavía is perfect. Or at least, perfect for tourists. In the Hostal Auñamendi I round off my evening drying socks with the hairdryer.

Ochagavía to Isaba-Izaba

The Senda has become a road and continues to be a road all morning. At first the gaps in the trees afford views back to Ochagavía but then the forest takes over. Regimented plantations. Trees, more trees. Lighter green, darker green. Tree blindness sets in. I was already walking in a kind of haze and the hot day makes me feel even sleepier. I make a point of stopping for wild honeysuckle, smelling it to remind myself that there is life beyond green. I am overjoyed to meet some very ordinary cows. I eat a snack in a small clearing.

"Boring," says Carlos when he overtakes me. "Boring," repeat María and Nuria in turn.

At the other side of the forest the undulating pastures are empty. Finally I can see again: jagged mountains in the distance, blue-grey. Three different groups of *Senderistas* warn me about the day after tomorrow: no villages, nothing except for locked ruins and a possible shepherd's hut.

The path slips back under the trees, but here the forest is delightfully disorganised. In the middle of it all, entangled in the undergrowth, is the Hermitage of Idoia, becoming overgrown again after its restoration, although the hydrangeas, geraniums, and marigolds are still being watered. As this church is also locked I head down through the woods to the village of Isaba. It too is picturesque, even though it has not yet featured in *'Mi pueblo es de postal'* like Ochagavía. Another difference is that Isaba shuns its river, clinging to the safety of the hill.

Left to itself the village would turn green: the walls are already splashed with ivy, the cobbles outlined in moss. The roofs are steep for snow and the doors well hidden under stone arches. I climb higher looking for the castle – there must be a castle – but all I find is a cinema. It is showing 'The Untouchables' and must surely be the last picture house in any Pyrenean village.

The church looks like a fortress and even has a coat of arms: a smiling man wearing a crown, and three mountains. The wording is ALDVRAMEN REY DE CORDOBA 1583. The folklore museum supplies the interpretation. The head really has nothing to smile about, having just been separated from its shoulders, according to tradition not far from here, but at a much earlier date. The Roncal valley has appropriated a big slice of history for itself, vaunting a role in the forced departure of the Muslims.

The mountains on the coat of arms might seem easy to interpret but they are not necessarily the Pyrenees. From at least the 9th century and probably earlier the *Roncalés* have been taking their livestock down to the Bardenas hills way south of Pamplona for the winter along what was to become the *cañada real*. Transhumance is a long tradition here.

The only significant events not alluded to on the coat of arms are the

Treaty of the Three Cows which settled a dispute about pasture rights in 1375 and which is still respected; and the timber industry mirroring that of the Chemin de la Mâture in France. The wood extracted was destined for the respective navies of the two countries.

In the evening in the hotel I look at my e-mail. The only message that matters is from a bookshop: they have just received the new corrected Prames guide to the Senda.

Isaba to Zuriza

The Senda descends past a little roadside chapel and along a wooded valley into a gorge. I spot a side path and follow it down to the river. At some stage the access must have been better organised, but now the boardwalk resembles the wreckage of a raft cast up on the rocks. I tread warily on the rotting lattice, climb a doubtful ladder making sure to keep my feet to the sides, and then simply sit on the river bank, contemplating the water pouring over the Cascada de Belabarze into its turquoise pool.

Back on the Senda, it is not long before the path acquires paving stones and the trees open out into a long valley, pasture trapped above the bottleneck gorge. Keeping my head down under the edge of the forest, I look out at the river meandering from side to side, measuring my progress by the regularly spaced granges, still in use: *borda de* Francisco Mayo, Valentín, Dronda, Francho, Esanoi, Paletas, Esparz, Txibarro. The grass is short but I can't see any sheep. In fact, in some places the grass is completely missing. These rectangles have exchanged fresh air and sheep for urban pollution and a lawn-mower.

Suddenly there is an explosion of noise which quickly resolves into bells and breaking twigs. A herd of sheep hiding from the sun like me comes careening round the corner, splitting into two streams to avoid me, and then stops abruptly. The heads go down and the munching starts again. Clean-cut, they are wearing fleece on their backs like a judge's wig, their bellies close-shaved. This used to be Camille's larder, raided when he got tired of French lamb; Neré was seen in the area a few days ago. By the end of this year Neré will have struck eighteen times, killing twenty-five sheep.

I have just entered bear country. I would like to see one, *I think*. As long as it isn't too close. But the chances are slim. Nowadays *'L'homme qui a vu l'ours* – the man who saw the bear' has a quasi-mystical status. (It isn't a question of *a* bear, any representative of the species, but *the*, an individual.) Since the reintroduction of bears from Slovenia in 1996 all encounters with these aliens and their local relatives have been logged; most of the eyewitnesses are walkers, shepherds, or staff from the Brown Bear Network which looks after them. The 523 observations in France have been analysed in detail. In 414 cases the bear simply went away peacefully. Only eleven cases of aggression are recorded, and in every instance it was a female accompanied by cubs and surprised at a short distance. The typical tactic was to charge to demonstrate her potential and then flee. Close encounters of the fourth kind are unknown.

Leaving the sheep behind in their blissful ignorance, I climb to the Arguibiela pass. Unexpectedly, real mountains appear on the other side of the valley in front of me. The hills have been getting progressively higher, but here the vertical scale has been exaggerated. This is where Navarre ends and Aragon starts. I'd expected it to be a mere administrative convenience but it's like stepping into a different land. Running all along one side of the long valley, the melodramatic white cliffs of the Sierra d'Alano should be a border wall.

Below, near the river, Zuriza looks very different to the villages of the last few days. For a start it is laid out on a grid with a score of houses and bungalows, a hotel, a hostel, a restaurant, a bar, a swimming pool, a supermarket, and – almost incidentally though this is officially a campsite – some tents. There must be 200 inhabitants, most of whom are sunning themselves. I have entered the kingdom of leisure, at least for an afternoon. At the same time I have left the kingdom of double-barrelled toponyms behind, at least as far as road signs are concerned.

I check out the dormitory, and take a 64-bed siesta. Afterwards, in the bar, I meet an American couple who are heading in the opposite direction. They ask me about the route but when it comes to describing the walking between Isaba and Ochagavía my mind goes blank. I hesitate, embarrassed, trying to summon up some fragment of useful information. I think I must have sunstroke until I remember the greenness of the Forest of Forgetting.

Jen is tall and thin, with tidy hair and a big smile; Brew is shorter, with a perfectly trimmed beard. Suspiciously clean and fresh for walkers who have come all the way from the Mediterranean. They must be reading my thoughts: Brew explains that they have been off-trail for three weeks. They hope to complete the Senda in a total of 30 days, finishing the section that took me nearly two weeks in under one. I suppress my scepticism: if they can do that they must live on a different planet. And I think no more about it until I look at a blog the following winter and chance upon a picture of them at Sorogain.

Following the links, I discover that they do indeed live on a different planet. Jen is the world record holder – not just the women's record holder – for through-hiking the Appalachian Trail. Brew was the support team.

As for my prospects for tomorrow, the receptionist tells me about a shepherd's hut at Aguas Tuertas, though she doesn't know if it is open.

I saunter up the valley and dandle my feet in the river, taking pictures of the mountains as the first clouds start sticking to their tops. Two men are coming along the track from the east, obvious *Senderistas*. One is stocky, brown-faced, and exhausted and the other is emaciated, pale, and exhausted.

"*¡Ya está!* – That's it. You've arrived," I greet them.

They just stare at me, nodding.

"Where have you come from today?"

'Candanchú.'

I've been studying the map this afternoon. Candanchú is a good two days' walking away.

They don't look as though they belong together. They don't even look as though they belong to the same century. The stocky man reminds me of the 18th-century preacher, John Wesley, his exuberant hair flying out in all directions on a windy day. The other man is sleekly 21st-century down to his rectangular rimless glasses and black shorts.

When it is nearly time to eat, I go back to the bar. Seeing the stocky *Senderista* sitting on his own, I talk to him. Jordi tells me that he has walked from the Mediterranean but that his friend has only just joined him. The friend likes to travel light, so he doesn't have a sleeping bag, which is why they have walked so far today. By the time Òscar arrives I have already been invited to dine in the restaurant with them.

"There's a hut at Aguas Tuertas isn't there?" I ask.

"The hut was shut but you could sleep in the shed," Òscar replies.

Paths crossing

Jordi has slept outdoors four times so far, because there weren't enough hostels.

We talk about the mountains we know. They have both climbed most of the Catalan summits from the south, just as I have climbed them from the north. I stayed in the Refuge de la Carança a few days before Òscar earlier this year.

When it comes to ordering, I discover that Òscar eats everything except meat and Jordi eats everything except gluten. They order a bottle of *crianza* for us to share.

When the food arrives Òscar hardly eats anything. It shows. I saw him going to the shower earlier, his ribs all plainly visible.

"He doesn't eat in the day, either," says Jordi.

It turns out that Jordi is a baker by profession despite being a coeliac. Òscar is an economist for the *Generalitat* but writes ski and mountain bike guides for pleasure.

"Don't you speak Catalan?" Òscar asks me. "It's just that I live Catalan... at home, at work, on holiday. I haven't spoken so much Spanish in a long while. I have to concentrate to make sure that I'm constructing sentences correctly."

Jordi questions me about the accommodation for the next few days.

"What's Orreaga like?"

"A factory," I reply. They look blank. It is true that Orreaga is mythic, bathed in the glow of history. So I search round for something equivalent in Catalonia, adding: "Like Núria."

After a second of hesitation as Jordi tries to understand what I mean, I can see him trying to compose a polite response. I look at Òscar who is betraying similar symptoms. I have time to understand I have been disparaging about *the* icon of Catalan *excursionista* mythology. It too is surrounded by a special aura.

"But the valley is beautiful," says Jordi having finally lighted on something we can agree about.

"Yes," I echo, thankful. "The views from Noucreus and along the ridge to Puigmal are quite something."

We talk about other hostels. Òscar says: "*Los españoles no son seriosos* – the Spanish don't take things seriously – you ring them up saying you are a vegetarian but they have forgotten by the time you arrive. Catalans *are* serious."

When we have finished eating Jordi offers me a Patxaran sloe-flavoured liqueur, but I have to go to bed to get some sleep in.

Zuriza to Aguas Tuertas

The first two huts are structurally unsound, the third even more dangerous, the fourth full of cow shit and although the fifth hut is just about plausible it is still too early. So by the time I am climbing the final slope up to Aguas Tuertas I am none too optimistic.

When I left Zuriza this morning, the moon was full so I didn't need my head torch. By the time I reached the first of the huts the sun had just started stroking the Sierra d'Alano in glorious pink. There is no wind, no clouds, nobody, only me and the path.

Just before the pass at the Cuello Petraficha something astonishing happens. Bells, bleating, then the leaders coming over the horizon. One thread, two threads, splitting into five, six. I sit down to watch. Long threads of sheep moving briskly head-to-tail across the top of the valley, making for the other side and the last of the dew. A simple but fascinating everyday rural story. They keep on coming but I ought to get moving again. As I climb the hill I can see further back. The denouement is still coming over the ridge, in a single line half a kilometre long. Sheep spin a good yarn.

It seems like a timeless choreography, but the reintroduction of brown bears in France has changed the tempo; the frontier is no barrier. If too many sheep are killed, carefree flocks like this could soon disappear. In any case the management of the hills is going to change. At present no shepherds watch over these sheep. They are not corralled into enclosures at night. Nor guarded by a *patou*.

Patous used to be a familiar sight in the Pyrenees and are making a comeback, though not apparently here. Superb dogs with long white hair, twice the size of a sheep when fully grown, they are brought up with lambs. As puppies they can be seen nestling up to the mother sheep side by side with the suckling lambs. If the training is done properly a *patou* receives minimal affection from the shepherd and nobody else will be allowed to approach him. As a result he will become suspicious of other people and other animals. He will bond with *his* flock and will defend it against a bear. If it came to

Paths crossing

Sierra d'Alano seen from near the Cuello Petraficha

a fight he would lose but mostly it doesn't come to that because the bear prefers easier pickings, berries for example.

Patous and all this extra care mean extra costs. Some are obvious; others less so. Corralling sheep at night means that they miss out on their main meals. Breakfast and supper, normally leisurely banquets in the cool of the day, become snacks grabbed as they commute to and from the pasture, often far away. On the other hand, the presence of a shepherd means that diseases – by far and away the main cause of losses in the *estive* – are minimised. If the economic balance is too negative, the sheep and these open pastures will disappear.

The pass marks a distinct geological fault. Now I am treading on purple conglomerate plum pudding. On the slopes the layers are less well stirred: interleaved, alternating white and purple steps. A few minutes later I meet a couple of day-walkers out to climb Planta Tortiella. While we are talking the man stops me and points to the hill.

"*¡Sarrios!*"

Cows in the valley above La Cantina

I guess that it must be some kind of animal.
"I can't see them."
"There, in the rocks. Look along my arm."
I peer in the direction he is pointing.
"I can't see them. Can you take a photo for me? Then I'll be able to look at it later."

The Refugio del Sabucar is occupied by two cows. In Guarrinza one building, labelled La Cantina on my map, looks promising. The door has been broken down but the inside is homely. Wooden panelling, bunk beds with dirty mattresses, a chimney, and even a bar, though all the bottles are empty and some are broken. I suppose it was the canteen for the squaddies stationed here. If I don't find anything further along I'll come back.

As Òscar said, the door of the Aguas Tuertas hut is firmly shut; when I try the handle it comes off. But I slot the rod back into the hole, turn the handle more carefully, push hard, and the door opens. Like the hut at the Collado de Aritxulegui everything inside is made of concrete. I will have to sleep on the floor. The Cantina would be more comfortable but it is too far to go back.

I spend a long while grazing – like the cows outside – and examining my feet. Sitting on the doorstep, I chat with day-trippers and then go in search of a spring high up on the other side of the river, as indicated by the staff in Zuriza. At the spring a little pool has been created by prising rocks out of the hillside, the unexpected gift of some anonymous shepherd.

The valley, viewed from my perch, is one of those unmistakable geological features: a glacial hanging valley, its exit blocked by a volcano of harder rock. The river above the plug is unreasonably meandering. (Aguas Tuertas is probably a variant on Aigüestortes (twisted waters), like the national park further east.) The subsoil where it shows in the banks of the river is a deep purple, the river itself rusty. The pasture is unreasonably flat and unreasonably green. The surrounding mountains add drama: a Pyrenean idyll.

The mist rolls in from the other end of the valley, catching on the horns of the cows but leaving the hills visible. I retreat to my hut and look at the photos of the *sarrios* on my camera. Blown up, they are easy to distinguish, all eleven of them. We call them *isards* – the Pyrenean relative of the *chamois*.

I sleep fine despite the hard floor, the pain in my feet, and the wind rattling the corrugated iron roof. I am particularly grateful for the detachable door handle.

Aguas Tuertas to Candanchú

The pleasure of being an itinerant is that each day is bright with the prospect of arrival and a different sunset. But it also contains the melancholy of departure. Shuttled between dawn and dusk, the Senda has wrapped me in its cloth. It has literally transported me from the ocean into the first mountains and metaphorically into a different land. In French it is known as *dépaysement* – the state of being elsewhere. In English it is known as the 'Lone Enraptured Male'.

But it is time to go back. I could continue for a few days more, but after Candanchú, crossing over to France becomes difficult. So this evening I will be heading home. The tension between morning and evening is stronger than ever.

Footprints on the mountains

The mist has cleared overnight. After breakfast by firelight I step outside the hut and almost squash a fire salamander. Above, Venus is just rising; the bull is already at work.

At the other end of the valley the Swiss roll geology is again lit up a joyous pink, but the clouds are menacing. I push on quickly over the pass as the clouds thicken and the first clap of thunder sounds to the south, but on the way down to the silvery Ibón d'Estanés, the very first lake on the Senda, the heavens stabilise. The campers on the shore are just getting up. The *marmottes*, on the other hand, are still in bed: many burrows line the sides of the path but no whistles are to be heard.

Various people say hello and I chat with a group of Basques who know Ituren. Then the path descends, slipping clandestinely into France and out again to the ski resort of Candanchú and its charmless out-of-season scarred landscape.

I hitch to Canfranc with the Basques. At the train station, a passer-by can't resist sharing his excitement with me: "*¿Es maravillosa, no?* - It's marvellous,

Pico Alto de la Portaza

isn't it?" I agree with him, but really it defies adjectives. Magnificent and monstrous would apply equally. Or simply big. Counting the windows and multiplying up I soon arrive at more than 300. I have the impression that the architect just kept on going adding identical modules until he ran out of ink.

At one end of the building there is a train, Hornby Dublo-sized in comparison. Having established that it will be stationed there for the foreseeable future I try to break into the building itself – enticing glimpses of art-deco are visible through the windows – but it is protected by a high wire fence and I have left my jemmy at home.

Imagine a mainline station rewritten as a fairy-tale, plucked out of central Paris by Google Earth and redeposited in a narrow mountain valley. Zoom in. It must be one of the biggest stations in Europe, but instead of serving some metropolis it now serves a village. Instead of the 2,000 railway workers initially planned there are just four.

It looks like something Franco would have created, but actually it was inaugurated in 1928. Originally it was designed to cater for international traffic through a tunnel under the nearby Somport pass. But apart from during the Second World War, when it was used to secretly pass Nazi gold in one direction and tungsten in the other, the line was never economic. When a bridge on the French side was damaged in 1970 the cross-border part of the line was closed.

The sad little train I have seen waiting in the station still climbs hopefully every day up to Canfranc but it is always disappointed. It will wait in vain for the fleeting kiss it used to share with its French soulmate. I'm not going to say anything that might upset it but they were clearly incompatible. The French system runs on tracks 1.43m apart with the Spanish on 1.66m. Which accounts for this mountain assignation, the phantom 2,000 workers, and the economic nonsense of the line. Everything had to be transferred. As far as trains were concerned, until the recent opening of the high speed link between Perpignan and Barcelona, the Pyrenees really were a barrier.

The station is just one of several monuments to the failure to create a viable crossing. The first attempt to negotiate *Summum Portus* (hence Somport) was by the Romans. A thousand years later, pilgrims gave the pass a new lease of life as the only Way of St James coming from France that avoided those nasty Basques. Then came the railway tunnel and finally, at the beginning of the third millennium, the road tunnel. The road is one of those ideas that looks great on paper, linking Toulouse directly with Madrid, but in practice most of the traffic on the tortuous route goes no further than the foothills.

My attempted burglary having failed, I walk to the entrance of the road tunnel and again use that much under-rated second millennium form of conveyance. Within twenty minutes I am being driven through the Somport tunnel and past the entrance to the Chemin de la Mâture on my way back home.

Water, snow, ice

Winter of discontent

November. Suddenly, I have a new spring in my step. Bad news. My left knee clicks and then springs as I walk. I'm not even in the mountains. Over the next few days I pay more attention. A definite clicking with every step, though it doesn't hurt. Bones catching against each other? Surely not.

A week later, crossing the Passeig de Gràcia in Barcelona, my leg collapses under me. My knees hit the tarmac, hard. I am lying in the road surrounded by hooting traffic, listening to the crocodile of time snapping at my heels.

December. My doctor sends me for a scan. Damaged meniscus. Surgery.

January. The surgeon says inoperable. The cartilage is also damaged. If he tidies up the meniscus I really will have two bones knocking against each other. He recommends hydraulic acid.

When I report this to a friend, she says: "Not hydraulic acid, hyaluronic acid. Botox."

Finally the knees which won the Boy Scout Knobbly Knee Kontest will have the beauty treatment they always craved.

February. I go to see a rheumatologist for my injections.

"Bend your knee," she says authoritatively. I do so easily.

"100%," she notes, pursing her mouth.

I can guess what she is thinking.

"If I can't do 20km and 1000m of climbing it doesn't count."

"Keep on walking," the doctor advises, "but stick to even surfaces. It is treading on pebbles and uneven rocks which does the damage."

Pointing to the book I have taken to read in the waiting room, she says: "The Way of St James would be better than the Pyrenees".

After the injection of 'Go-On' I ask if I can walk the two kilometres into town.

Footprints on the mountains

"It's a long way you know," says the doctor.
"Not really," I reply.
"You must catch the bus."

Following the visit to the rheumatologist, I double dig the garden, and then start walking again, testing. After two months I reach Carcassonne. I have never walked so far since I was a Scout. In the week before my departure, I fill my rucksack with ten litres of water and climb the mountain behind my village at dawn every day.

The second part of my preparations wasn't part of the plan either. It consists of a fleece, gloves, crampons, and an ice-axe. After fifteen years of walking twice a month in the Pyrenees, I thought I knew what to expect. By 22 June the snow will be gone. Will I even need long trousers? But the 'once-a-century' winter has changed everything.

I have little experience of using crampons. So I prepare by watching videos and practising secretly when Veronica is out of the house. I put a fluffy snow-white towel on the bedroom floor, lie on my back ice-axe in hand, and shut my eyes. I'm slipping down an icy slope, out of control. I grip the axe tightly, stick the pick end into the towel and, as my speed increases, find myself pulled violently over onto my chest. I raise myself up with the ice-axe firmly implanted in the towel, balancing on my knees so that my crampons don't stick in. It works perfectly.

The third part of my plan is to take my weight more seriously. I have put on eight kilograms over the last ten years. It just so happens that this is nearly the weight of my rucksack when full. If I can lose all that fat before the summer, I won't notice the weight on my back.

Thinking about my weight has also made me reconsider the contents of my rucksack: what should go in, what can be left out, and above all how to measure it. It is the culmination of a process started many years ago when I first began walking in the Pyrenees. At that time I was impressed by those hikers with colossal sacks on their backs, overflowing with tents and foam mattresses, dripping accessories. They were my heroes. In order to walk day after day in the mountains, you had to be strong. The more they carried the more heroic they were. I built up my muscles. I too flaunted a giant rucksack.

Later, I started going on walks with professional guides. Their minimalist rucksacks were much smaller than mine and not even full. I started weighing my toothbrush. I replaced water with water purifying tablets, bought an ultralight rucksack, and halved the weight on my back. But how far could I go? What equipment was really necessary?

How long could I survive with a broken leg in the hope that someone would stumble across me? A sleeping bag would add twelve hours. A tent another twenty-four. I decided to put twelve hours in my rucksack and no more.

For several years that was my philosophy. What went into the rucksack was measured in survival-hours. But then I read the immortal Jean-Christophe Ruffin. The contents of a rucksack, he claims, should be measured not in grams, not in hours, but in terms of fear. When you weigh your rucksack you are not only weighing the things it contains. You are also subconsciously weighing up your fears.

With this in mind, fear suddenly becomes measurable on the kitchen scales. That fleece corresponds to 574g of cold fear. That first aid kit: accident (246g). That mp3 player: boredom (45g).

Fear-grams have become my unit of choice.

Not stopping at my rucksack, I realise that the philosophy can be transferred to life beyond the trail. Do I really need all those possessions? What am I afraid of? I go through the house systematically discarding anything unused in the last ten years. The effect is so radical that Veronica asks me what I am doing and I am obliged to explain. She asks me if she is part of the unwanted baggage.

Canfranc to Candanchú

By June I have shed six kilograms in body weight but the prospect of snow has added 1526 fear-grams to the load on my back.

As the day of departure approaches I keep checking the webcams at the hostels. Vast areas of white. On the first of June, the ski resorts at Porté-Puymorens and Artouste *reopen*. The snow is not melting. What about the day between Góriz and Pineta? According to all accounts the path is impressively steep even when dry. And with snow?

On the day itself, the train is full of rucksacks: the annual pilgrimage to the Pyrenees has started. The guard informs us that the train will be terminating at Lourdes, not for benediction but because the track beyond has been damaged by flooding.

Sometime later that afternoon I am sitting on the terrace of a café in Canfranc-Estación under a parasol, hiding from the scorching sun. It is difficult to believe that snow could be a problem.

Ordering an ice-cream and looking around I notice that Canfranc has none of the seedy ambivalence of a frontier town. La Jonquera, further along the Pyrenees, hosts emporia selling cut-price cigarettes, car parks, and traffic jams. Here there is hardly any traffic at all, just quiet cafés.

But it wasn't always like this. In the Second World War, after the Nazis took over running the station, Canfranc resembled 'Casablanca', the film. Rick's café had its twin in the Fonda Marraco. At one table you would find Albert Le Lay, a hybrid of Rick and Victor Lazlo. At another Mariano Aso, head of Customs, playing Captain Renault. Spies, Jews escaping persecution, pilots shot down in France, Resistance agents, they all passed through.

Now, nobody passes through Canfranc-Estación. The new road tunnel avoids it completely. In summer the only tourists seem to be walkers and people visiting the railway station.

I start to walk to Candanchú where I left off last year but only get as far as the col de Ladrones. Unfortunately somebody has filched the path; so I hitch-hike.

"We're not going to Candanchú," says the driver of the very first car that comes by, "but we'll take you anyway."

They drop me at the edge of the village, leaving me to walk through the dismally empty tower blocks built for skiers. I look up, scanning the windows for signs of life. Is that a modern Themroc lifting a sledgehammer? How long would the walls resist his troglodytic conversion? Would Michel Piccoli like to star again?

In the middle of this monotony, one building stands out from the crowd: a chalet, one of the relics of the earliest days of skiing, opened in the winter of 1934/5. The president of the French Ski Federation in his inaugural address went as far as to claim: "*Ya hay Pirineos* – Now the Pyrenees exist".

Yet another Frenchman appropriating the Pyrenees! I review the list of propagandists: Ramond de Carbonnières, Russell, Packe, Schrader, Brulle,

Water, snow, ice

Tchihatchef, Franqueville etc. The 19th century was full of them. Not one of them is Spanish.

The only Spaniard ever to get a mention is Vincente de Herida for the maps he drew of the border, along with his French counterpart, Junker. He may even have climbed Monte Perdido – the famous 'lost' mountain – a decade before Ramond. But records are sparse and his legacy surprisingly small. It is almost as if he never existed.

Turning away from the chalet, I walk up to the huge, empty car park. The valley is wider here and the snow on the peaks visible. I put on another layer.

Back in the village, the Aguila hostel is one of the very few businesses open. I am the only hiker this evening, though a group of German photographers has been staying for several nights.

Later, as the chef offers me a glass of Patxaran to round off my dinner, we chat. I am the first, he tells me. Normally he would have seen dozens by now, but nobody is walking the Senda this year. Will there be snow? Will I need crampons? Yes, on both counts. But I won't be alone to start with. The Canal Roya is where you go on a Sunday.

Candanchú to Sallent de Gállego

I put on my crampons, unfasten my ice axe, and step onto the slope, still icy from the night. Within a few steps I have caught one of the crampons in my trouser leg and tripped over. I have practised how to fall on snow and how to self-arrest but not how to walk. The chef was wrong: I am alone.

Much to my surprise, I had spent the night in the company of two Capuchin nuns. They had arrived very late and finding nobody still up had knocked on my door. They were a little shy at first but the bottle of Patxaran helped and things were just beginning to get improbably interesting when I woke up.

After breakfast I tell the chef I will ring from Sallent to let him know the conditions. A few minutes later, stepping out of the hostel I am still hazy, as is the atmosphere, but there isn't too much wadding in the enveloping cloud.

However, the greyness persists, so it is not the scenery which attracts my attention but some graffiti on an isolated building: 'ARAMÓN YE NAZIÓN' accompanied by an anarchist (A). The language is Aragonés. Aramón is an expanding skiing company hovering like a vulture over the struggling Candanchú site. The company is talking about linking Candanchú to Formigal, thus creating the largest resort in the Pyrenees and cutting through an important wildlife corridor. Beware: *Aramón* is invading. Indeed, one of the reasons I have chosen the Canal Roya today is to reduce the time spent in areas blighted by ski infrastructure. Today, I'm an anarchist.

In a clearing in the Canal Roya I crane my neck at an impressive chimney, the last remaining element of a forge. Red (*roya*) in the name means iron in the rocks. Factory workers here made combs, knives, and buttons. There was a *venta* for travellers. There were no trees at that time, now there is little else.

The path has become a track heading cautiously up the valley. It's a classic walk but I've yet to see anybody, never mind the predicted hordes of day-trippers. So the edge of the dark forest is a revelation, a classic glacial valley of lush mountain pasture speckled with buttercups, blue gentians, and white asphodel, sparsely populated by cows. Bucolic, except for the river: an angry torrent sweeping under the bridge, its white teeth chomping at the banks.

Finally the cloud starts to lift and I see two walkers on the opposite side of the valley. They cross the river at a second bridge and our paths converge. A rush of relief surges through me. Carlos and Carlos are going to climb the Anayet following the Senda as far as the *ibones* (lakes). They are half my age so I have to walk rather fast in order to keep up with them. We cross various snow drifts and arrive at the end of the valley. Ahead, the path disappears into a wall of snow: it looks dauntingly steep and very white.

On the last of the flat, three men are just finishing packing up their tents before going back down the valley.

"We tried to go up to the lakes yesterday," one of them tells us. "We got to about twenty minutes from the top but it was too steep and we had to come back down." He pauses. "*Tenía miedo. No tengo cojones* – I was afraid. I don't have the balls," he smiles, putting a hand to his throat to show us where they are now.

"Do you have crampons?" I ask.

"No. With crampons, no problem."

Carlos and Carlos have a hurried discussion. They decide to look more closely so we continue to the edge of the snow. We meet a couple who have just turned back. Carlos and Carlos, not having crampons, turn back as well.

Alone then. After my false start catching my crampons, I tuck my trousers into my socks, turn out my toes, and walk up the icy slope like a duck, keeping my feet well apart. I aim for the nearest patch of heather, pull myself onto it and trampoline up the mattress. The slope gets steeper, the heather thicker and I'm not sure if crampons help. Now, the ice looks a better bet. I zigzag, stamping into the crust with each step, which I should have been doing all along. I take a break on an outcrop of dull purple rock. Down below Carlos and Carlos are fast-disappearing specks.

The next section turns out to be relatively easy – perhaps I have stumbled on a better route than the others – with patches of *gispet* grass, still grey after the months under the snow, to take advantage of. Even so, by the time I arrive at the top I am trembling. I remember the spin dryer from last year. Thankfully nobody turned it on.

I sit down carelessly, just missing an oxlip. The area is not as empty as I had thought. Some walkers are descending from one of the ragged peaks which surround the volcanic plateau. Others are criss-crossing the snowy plateau. A far-off figure with an optimistic fishing rod is dipping into blue crescents – when the snow melts this hanging valley must look just like Aguas Tuertas. Beyond, to the north, I can make out the Pic du Midi d'Ossau, also volcanic. The clouds have all-but disappeared.

I put my black fleece on over my anorak to be warmed by the radiant sun, and sit down on a rock. Two walkers come up behind me. They've been following me all the way from the Canal Roya though I didn't know it. With crampons, of course. All the others must have come from Formigal, where I'm heading.

Sauntering across to the other end of the plateau I look over the edge and see a string of walkers, some going up, others already going down. I can see from the way they are tottering across the snow like two-year-olds that they don't have crampons, but I'm not going to take mine off. I strut past them.

Below the snowline, the path is a purple slit in the grey grass. Lower still, the river is in full spate, crashing over the rocks but also meandering lazily across the flatter pasture and its marsh marigolds.

I race through the deserted ski lifts at Culivillas and along a road to the village of Formigal, walking ever faster to eclipse the boredom. The grass on the other side of the valley is an unnatural velvety green, unnaturally even, and unnaturally weed-free, like artificial turf. It has been cleaned up, I suppose for the purposes of skiing. But why isn't the Senda over there instead of here on this dull road?

Aramón has been unrolling its carpet in the Gállego valley. The lifts have a capacity of 30,000 skiers per hour. For a ski resort it's surprisingly unscarred, although the infrastructure at Formigal is less attractive.

To be fair, Aramón is not some wicked capitalist stepmother who has beguiled an ageing widower in order to steal the family treasure. She is the offspring of the marriage of the Aragon government and the bank Ibercaja. She doesn't only fill her coffers with the white gold of skiing; she also provides employment. The population of the valley increased by 50% (to 1522) in the first decade of the 21st century, as did the number of buildings. Average wages doubled!

But some things seem to have been forgotten in this new Klondike. Like shit. At the end of the decade all the waste water from Formigal was still going directly into the River Gállego.

The landscape is being transformed. Again, I say to myself. Since the last glaciation the main agents have been sheep and cows. By the way, where are the sheep?

Once it has bypassed Formigal and its apartment blocks, pizzerias, and petrol station, the Senda finally leaves the road and cuts over a hill to Sallent de Gállego. Viewed from the top, Sallent is all higgledy-piggledy grey slate roofs with terraced fields beyond, small green parcels beribboned with dark hedges. Everything is on a different scale. Sallent is for *people*; Formigal is for the *masses*.

I've arranged to meet Phil here and have booked the Hotel Almud on his suggestion. The coat of arms above the door sets the tone. The interior décor corresponds: comfortable antique furniture, ornate candlesticks, glass-topped tables displaying rusty keys and locks, and elaborate carpets. I take my boots off. Sitting behind the reception desk, Maria-José isn't at all disturbed by my appearance. Phil won't arrive until tomorrow morning, she tells me.

In the early evening I go out for a walk around the village. The houses are built in stone: grey, grey-pink but mostly honey-coloured. Looking up, I spot a chimney equipped with a medieval burglar alarm – *espantabrujas*, fancy finials said to scare witches.

Not everything fits into this traditional framework: like the monstrous painting of a fat butcher with a huge meat cleaver and a sinister expression in the process of massacring a large ham, on the shutters of a shop unconvincingly labelled *'Tu carnicero amigo* – your friendly butcher'. Or indeed, just around the corner, a wall painted bright blue in a mock-cubist representation of a ruined megalithic city. Although the effect is three-dimensional the wall is flat. Except, that is, for the plastic excrescences bolted to the surface. A notice insists that users must be members of a mountaineering club but safety features are not much in evidence.

When the time comes to eat I go down in my walking socks, thinking that the restaurant is in the same building. But María-José tells me and the other guests to follow her, speeding off down the road. I have to rush out behind them, and try to keep up but the restaurant is several streets away. The other guests don't say anything when I limp in but nor do they invite me to their table. I have great hopes having seen posters for milk-fed lamb, a local speciality, but it is not on offer. We get steak and *crisps*.

Sallent de Gállego to Respomuso

I first contacted Phil a month ago because he lives near Sallent all year round. Could he tell me what the conditions are like? He did even better. Come and join us for a couple of days, he replied.

I go down to breakfast wearing two pairs of socks this time, just in case. The other walkers in my group all arrived late yesterday evening, well after I'd gone to bed. Phil appears with a smile and four other guides. We are only six walkers; why so many guides?

"Change of programme," says Phil. "We're not going to the Ibones de Arriel because it's too dangerous. Too much snow."

We pile into various vehicles and are driven to the top end of the Sarra dam. I'm a little disappointed that this will skip three kilometres of the Senda and also miss the waterfall from which Sallent takes its name, but I'm not about to complain.

The walk starts with introductions and a group photo. Afterwards I inspect the notice erected on the other side of the bridge by the Aragon government:

> The Pyrenean glaciers constitute the most southerly examples of ice in Europe… the singularity and fragility of these small but immensely beautiful relics of the Ice Age makes them of great scientific, environmental, cultural, and landscape interest.

The banality of the description leaves me completely unprepared for the next earth-shattering sentence: 'The glaciers are protected by law No. 2/1990 of 21 March.' It appears that the Aragon government has found the solution to global warming.

The path is well trodden, passing through shady forest. Phil indicates the flowers: "Normally on this route people are not that interested. But on the lower level walks they are always asking. I'm compiling a booklet."

He points warily at a *grasilla* (*Pinguicula vulgaris*), a carnivorous plant clinging to a rock. He is less timid with a wild rose hip. "The locals call it *tapaculo*. It's supposed to cure diarrhoea." The locals have a sense of humour. *Tapa* means 'cork'. He doesn't need to explain what *culo* means.

"I found a viper last week," Phil continues. "It was cold so the viper was lethargic and didn't slither away like they usually do. I was really excited to be able to take a photo but nobody else was very keen."

We walkers are a mixed bunch. Three sporty friends have flown in from Guernsey: Claire and Martine have recently climbed Kilimanjaro but John is more at ease on a surfboard than a mountain. Following them is a man with a thick Scottish accent who claims to be a New Zealander, and his wife.

"I left the kiwis at the age of five months," Colin explains, "on the first ship bringing refugees home, in September 1945. I lived in Scotland until I retired and then went back."

That makes him nine years older than me, at an age where the years really begin to count. Normally he and his wife Lynn walk on spongy Middle Earth tracks on North Island. This will be a challenge, he says.

We arrive at the first patch of sloping snow. I unhook my ice axe from my sack though nobody else bothers.

"Are you alright?" asks Claire.

Water, snow, ice

We cross several more patches of snow, the last remnants of winter avalanches.

That's the dilemma of the Respomuso hostel, Arkaitz, one of the local guides, tells us. All the paths to it cross avalanche zones. If walkers ring up, the managers are often obliged to turn them away, but their contract with the FAM (the Aragon Mountaineering Club) obliges them to stay open all year. One winter the avalanches even engulfed the hostel itself and the managers had to be evacuated.

Someone asks what the river is called. "Aguas Limpias," says Hannah. "It means clear waters." Not after it's been through Sallent.

My knee has started clicking again. I don't mention that either.

We arrive at the hostel under a blazing sun, but despite that and the date – 24 June, officially summer – we meet two skiers just outside. An Alsatian dog, having investigated the skiers, comes up to sniff at me. The only time I was ever bitten it was an Alsatian. I back away.

"He's just doing his job, checking out how you smell," explains Arkaitz. "He's the hostel's mountain rescue dog."

I recall my physiotherapist's story of a woman who slithered 300m down a snowy mountain. By the time the search party arrived with their dogs later that same day only the bones were left: she had been eaten by vultures.

I ask what's in store for us.

"It isn't more difficult with the snow. You just have to adapt," Arkaitz claims.

"In guide training," Hannah adds, "they note how well you adjust to the situation. You can't just say 'I did it like this last time, so I'll do it the same way again.'"

"How many guides would you normally have?" I ask her.

"Just me," she replies brightly. "And Arkaitz when there's snow."

The other guides have come to learn the route or practise techniques.

Phil sketches in his background in the Scout movement where he got his first mountain guide qualifications. He and his wife Anna started the business in 2008. They wanted to live in the Pyrenees, not London.

"I put the website online and somebody rang the same day. I had to bluff my way through the booking process."

I select a pair of sandals provided by the hostel and take off my boots.

Footprints on the mountains

View from the Respomuso hostel

My feet are playing up: hardly surprising with twice the normal number of socks.

The others go off for the afternoon to learn ice techniques. I want to conserve my strength so I only take a short walk to a nearby lake.

Suddenly I hear a whistle. At first I can't see where it is coming from but I then locate a silhouette at the other end of the lake. An animal walking with all four legs stretched out as long as possible, like a cat on a hot tin roof: It must be a *marmotte*. Normally *marmottes* hug the ground. Normally they don't find their world still frozen when they come out of hibernation.

The *marmotte* is sensibly keeping to the edges. In the middle, the ice looks like a smashed window pane. Mini icebergs have detached themselves and are spreading imperceptibly across the vivid turquoise surface.

Back at the hostel the dials on the barometer indicate an atmospheric pressure off the top of the scale. Good weather for the foreseeable future then. The hostel manager goes down to the dam carrying a fishing rod. He doesn't stay long; a saw would have been more useful.

The others come back just before dinner and while eating we learn more about our guides. Arkaitz spends much of his time working in Antarctica, ensuring the safety of the scientists when they venture out of the huts. Claire asks what he does on his holidays. Travels to climb, is the reply. He goes to a cliff, climbs it, and then comes back again. When he is not doing that he takes part in climbing competitions. You have a choice of routes, each worth a certain number of points. You climb as many as you can in a specific time and the team with the most points wins.

"You're mad," concludes Claire.

He's modest about his skills, as are the other guides, but it quickly becomes clear that they are all seriously overqualified for this outing.

In the dormitory later it is a question of who will sleep next to whom: the beds sleep five people side-by-side.

John is next to Claire.

"I might turn over and kiss you in the night," he says. She pretends to be horrified.

"By mistake," he adds.

Colin points out that he is on the other side.

"If you kiss me," he says seriously, "just remember: *no tongue*."

Respomuso to Baños de Panticosa

The next morning Colin comes down to breakfast visibly in a state of confusion. He is wearing a bright-blue pair of what must be Lynn's leggings under a pair of beige shorts, and a burgundy red tee-shirt. But his clothing is the only thing which is bright. He looks glum, eyes half shut.

"I didn't sleep a wink. In fact, I've never slept so badly in all my life," he confirms. "I'm really tired. But if I don't do it now I never will."

He notices me looking at his legs.

"I haven't brought any long trousers," he smiles.

As we are packing our rucksacks Claire looks at me strangely and says:

"Are you alright?"

"Yes," I reply.

"Do you want to do your own thing, or tag along with us?" Hannah asks me.

Footprints on the mountains

"Tag along if that's OK."

We put on our crampons after a few minutes' walking and don't take them off again until we are in sight of the new Bachimaña hostel, late in the afternoon. The ascent to the Col de Tebarray is hard work, even in the few places equipped with footprints. The snow is icy and the crampons don't grip well, but being roped-up takes the fear out of it. At first Colin struggles but then he summons up strength from who knows where.

We take a rest by a small lake and look around. It is a harsh landscape, duotone, only one colour permitted – blue – in the fissured surfaces of the ice-locked lake. The few other colours are artificial: the vivid reds and greens of tee-shirts and trousers, the orange climbing harnesses.

At the pass we take a break. Hannah asks me: "Would you have done that if you were on your own?"

"No," I reply.

Then my rucksack explodes as I am repacking it. Less dramatically than the last time, but it's more difficult to fix. I'm going to need a new frame.

"Have you got some Duck tape?" Hannah asks in a matter-of-fact way.

This is the one thing every serious walker has. I don't. She extracts some from her sack.

After the pass everything changes. The descent is a joyful romp, circumnavigating turquoise lakes still blockaded by icebergs, gambolling like newborn lambs down the slopes. The snow has softened up; almost slush in places, pink with algae. Inexplicably, Claire keeps slipping and falling over, but she doesn't injure herself and just gets on with it. I look at us, six walkers tied to the guides two by two. Gulliver pulling ships behind him.

At the second pass, following Claire's instructions, John takes off his tee-shirt and rolls in the snow for a photograph. We also snap the Glaciar del Infierno (Glacier of Hell) before it disappears, victim of the unequal competition between the fires of the Underworld and the Government of Aragon.

At the spanking new Bachimaña hostel, whilst everybody else is taking their boots off, I ask the manager for advice. The Senda is passable, he says. He was there two days ago.

The others are staying here and having a day's rest tomorrow before attacking more mountains. But I am going on to the hostel in the Baños de Panticosa, down in the valley, accompanied by Arkaitz who is going home

Water, snow, ice

for the night. We pass a couple of *sarrios* bounding across the snow and a sign warning of avalanches, all the more convincing for being half-buried in a drift, bent over by the weight of the snow which hit it. The principal access to the Bachimaña hostel, like that of Respomuso, is not to be recommended in winter.

Dropping down the valley, off the snow now, green is added to the spectrum. Then yellow: flowering gentians trumpet the arrival of spring. Here, the path shows signs of deliberate maintenance. Here, the viewpoints all have balustrades, all the better to safely admire the spa facilities of the Baños below.

We stop at one of them. Somebody is repainting the cladding of a pavilion, all indulgent wood and tracery finials. Three tourists are walking past an austerely rectangular 19th-century hotel. But another building, all curves and silvery reflections, looks as though it belongs on a city computer screen rather than in a mountain valley. Then Arkaitz points out the ruins: old stone ruins which have lost their roofs and new concrete ruins which have never had them, wreathed in steel, grass, and trees.

One building doesn't fall into any of these categories. The Casa Piedra (stone house) hostel has an intact slate roof. It is old but not ruined.

"The owners of the spa don't like the hostel. Spa, casino, luxury hotel, dirty walkers. No! It was going to be replaced by Bachimaña. But the spa isn't economically viable. They never got round to knocking the Casa Piedra down."

"So now the two hostels compete against each other?"

"No. They're run by the same management."

What I can't see from my aerial viewpoint are the Roman coins found here, marking the spa's origins. Its heyday was in the 19th century; at the beginning of the 20th century Alfonso XIII came to visit. But a hundred years later 60 million euros were needed to renovate it. It was re-baptised 'Panticosa Resort' – in English. Then came the crisis.

At the hostel we sit outside on a log bench drinking beers.

"If I set out late the snow will be softer and my crampons will stick better, won't they?" I suggest.

Arkaitz looks at me doubtfully: "What do you mean by late?"

"Eight o'clock."

"I thought you meant ten. People here think eight is early... You should set out as early as possible. It's not the climbing that will be difficult but going down the other side. It faces east and will have had the sun all morning. It will be soft."

"Is it easier than what we have done today?"

"About the same, but I'm not worried. I'm not afraid for you."

He continues: "Keep to the left, don't forget. You will come to a little hut just below the dam where the pipe comes out."

Inside the hostel I ask about drying my boots and socks and am told to turn the radiator on in the dormitory. I also learn that a company of soldiers left the Baños this morning and said they would telephone with news when they arrived at Bujaruelo, the next hostel on the Senda.

Baños de Panticosa to Bujaruelo

Still wet. The socks have fallen off the radiator in the night. I stuff them into the net on my rucksack so they can dry off and put on a spare two.

The soldiers still haven't rung so the manager contacts Bujaruelo. They haven't arrived.

Crossing the deserted esplanade, I walk up the steps to an octagonal building which has seen better days. Water is flooding out of the bottom of the door. '*Fuente en rehabilitación* – spring being renovated,' claims a weather-beaten notice.

The Senda zigzags up through the forest and then out onto the open flank of the mountain. It meets up with a rusty water pipeline; then the pipeline diverges, striking off up the slope. Where the snow has melted the path is obvious; on the snow it is not even marked by footprints. At the Ibón baxo de Brazato I strap on my crampons, stamping my feet into the solid white crust. A red-and-white waymark on a rock indicates the route and I stagger up the side of the mountain. At the top I rediscover the pipeline. If I had only followed it all the way the climb would have been that much easier. Left, he said, left.

This time I stick to the pipeline, which runs through a channel carved out of the solid rock to a bunker tucked in an overhang. Five or six military kit bags lie abandoned on the floor; this must be the hut Arkaitz talked about. It is also the end of the channel so the only way forward is to climb the vertical metal ladder attached to the outside wall.

A few seconds later and I am walking along the top of the dam of the Ibón derro Brazato. The reservoir is mostly covered in snow but near the edges blue water shows through, like streams slinking in voluptuous curves across a sandy estuary. Although the colours are arranged in the same duotones as yesterday the effect is quite different. Yesterday the ice on the lakes was almost bereft of snow: sharp, angular shards of broken glass, flotsam crashing against a rocky shore. Here the reservoir is clothed in fur. Looking around, it seems that everywhere is clothed in that same white fur. Soft and sensual; but dangerous, like Venus.

Getting around to the other side is easy. You only have to follow a clear track in the snow a few metres above the surface of the reservoir. Many people – the soldiers perhaps – must have walked along the track but it continues around the edge in the wrong direction. I need to climb the snow-filled coombe without tobogganing into the water. Nobody else has.

I take a historic last photograph and turn to face the slope. It is steeper than yesterday and there are no footprints here, no rope. Here at the bottom of the slope nothing distinguishes the walker who will get to the top from the one who won't. Going straight up isn't an option, so I traverse diagonally, mentally practising a self-arrest.

I invoke Cheryl Strayed and her book, *Wild: From lost to found on the Pacific Crest Trail*. If she can walk the PCT with no experience whilst making all kinds of basic mistakes, some of which should have killed her, then…

Cheryl Strayed doesn't get me very far. She works very well on a rational plane, but that's not where I am. I need instinct. No, not instinct: action.

Left foot, right foot, ice axe. Stamp, stamp, stab. *Slower.* Always two points of contact. Stamp, stamp, stab. Get a rhythm going. Lift, stamp, lift stamp, pull stab … Turn. I don't like that. Passing the ice axe to the other hand. I don't like it on my left either. Stamp, stamp, stab…

I'm tiring but can't stop even though that would give me the reassuring stability of a three-legged stool. If I stop and let thoughts trickle into my mind I won't be able to move again, either up or down. I continue…

I'm now well above the icy water and unconvinced that a self-arrest will work: the crust here is too hard to pierce properly. A little higher and the slope starts to slacken off. I balance myself carefully, leave go of the ice axe

Looking back at the Ibón derro Brazato

and take my camera out of my pocket. At the top I collapse behind a rough stone wall and eat a snack. It is cold, but there's no wind and the sun warms my black trousers.

After eating, I traverse around what must be the Ibones altos de Brazato, though they are completely covered in snow, to the Puerto de Brazato. The Batanes valley on the other side, another glacial U, is white apart from a few slivers of iridescent blue and a few patches of grey rock. The snow is just that bit softer.

I'm beginning to appreciate what Arkaitz said about the afternoons. Even though crampons don't penetrate far in the mornings, they do stick. Now my feet keep slithering. But I'm no longer unduly concerned. Except about avalanches.

At present, walking on snow seems so much easier than walking on rock or even on grass or gravel. With crampons you – I was going to write you just slide down it, but that's not actually true – you don't. Perhaps snow is not such a bad thing.

Half way down, the valley narrows and I have to climb up above the river to avoid a cliff. I sit on a rock warmed by the sun and change my wet socks, taking my boots off carefully, remembering Cheryl Strayed again: the passage where she takes one off and then knocks it only to watch it disappear into the void.

Here, the sound of the river is deadened by its snow shroud. I have seen a few *sarrio* tracks but no animals, not even any birds. Here, there is no life except for me. Yet, this is *the* place to be. This is the centre of everything, the centre of the world. It must have been like this for Dalí who also reported once finding the centre of the world. His only mistake was to situate it in Perpignan railway station. In the men's toilets facing a urinal, according to urban legend.

By the time I reach the bottom of the barranco de Batanes the river has swollen into a torrent. It cartwheels into the river Ara at the same point as another tributary. Both are marked with a dotted line on my map, but there is nothing intermittent about them today. Whichever way I turn, I need to cross at least two rivers to get to the path on the other side.

So that's why the manager at the Casa de Piedra was more concerned by the rivers than by the snow. At the time, I didn't take in what he said. But he's right: the same storm which destroyed the railway track between Lourdes and Pau has started melting the snow.

I hurl the biggest rocks I can carry into the Batanes in the hope of creating stepping stones. But although this creates some footholds the stones have the effect of damming the river, channelling it deeper and faster. I destroy my engineering and, leaving my rucksack on the bank, test out the waters. It's too cold and uneven to take my boots off. The water comes above my knees and I have to lean into the current to maintain balance, grabbing hold of submerged rocks to avoid being swept away. But the test is conclusive. I rescue my rucksack and plough across. My feet are freezing and even wringing out my socks makes little difference. They immediately soak up the water from the boots.

There is still another river to cross, the Ara, but my map shows a bridge lower down. I can see two walkers on the path opposite but it isn't worth trying to ask them: they won't be able to hear me over the deafening waters.

This side of the river is more grass than scrub so the lack of a path isn't a handicap. Colour has returned: purple and yellow, palest blue and fluffy pink: pansy and orchid, forget-me-not and kidneyvetch. Those white golf balls in the grass – *pedos de lobo* (wolf's farts) – might be of interest to the cook at the hostel, so I pick them.

Seen from a distance, the predicted bridge looks broken in two but what I took for damage is only a washed-up tree trunk at an incongruous angle. After the bridge I think I am finally safe and have just about dried out my socks when the path crosses another dotted blue line. I count four in total, all overflowing.

At the point where the path turns into a track a trilingual sign warns walkers coming in the other direction of the risk of tumbling from a cliff. It says nothing about being able to swim. Another one explains that cattle have priority. I haven't seen any cows although the pastures look ready. Perhaps the farmers are waiting until the streams are easier to cross.

Further down the valley at the Ordiso hut two camouflaged Sanyana Land Rovers draw up. A score of squaddies emerge from the hut, finishing the packing of their colossal rucksacks. By the time I arrive they have rucksacks on their backs and machine guns slung over their shoulders carelessly pointing in my direction.

'You were at the Baños de Panticosa yesterday, weren't you?' I ask.

"Yes."

"The manager told me. I've been following you since Respomuso."

One of them wants to practice his English and asks me where I come from but before I've had time to reply he is told to get a move on. They bundle into the jeeps, guns and all, a more macho version of one of those competitions to see how many teenagers can fit into a mini.

It is a long walk down the track through forests of Scots pine, across meadows, through groves of rowan and yew trees. Then all that disappears and the Senda plunges into a maze: a forest of box, three times as tall as me, stretching vertically for light. I have arrived at Bujaruelo.

At the iconic stone bridge a fingerpost sign reads 'Baños de Panticosa: 6h30'. I have taken twice as long. Another finger points out that France is only three hours' walk away. Gavarnie is just a couple of hours further.

The path to Gavarnie is one of the classic routes over the mountains, like the St-Jean-Pied-de-Port pilgrim route. There was a customs post here and another in the valley on the other side. The alternative route runs through the gap tooth in the Pyrenean jaw at the Brèche de Roland. Six hundred metres higher, it was the smugglers' choice.

There have been several projects to improve communications, but they have come to nothing. One was a railway tunnel linking the Cirque de Gavarnie to the Ordesa valley. The hard winters of 1860–65 put an end to that idea. More recently, in 1965 the chief engineer of the province of Huesca proposed a road tunnel with an underground car park and a 1000m lift which would have rocketed tourists up to the Brèche de Roland!

Inside the hostel the four staff are pouring beer for the dozens of walkers sitting at the tables. I say that I want to stay the night and take the *pedos de lobo* out of my rucksack. They smell of earth and aniseed.

"What are they?"

"*Pedos de lobo.*" They look blank. Perhaps I've said the wrong thing. "Mushrooms. They're edible."

"The chef wouldn't know what to do with them."

A woman standing at the counter next to me says: "He's right. I recognise them. You can fry them in oil with parsley and garlic."

The chef wouldn't know what to do with them. The staff have some difficulty in organising me a bed so whilst waiting I telephone the Baños de Panticosa to tell them my news.

"I'll put it on our blog," says the manager.

Back at the bar, I order a drink.

I say to the woman: "You can have the mushrooms if you like."

"I'll cook them when I get home," she replies.

"If they are brown inside don't eat them," I instruct. They are called wolf's farts because they explode when they are over-ripe, releasing a dense brown cloud of spores into the atmosphere.

She is drinking a glass of beer standing at the bar. She is about my age. This is quite remarkable. In Spain, women of my age do not go to bars alone, and certainly don't stand at the counter. It's just not on.

"What have you done today?" she asks looking at my rucksack slumped on the floor.

I just tell her about the snow and the rivers, but secretly I think: 'I've lived.'

Dinner is served in the *comedor*. The squaddies are eating at a big table reserved for them and say hello as I pass. Apart from them, about sixty people are tucking in. It's not quite a factory like Orreaga but the noise is infernal and I can hardly understand the others at my table. The meal is good and filling, if lacking in local inspiration.

Even so, you can't get much more authentic than Bujaruelo. The hostel had *already* been sheltering travellers for over 500 years before Ramond de Carbonnières stayed here.

> There was considerable commotion in the hostel, *he wrote*. Mule drivers, merchants, smugglers, and customs officers: all going about their business in their own way. Some swearing loudly, others whispering quietly, this one running away, that one robbed, others chasing their prey across the precipices of the Taillon.

The book, published in 1792, brought the mountains to the notice of the world (Paris). So Bujaruelo was one of the midwives present at the 'birth' of the Pyrenees. But, in contrast with Gavarnie, the other half of the team, it has remained a modest hamlet.

A walk in the Park

Bujaruelo to Torla

In the morning I look at the sparse remains of the Romanesque chapel, where pilgrims gave thanks for their safe crossing, and where some centuries later soldiers shot at the windows, leaving them pock-marked.

The Senda crosses the medieval bridge over the River Ara and turns downstream, into the pine forest. *Merde*, another river. Up to my knees. Very strong current. So that explains the Japanese couple, an elderly man and perhaps his daughter coming in the other direction at an improbably early hour. They must have set out from Bujaruelo and turned back. However, I reach the bridge back over the river Ara and onto the road without further ado. On the other side two soldiers are filling the recycling bins with beer bottles. They get back into their vehicles. The 'RCZM 66' on the door identifies them: the Regimiento de Cazadores de Montaña 'América' 66.

A little further downstream the Senda leaves the road to climb up to the Escalas, the former path to Torla used before the road was built in the valley. In places it is narrow with a cable attached to the cliff. Also hanging on is a small clump of *ramonde des Pyrénées* (Pyrenean violet) named after Ramond. It is lost: the rest of the Gesneriaceae live in the tropics. Thirty million years ago its ancestors had family all around; now it is home alone. The other reason it is here on this cliff is its ability to withstand drought. In the heat of the summer it shrivels, only to revive with the first rains.

I am taking a photograph of it when the sound of singing drifts into my consciousness. I tune my ears, incredulous. Somewhere down in the valley a male voice choir is in full song. But I can see neither churches nor houses, only the steep forested slopes, the river, and the road. Then they come round the bend and from my vantage point I see two parallel lines of soldiers marching like pine processionary caterpillars – dressed in the same mottled browns and following nose to tail. Not chained together but they might as well be. Inexplicably one of them trips and falls on his face. His colleagues merely step over him, still singing, until he rolls out of the way, picks himself up, and slips back into the line. I take a photo of the phenomenon and just at that moment another of the soldiers steps out of line and points me out to an officer: "There's that spy again."

As it happens I don't need to spy at all. The regiment's website contains a report on the exercise: six days in the mountains, in conditions much more extreme than those I encountered. It concludes:

> In exchange for all that effort the mountains give us the possibility of savouring the taste of victory over our limitations. As the old mountaineering adage goes: 'It is not the mountain that we conquer, but ourselves.'

I look at some other pages. The first thing in the listing of their principal activities is a photo entitled '*Homenaje a los caidos* – homage to the fallen'.

Back on the Escalas I grip the cable. At the end of the 'delicate' passage the valley opens up. Between the vegetation the rock surface is rippled like tidemarks on sand. To the left I can see the start of the Ordesa valley, it too marked by geology.

A chainsaw makes itself heard. Four men are working with strimmers. They stop to let me pass and I thank them for clearing the path. A few minutes later I open the door of the Hotel Ordesa. I have hardly started walking today but have already arrived at my destination.

The first thing I do is ring the Compañia de Guias and ask about the path between Góriz and Pineta which is looming up ahead of me. It is snowy, steep, and downhill which is more difficult than climbing, says the guide. But all the staff are out with Japanese clients for several days so I'm stuck.

I study my maps, then ring Phil.

"Can I cut off the corner from Góriz into the Añisclo canyon?"

"Don't do that. The path on the map doesn't exist anymore. A few years ago a woman was lost there for eleven days." The hotel has internet access. The woman wasn't alone, as I had assumed, but part of a group of fourteen. They stopped briefly but she continued, thinking she was going in the right direction.

A walk in the Park

Apart from taking a rest I want to visit Torla, 'the gateway to the Ordesa-Monte Perdido National Park'. As I walk down the road, dodging cars on the bypass, one of them pulls to a halt. It is Arkaitz on his way to Góriz to meet up with Colin, Claire and company. Tomorrow they will be climbing Monte Perdido, the second highest mountain in the Pyrenees.

In the centre of Torla, on one side of the road a neon sign advertises the Arco Iris Pub (Rainbow Pub) but it is closed. Opposite it the As Proas discotheque doesn't look as though it has done any business for some time. Further down the Bar-Frankfurt la Gruta (the Grotto) is also closed. I head for the ethnological museum but it doesn't open until July.

In any case my main interest is not the village but the National park visitor centre. I expect some kind of museum; what I get, on the outside, is a smallish chalet. But walking through the door is like walking into a Tardis. Where there should be a floor there is a gigantic hole with a vertical cotton tube, now purple, now blue, now red as the lighting changes. Apparently, at one time it even had a luminous cylinder in the centre, though it didn't move up and down. The cotton tube is part of a series of installations called '*Castillos en el aire* – castles in the air'.

> In this work, the unattainable, immeasurable, remote mountain, once it is brought down to size, is converted by artistic expression into a homely palpable object.

At the information desk, the receptionist is talking on what looks like a radio-telephone.

"… helicopter… accident…"

When she has finished I ask her what has happened but she is evasive.

"When you ring 112 does it come through to here?" I have difficulty in imagining her organising the emergency services in between selling souvenirs to tourists.

"No but we are involved in the coordination."

I ask about sheep. Is the transhumance late? No, she says, they no longer come.

A helical ramp suspended from the walls of the spaceship descends into the hillside, leading me through an exhibition, reading quotations as I go:

Torla

It is the path to the top which gives meaning to the summit. Without the experience of the voyage, the top is meaningless. It is only a viewpoint. The path up the mountain fuses the sensations and experiences of our inner voyage with the grandeur of the exterior.

'*La cumbre mística*', Revista *Voluntad*, 22, 1 October 1920

When the mountain has stolen your heart, everything comes from her, everything leads to her.

Franz Schrader

At the bottom of the ramp is a picture window. This must be the feature around which the whole edifice was designed. Conceptually, the building is not an interpretive centre but a camera, its lens pointing at the town with the undulating snow-capped cliffs of the Peña Mondarruego as a backdrop.

This is *the* photo of Torla, the one you see everywhere. The perspective gives the impression that the cliffs overshadow the town and that the slightest rock fall could land on the head of some unfortunate villager, though in reality they are separated by some 5km.

But the main attraction for me is a new exhibition on the Pyrenean ibex (*bucardo* in Spanish, *bouquetin* in French, *steinbock* in German). And the star is Laña (also known as Celia), the very last of the species, in a glass case, looking remarkably perky. She died on 6 January 2000, victim of a falling branch. The Pyrenean ibex was extinct, the first recorded extermination of the 21st century.

But that isn't the end of the story.

Pyrenean ibex: the return

Despite the death of Laña, only two years after I walked through Torla ibex kids were again being born in the mountains. Their parents had travelled from central Spain to be released on the French side. The return of the ibex is part of the 2011 *Stratégie Pyrénéenne de Valorisation de la Biodiversité* (Pyrenean Strategy for Biodiversity Enhancement) a vast rewilding protocol signed by Spain, France, and Andorra. It could change the face of the Pyrenees.

As far as the ibex is concerned, it first emerges from the Pyrenean mist some 13,000 years ago on the walls of the Black Room in the caves at Niaux in the French Ariège. One painting shows a male, looking like a fat goat with dark fur on its back and a lighter belly, its long horns arching backwards. The only thing missing is the characteristic twist of the horns seen on its descendants, and a sense of scale: males weigh 90kg.

The next mention is in Gaston Fébus' hunting manual written in the 14th century. One day he saw more than a hundred. Not interesting, he wrote, too easy. And indeed, with the invention of firearms it became far too easy. As early as 1825 the Pyrenean ibex was reported to be extinct. In reality, there were still a few holed up near Torla.

In the 19th century the area was more accessible from the north than from the south. Britons like Sir Victor Brooke wrote about their exploits, though other nationalities also competed for the prized horns. The last two ibex seen in France were killed by a hunter's bullets in 1910.

Footprints on the mountains

In the same year, when Russian prince Teodoro de Tchihatchef, an early ecotourist, came to observe ibex near Torla he was disappointed. After two weeks he was about to leave when local guides persuaded him to stay for just one more day. Miracle! For the first time, when he scanned the cliffs with his binoculars, he saw an ibex: on the Faja de Pelay, over a kilometre away. He insisted on going to look. Naturally, by the time he arrived the animal had disappeared, even though it was stuffed. But the prince was so pleased that he engaged the guides for another two weeks.

In 1918 the creation of the Ordesa National Park should have given the ibex a measure of protection, but the inaugural speech gives a clue to the subsequent failure:

> "It is really unfortunate that from 15 July to 15 September, which is the tourist season in the region, the French frontier of our National Park is full of tourists and constantly visited by motorists coming to contemplate Gavarnie, whilst only enthusiasts who dare defy the problems of an excruciatingly difficult journey reach the Ordesa Valley."

The result was new roads and an increasing number of visitors. There was even a plan to build a hydroelectric dam in the valley in 1919. Thankfully the inhabitants of Torla managed to fight off the idea.

Although hunting in the Park was now illegal it continued to a lesser extent. And during and after the Spanish Civil War famished soldiers and *maquis* shot whatever came into their sights.

Conservation was not the spirit of the age, as one anecdote demonstrates: in a single day hunters from the American airbase in Saragossa killed 30 or 40 *sarrios*. With machine guns. Those ibex misguided enough to stray beyond the Park's boundaries were 'intensely persecuted'.

Even so, one estimate in 1980 suggested that thirty ibex remained. But by then the damage was done, and only three lived on into the late 1990s.

A plan to mate the survivors – all female – with males from outside failed because of their poor health. Although two of them became pregnant there were no live births until *after* the last of them was dead.

That was in 2009. The kid only survived a few minutes because she couldn't breathe properly. She had been cloned from cells taken from Laña: a first for an extinct species. But even if she had survived, she would have

A walk in the Park

Laña, the last Pyrenean ibex

had to contend with a poor genetic heritage. Studies of Laña's DNA showed a high degree of inbreeding.

Previously there had been two more conventional attempts to strengthen the population. In 1970, the owner of the Baños de Panticosa spa imported between eight and twelve ibex from Gredos but the initiative had no lasting impact. Later another collection was established in the nearby Sierra de Guara. Although they were kept in large enclosures, most escaped and some are still living there but don't seem to have migrated to the Pyrenees. These were private initiatives, so no impact studies were undertaken.

Then there were several official French projects which came to nothing, until 2014 when the first ibex were imported. In 2015 another batch arrived and the first ibex to be born in France for a century was spotted in the French Ariège. Its mother had arrived only a few weeks previously, already pregnant.

Soon after the birth, I went to look for the newcomers with Jordi Estèbe from the Parc Naturel Régional des Pyrénées Ariégeoises. A shepherd had seen a second young kid just on the other side of the frontier in Spain. This would be very good news as the births so far this year have been disappointing: the one in the Ariège and another in the High-Pyrenees.

We have arranged to meet at Ossèse. Whilst waiting for him a gaggle of Catalans passes by; I fear that they will frighten the ibex. But when Jordi arrives he tells me that however quiet he is, by the time he has focussed his telescope the ibex is already looking at him.

"My camouflage tee-shirt won't make any difference then?"

"You'll stand out less. But all *bovidae* are colour blind."

Like bulls. So the dull green anorak I have bought for the occasion is no more appropriate than my red one.

When ibex *do* see you their response is to climb. They are happiest on exposed slopes of 55–80 degrees which saves them from most predators, but makes them easier to shoot.

Although ibex also suffered from loss of habitat and inbreeding, it is clear that hunting was by far the most important factor in their disappearance. When Alfonso XIII created a royal game reserve in Gredos near Madrid in 1905 there were only a few hundred ibex in the whole of Spain. The best local hunters, destined to become the best local poachers, were recruited as gamekeepers and the population soared. If it were not for this initiative there would probably be no ibex in Spain today: but as a result the population stands at about 50,000. But still, despite theoretical protection, the Pyrenean sub-species didn't survive.

Nowadays, hunting ibex in Spain is big business. Taking home a pair of horns from a dominant male can cost up to 20,000 euros when all the expenses of the hunt are taken into account. Exporting live ibex was made illegal to preserve the monopoly. So when the first official requests were made for ibex to repopulate the Pyrenees the Spanish were suspicious of the motivations, particularly as the hunting associations were the big guns behind the scenes. It was only when the French government outlawed hunting that they relented.

If habitat was a relatively small factor in the extinction it is because ibex are remarkably adaptable. In Spain they can be found near the southern shores of Andalusia (45 degrees Celsius in summer) and in Cantabria (minus 20 in winter). The rainfall varies from 200mm to 2000mm. Once hunting

A walk in the Park

Two-year-old male ibex with tracking collar
© *Jordi Estèbe - Parc naturel régional des Pyrénées Ariégeoises*

stopped they colonised areas where they had been unknown. Those living in nature parks have lost their fear of humans. A friend walking in the Alps came across a herd recently. She lay down and let them approach, spending an hour watching them graze only a few paces away. But the newcomers in Ariège are still timid and stick to the heights.

"The cliffs also mean they can find food in winter because the avalanches expose the vegetation," says Jordi.

It is a dangerous strategy: two were killed last winter. But this choice of habitat was one of the considerations for reintroduction. They are not in competition with *sarrios* at a critical moment in the annual cycle: *sarrios* more sensibly descend into the woods.

We quickly overtake the Catalans in the forest, coming to a stop at the Plat de Lauze. Jordi extracts a folding aerial from his rucksack and starts waving it around his head, like a 21st-century divining rod. The ibex, he tells me, wear earrings and necklaces. The earrings are cheap coloured plastic ID tags but the necklaces cost 2500 euros each.

Footprints on the mountains

"There's a female up there," he tells me pointing to some crags way above us. "I know where she was last night. The necklaces send a GPS signal four times a day."

Looking at a chart and tuning his radio, he rotates the aerial until the beeps are at their loudest: exactly opposite to where he was pointing.

"It's a reflection," he explains. "The radio is better once you are in the field but not totally reliable."

Even if we don't see her we might spot one of the other nine without necklaces which could be anywhere.

The clouds are masking the top of the crags but lifting slowly. We scan the zone with our telescopes. Two and a half hours later, the only thing we have seen is vultures circling on the thermals. The Catalans and various other walkers have long passed by.

We climb further up the valley and eat lunch, looking all the time but seeing nothing. I have to return to Ossèse but Jordi continues into Spain.

I'm disappointed, despite going to see a stuffed ibex at close quarters in an exhibition in Seix, part of the campaign to make sure locals know what they look like. But Jordi must be more so. When he is back at base two days later he sends me an email. Despite all the technology he has not seen a single ibex. It's like that one time in four.

Two weeks later the kid Jordi was looking for is making appearances on television, caught on video scampering joyfully next to his mother near the head of the valley.

The media talk of success, and it is true that the renewed presence of ibex in the Pyrenees is a success in itself. But the number of births is disappointing. According to official criteria success is defined as an annual population growth of 20–30% with 0.8–1.0 kids per female of two years or more. Both of the kids born in the Ariège this year were conceived before their mothers arrived. None of the 2014 females have produced offspring.

"Are you aiming for a certain population?" I asked Jordi.

"There's no figure. One hundred would be fine as long as they don't have a problem. But you need 500 to be safe from epidemics. The same as for any wild species."

I don't ask him if the figure applies to bears also.

A few weeks after my expedition with Jordi, I am in Spain walking with a biology teacher. When I talk about the *bucardo* being reintroduced he corrects me.

"They're extinct. The new ones are *cabra montes*."

"Isn't it the same?"

"No, the *bucardos* only lived in the Pyrenees; the *cabra montes* further south. They are different sub-species."

So while foreigners can be content that the ibex/*bouquetin*/*steinbock* has been reborn, the Spanish are still lamenting the definitive loss of the *bucardo*.

If the reintroductions are successful, the ibex will munch their way across the mountains, like goats eating not only grasses but also woody branches, opening up the slopes. Very young they will interest foxes and eagles. At the other end of their life cycle griffon vultures will pick the flesh from the bones as bearded vultures hover above awaiting their turn.

Life is hard.

The Pyrenean ibex is dead. Long live the (Pyrenean) ibex.

Torla to the Pradera

Today is supposed to be a day off but I can't stop. I walk along brushing flowers with my hand and bending down to smell them. At the Puente de los Navarros the Senda descends to the bubbling river. On the other side, at the edge of the Ordesa-Monte Perdido National Park, a panel lists the eighteen mortal sins: camping, lighting fires, picking flowers, etc.

From here, close to, the Ordesa valley glimpsed between the trees looks less impressive than when seen from Torla. Under the forest canopy, it is dark. The tree trunks search for the sun with disciplined verticality; their roots in search of water squirm across the path.

To one side there is a large stone monument. A bearded, balding man with a lorgnette looks back at me from the plaque. He looks studious.

To Luciano Briet
died 4 August 1921
A tribute of admiration and gratitude
to the man who sang of the Ordesa valley.
15 August 1922

Footprints on the mountains

I have only just discovered the existence of Monsieur Briet, whose Christian name, incidentally, was Lucien not Luciano. (It has to be said that the Spanish have no respect for first names. The son of the carpenter living next door might be called Jésus. For them, the queen of England is Isabella II. And I get called Estive, like the pasture.)

Lucien Briet is virtually unknown in France and certainly not to be considered in the same breath as the 'Pleiades', the seven stars of the Pyrenees: Russell, Wallon, Lequeutre, Schrader, Gourdon, Saint-Saud, and Prudent who mapped, studied, and popularised them. But here he is a hero. The video I watched in the visitor centre yesterday started with a tribute to him.

His photographs taken at the beginning of the 20th century are a unique record of the Pyrenees at that time. But more than that: the inhabitants *liked* him. Lucien was one of them. The 'greats' were too distant. Unfortunately Briet made the mistake of accusing one of those 'greats', Schrader, of cartographic plagiarism. The subsequent ostracism could be one of the reasons for his low profile north of the border.

In contrast, in Spain, his work was decisive in the creation of the Ordesa National Park. (In 1997 it became part of the Monte Perdido World Heritage Site.) This is the greatest homage to Briet.

Still, I ask myself, where were the Spanish? Did they really leave the 'discovery' of the Pyrenees, the creation of the 'modern' Pyrenees to the French? Skipping a century, the reintroduction of ibex and bears are French initiatives. Even the idea of long-distance trails was imported from France. Is this all part of the same legacy?

At the Pradera the trees thin and the path gains a concrete border. I meet a young couple with their baby in a pushchair.

I am once again confronted by a panel reminding me of the eighteen mortal sins, in the event that my memory has become unreliable. And, just in case I was thinking of enjoying myself, it also warns me of the nine deadly risks. The road sign iconography – red triangles for the warnings, red diagonal lines crossing out the prohibited activities – is appropriate. The Pradera, although it means 'meadow', is a gigantic car park.

I was going to walk a little further up the valley but the path is barred by red-and-white-striped hazard tapes backed up by three men in uniform. The sign which says 'Refugio de Góriz' has been partially masked.

A walk in the Park

"But I want to go to Góriz tomorrow. I've booked in," I protest.

"It will probably be cleared by then, so there won't be a problem."

The Sarga agents are working hard to eliminate two of the nine deadly risks: trees or rocks falling on heads.

So I walk through the car park, stopping only to admire the souvenirs in the shop, and then station myself by the side of the road. The first car stops.

On the way back to the hotel I bump into four French hikers who have just finished a circular walk. Their thirty-something shaggy-haired leader tells me that they had intended to camp next to the Góriz hostel:

"But we took a wrong turning and ended up at a *via ferrata*. We weren't equipped for it and it was getting late so we just camped until the next day. From Góriz to the Sarradets it was snow all the way. We don't have crampons or ice axes but it was OK.'

The others just moan.

La Pradera to Góriz

In the morning when I get on the bus back to the Pradera nearly all the passengers are male. A few earthy rugby songs would be in order but the atmosphere is surprisingly quiet and studious, the conversations whispered. The only normal talking comes from the driver communicating with his colleagues by radio to ensure that they meet up at the passing places.

At the frontier of the National Park a sentry wearing the characteristic red shirt of the Sarga Agency waves us through. Access is limited to 1800 people at any one time.

At the Pradera the contents of the bus disperse and I head up the valley. The hazard tapes have gone. There's no wind in the forest, but out of the sun I shiver.

Higher up, I stop to look at conical bivalve fossils and the Cascada del Estrecho with its private rainbow. Above this geological plug the valley widens into meadows with patches of asphodel; the vertical cliffs at the end are visible for the first time.

I am in the middle of asking a Sarga agent about the appropriateness of concrete for holding the path together when Colin and Lynn come the other way. They had snow all the way up from the Lago Helado (Ice-Cream Lake).

"I was fine until I tried to get into bed in the evening afterwards," Colin explains, "but I banged my ankle on the frame and it swelled up. So we're going straight down. I'm not feeling strong enough to walk the Añisclo with the others."

When they have gone the agent finishes explaining that erosion is a problem given the number of visitors. Walking poles have made it worse – nobody used them thirty years ago, he claims. In order to save the rest of the National Park, the Ordesa valley has been 'sacrificed'.

In the forest the river was crashing wildly over the rocks; here it winds lazily in a wide basin. Alongside it, the rough stone paving snakes between fresh cow pats.

Nearly all the walkers are going in my direction, crowding together as we approach the liquid curtain of the Cascada Cola de Caballo (Horse's Tail Waterfall) which marks the end of the valley.

Most of the others stop here but a few continue and I watch their progress trying to discern how they can possibly make their way through the cliffs. The most obvious path is the signposted *Refugio Góriz por las clavijas* but that must be the way the French group tried. So I choose *Refugio de Góriz por sendero*, which appears to be going in completely the wrong direction.

The path climbs steadily, twisting, approaching the impossible cliffs cautiously; and then it sneaks through like a smuggler. Once above, it levels out and the view opens up. A squadron of yellow-billed alpine choughs dives in to inspect me and then soars back up into the air.

From this elevated viewpoint I can look down on the Ordesa valley and see the logic of it all. I spread out my map. My itinerary visits five valleys. The Bujaruelo and the Ordesa I have already walked; the Añisclo, Escuain, and Pineta are still to come. Five valleys, five arthritic digits deformed by the millennia, pressed into the mountains. God's handprint.

That's looking down. Looking up, to the north I can see a peak covered in snow: Monte Perdido. As Ramond was the first to remark: 'After Mont Blanc you must come to Monte Perdido; when you have seen the principal granitic mountain, you have still to see the principal calcareous one.' He found fossil seashells at 3000m. With a single blow of his geological hammer Ramond had knocked the glory of creation from God's grasp. But Ramond was more

A walk in the Park

Ordesa

a botanist than a geologist so it was Lyme Regis rather than Monte Perdido which went on to rewrite the history of the world. In stone.

The porosity of the rock explains the dry plateau and the fissures here. Ancient glaciation explains the rest. But scientific explanation is inadequate. The emotional appeal is all about scale. How can the canyon be so deep? Two Shards would fit into it one on top of the other – 1.9 Eiffel Towers, if you prefer metric units. How can the mountain be so high? Despite the climbing I have done today, the summit is still five Shards above me.

Four youngsters are coming in the other direction. I'd say they are about fifteen years old.

"Can we get back down this way? We've come up the *clavijas* and we don't want to go back down that way."

I look at them. They're not equipped for a *via ferrata*.

Further along, my walking pole taps against a rock which rings hollow though surely it can't be. I tap others. Some are hollow, others not. Nearby, another mystery: a single wild daffodil.

Footprints on the mountains

Arriving at the Góriz hostel I squeeze past walkers brushing the geology off their shoes. An Italian man and his son have just finished checking in. A disorderly queue builds up behind me. Those walkers who have finished the hard part of their day are eating lunch. Dressed in a rainbow of tee-shirts and talking a Babel of languages, they are jovially rowdy, quite different from their morning shadows.

The pandemonium is swilling around like waves when a storm blows in to a badly designed harbour. As on the bus, most of the walkers are men – only one in ten is female. Everybody, but everybody, is white, including the two Australian women propping up the bar. This is generally the case – not the Australians propping up the bar, but the predominance of ethnic whites. The Japanese are the only noticeable exception to the rule. In the whole of my walk I will meet just one black man.

When the squall has calmed down I ask about the GR11 to Pineta.

"The *fajas* are too icy," says the manager, "and even if you go round them you will still have the Collado de Añisclo on a downhill in full sun."

That settles it then. I'll go the long way round, three days' walking instead of one.

"You would need crampons," he adds.

"I've got crampons."

"I didn't know you had crampons. Of course you can do it."

"But I've booked in to the hostel in Bestué."

"I'll ring them up for you to cancel."

"No thanks. I'll go to Bestué."

"It's a long way. It will take you ten hours," he warns. "You won't see anybody. It's very empty, very wild."

I am about to enquire if there be dragons when he adds: "I've never been that far."

Instead I ask: "What about the rivers?"

"No problem. I went down to the river in the *barranco* yesterday for a bath. It's fine."

Upstairs in the dormitory the bunks are stratified in three layers with nine mattresses on each. Whilst arranging my space I look out of the window. On the concrete terrace below the hikers are trapped in Brownian motion, sitting down and then getting up again, fiddling with their rucksacks. I take a siesta. My legs are jittery too.

A walk in the Park

Near Góriz

I wake up when an avalanche of walkers bursts through the door. Downstairs the activity is still frenetic but outside it is calmer. The first tents, colourful molehills, are popping up. This is one of the few places in the National Park where they are permitted; overnight only.

As well as the tents, there are other signs of construction, but this set of scaffolding is completely bereft of workers. The unfinished extension to the hostel is a rural victim of the urban economic carnage. The main aim is medical: the plan is to inject tranquillity into the hostel. When completed there will only be eight more beds on top of the 72 existing but the space will be doubled.

For now, the main effect is that the sanitary block is outside, in a porta-cabin. There has never been hot water here and I don't fancy a cold shower especially after someone explains the reason the taps run continuously: to stop them freezing.

On the other hand the cubicles are stocked with vast quantities of toilet paper – in France you have to bring your own. Then again at Góriz you have to put it into a bucket, an ecologically sound idea which would be completely unacceptable over the border.

At dinner six of us have been allocated to the blue table, all the others being Spanish. Three are going to climb Monte Perdido; the other two have just returned from Casco. As far as I can make out I am the only solitary walker. Later I ask the people within earshot, but nobody else is walking the Senda.

We all go outside to watch the sunset. Those already sitting on the edge of the terrace look as though their legs are dangling over the cliffs of the Ordesa canyon although it is some distance away. Someone says that a week ago you needed crampons to come up here but no one is really saying much. Silently, with our backs to the hostel, we watch the sun go down over the geological fingerprints outlined by the snow.

As soon as the sun drops below the horizon most people go to bed. In the dormitory the lack of hot water makes itself known. I set my alarm.

Góriz to Bestué

It keeps me awake all night: not wanting to disturb the twenty-six other people in the room I am continually rousing myself to look at the time, hoping to catch the alarm just before it goes off. Finally a combination of peer pressure and cold feet gets me out of bed.

Outside, in the light of the half-moon, the early birds are tweeting. It must be four or five degrees. Inside, three walkers are eating by the glow of their head torches: they must have brought their supplies with them. The rest of us – a dozen sleepwalkers – will have to wait.

Finally the lights come on and a woman opens up the counter. Amongst the others waiting to eat breakfast is a couple I noticed yesterday. The woman, about 50 years old, has long jet-black dyed hair. An archetypical Spanish mama, she is noticeably outsized. The man looks like a walker.

"Where are you going?" I ask them.

"I'm taking her up Monte Perdido," the man replies. "We're setting out early so we can go slowly."

The poor woman looks resigned to her execution. It is going to be a long day for me too but I'm more optimistic.

A walk in the Park

Path down the Barranco Arrablo on the way to the Añisclo canyon

Outside again after breakfast, the sun is starting to brush the snow on the peaks a violent pink. I head across the crumpled rocks, negotiating the minor patches of snow without crampons. Ahead of me four walkers are striding along so fast that I have no hope of catching up with them.

At a fork in the path I realise I'm already hungry again and sit down to eat, watching the others climb up towards the *fajas*, the icy ledge on the cliff face. Afterwards, I repack my sack, take two steps and then turn around for the habitual inspection. I have left a bottle out.

From the bifurcation my route descends into a ravine. My eyes follow the path as it crosses the sloping terrace to a cliff only to reappear in another prairie at a lower level. The nearer I get to the cliff, the more improbable the trajectory seems. Five minutes of adrenalin later and I am on the second prairie. And so on. At the tree line a waterfall spurts out of the cliff face: the Fuen Blanca is a long white beard.

The ravine joins the Añisclo canyon. Standing at the other end of a bridge is a white-haired man, hands in pockets. Apart from the fact that he is wearing a blue fleece and walking boots, he could be taking a morning stroll in his home town. I didn't expect to see anybody here.

I say "*¡Hola! ¿Qué tal?*" and shake his hand warmly.

He looks startled by my enthusiasm.

"*¡Hola!*" he replies after a short pause, continuing in English, "I don't speak Spanish."

"How did you get here?"

"We came up the valley yesterday."

He's German, camping nearby with his fifteen-year-old son who is on his first expedition. We compare maps. My path is not marked on his map and the path he took yesterday is not on mine.

"Do you have a gas canister by any chance?" he asks me. "I bought the wrong one. Luckily there was a couple camping a kilometre further down so we went there."

"No, I'm sorry."

"Never mind… I must go and wake up my son."

I take the German's path, initially right next to the torrent then climbing through mixed forest and box. The Añisclo is much narrower than the Ordesa though just as deep and although it starts out straight it soon falls into pleats, gathered like a curtain pushed to the end of its rail. The vegetation scrabbles to keep its hold on the cliff face. The river cascades from white waterfalls into small but stunningly blue pools and then off again over boisterous cataracts.

I meet no more walkers, although the path is well worn. Sometime later it climbs up one of the folds out of the gorge. From the top, peeking over the canyon, I can see two disconnected landscapes. Above, one which reminds me of England, the South Downs. Take the green serge of those rolling hills and pull. Harder. Until the cloth rips to reveal a second landscape: trees *under* the grass. That's it, the Añisclo canyon, colder and wetter at the bottom than at the top.

On the plateau a third landscape comes into view behind the rolling hills: Pico de Añisclo (Soum de Ramond) and beyond it Monte Perdido, two of the 'Three Sisters' as they are called (Cilindro is just hidden from sight).

Then, within the next few minutes, I encounter twenty walkers, thirty

A walk in the Park

On the way to Bestue, looking back over the Añisclo canyon. From left to right: Monte Perdido, Pico de Añisclo and the Punta de las Olas

horses, and forty cows distributed along a cart track. All have their young with them, wandering or grazing in the bucolic surroundings. The foals try to feed from their mothers who want nothing to do with it. The area is anything but 'empty', anything but 'wild'. And, except perhaps for the man who has just stopped to light up a cigarette, nothing could be remotely considered to be breathing fire.

I take a wide berth round the cows, made wary by a friend's recent experience. Louis made the mistake of getting between a cow and her calf and was gored in the leg. At the hospital they told him he had been one centimetre away from a punctured artery.

One car comes by, then another but I ignore them. I *must* walk. So it's a long stretch of road and a short but pleasantly flowery *vereda* that bring me to Bestué (pronounced 'best way'). It has taken me ten hours as predicted, most of it descending, and I am still 1230m above sea level. Safe for the day.

Añisclo canyon viewed from the south (near Vio)

Bestué is deliciously decrepit. What I like most is the anarchic layout and the narrow streets, some hardly wide enough for a wheelbarrow to pass, completely untended. There may be stones somewhere below, but on the surface the streets are merely earth and weeds. Even so, the wheelbarrows *are* passing, and in a few years Bestué will be a quite different proposition. The authorities have recently invested in new paving for the main square and the process of gentrification has begun.

Bestué is one of those places you can only discover by chance and I have arrived at just the right moment. Between 1950 and 1980 the population of Upper Aragon decreased by an astonishing 60% and Bestué was no exception. Twenty years ago it was decaying. In ten years it will look like a chocolate box. Now it is perfect. At least that is what Enrique, the owner of the hostel tells me. As yet the number of inhabitants hasn't changed since he first came here. Twenty-one, twenty-two for decades. Old people die, young ones move in. The only thing that has really changed is that the sheep have gone.

A walk in the Park

The houses have sandstone walls, stone roofs, and name plaques. For the moment *espantabrujas* are more numerous than television aerials. One of the houses looks like a fortress. Set into the arch above the door, the family's arms are four bars for Aragon, a bear for strength, and a 'B' for Barrau.

The church is also fortified. Further down the hill, the 'hermitage' is not in some wild woods but just at the edge of the village. It is dedicated to the Virgen del Barrio (the neighbourhood virgin, a curious choice, but it could hardly be dedicated to the village bicycle).

Around the edge of the settlement, former terraces now in retirement wrinkle the hillside. No longer cultivated, they have become pasture. Stripped of their original purpose, striped by the low sun, they remain stupendously beautiful even at the end of their long lives.

In the hostel bar the television is tuned to a Catalan channel. I am the only customer. The first course is *escalivade*, charred, caramelised Mediterranean vegetables perfumed with garlic and olive oil. This is followed by a green salad accompanied by a dumpy sausage. When I have eaten it Enrique comes to take the plate away.

"It's pig's intestine stuffed with rice and herbs. It's a local recipe," he explains looking closely at my empty plate. "I make them myself…" he trails off.

I look at him. His lips are quivering, his eyes wide open. He looks worried. When he manages to compose himself sufficiently he splutters:

"*¡Has comido la aguja!* You've eaten the needle!"

One word flashes through my mind: hospital. The nearest one must be ages away and the roads are horribly inadequate. I'm reeling. Suddenly all my certainties have disappeared. My world has been reduced to a needle in my guts.

"Never mind," he adds. "*No pasa nada.* It'll come out at the other end."

I sit there, mouth open but unable to speak, looking at him. How can he be so unconcerned? How can a needle pass through without doing indescribable damage? Why isn't he phoning an ambulance? It is a long minute before I realize it was all a joke.

After several more courses, over coffee he tells me that he is Catalan, which explains the television and the *escalivade*. He spends winter as a ski instructor near Puigcerdà on the other side of Andorra. He settled here *'por romantismo'*. It is a good place for romantics: he met his wife in a neighbouring village.

Footprints on the mountains

Bestué to Bielsa

A dozen of the horses I saw yesterday have descended from the pastures overnight, blocking the way; though some are palomino-coloured and the others bay, they have a strong family resemblance. As I approach, they start to panic and I have to slow down and keep well away. They try to escape but on the right the slope is too steep and on the left a barbed wire fence stops them from disappearing into the forest. So I walk behind them. Then suddenly one of them shies for no apparent reason forcing its way through the fence, and the rest follow.

I have just left the village, in high spirits having slept well. Today I will follow the GR15, parallel to the Senda but in the foothills.

Up and over the pass and into the next valley and I am soon deep in forest, convinced that the path must be only a few metres away. Yes, this must be it. Then it dives into the undergrowth through a hole just big enough for a hare. I put my long trousers back on to reduce the scratches from the brambles and break my way through.

The trees have been planted on terraces with a 4-metre drop between each level. Scrambling down one of the drops, I trip and tumble onto my hands. What if I break a leg? I'd be stuck, not found until the forest was cut down. So embarrassed. The Senda must have been rerouted.

Back on the correct path, in another forest, I hear voices talking in French. And then they appear between the trees: a line of six men and one woman in their underwear. Hers is bright red, the men's is black or navy blue. They have walking boots on their feet and rucksacks on their backs but they don't look like any walkers I have ever seen.

"*Bonjour*," I say, hesitantly, wondering what kind of situation I might have stumbled into.

"*Bonjour*," says the leader who then explains that they are going canyoning in the nearby River Yaga. The others say embarrassed '*bonjours*' and pass by. When I look back at them I see that their rucksacks are really wet bags. Some are carrying crash helmets.

Out of the forest, I return to the heat, up and up a long hillside, stopping to scoop up water from a stream and pouring it over my head. Ecstatic thrill: cold water running down my spine. I fill up my water bottle.

The cloud is thickening on the peaks, its shadow sweeping down the valley trailing a haziness which looks like rain. So when I get to the dolmen de Tella I consider sheltering under it until the storm passes but the site is somewhat exposed and the capstone wouldn't offer much protection. Nearby, an interpretive panel looks interesting but instead of reading it I take a photograph and press on to the village on a tarmac road. I drink the rest of my water.

Tella is at the very end of the road, like Bestué; but Tella, which is higher up the mountains, must also have been higher up the grant queue. In consequence, the entrance to the village is marked by a visitor centre. Just as I arrive a man comes out, locks the door and drives off in his 4x4 labelled Sarga Agency.

A woman approaches me timidly asking if I have any change, pointing at a big orange vending machine which must be taking a holiday from its normal job in a railway station. It sells orange juice and bitter lemon. I don't have anything easily accessible but eventually she finds some smaller coins herself. It spits them out. I try a technique learned studying engineering, but even kicking doesn't work. She scuttles back to her car and speeds off down the hill.

I am thirsty too. I walk down the single street which makes up the village. A San Miguel *cerveza* advert looks promising and the bar even has a sign saying '*¡Entra y navega!* – Come in and surf' but the door is firmly locked. Further down the street the '*Casa de la bruja* – the witch's house' is also closed. The fountain is much more welcoming: above one of the taps some child has written '*bienvenidos*' accompanied by a drawing of a mermaid.

On the way out of the village the sundial on the church tower indicates the time. It must be some years since the painted numbers faded but the shadow is vertical. So, even without looking at my increasingly unreliable watch, I can see it is mid-day, two o'clock. Far too late for my planned walk over the hills to Bielsa given the still-brewing teacup.

Hitching, however, looks an equally difficult option given the non-existent traffic. Hopefully, I walk down the road, chatting with a Dutch couple who are sitting on the verge in the shade next to their car. It pays off. Six cars pass, indifferent; but the Dutch couple stops. When I tell them I am going up the valley to Pineta tomorrow they warn me about a broken bridge and the long detour they had taken to cross the river.

Footprints on the mountains

In Bielsa the rain finally catches up with me and I take refuge under the arcades of the town hall, a *lumpen* building with a surprising renaissance-style corner turret. The building also houses a museum. The door is locked but a notice says that a guided visit is about to begin so I sit on one of the stone benches under the arches. A hulk of a man comes over and sits down next to me. After a quarter of an hour of desultory conversation and mutual incomprehension he takes a key out of his pocket and opens the door, takes my money, and then disappears.

I study panels on the mines and the sheep, and am just looking at some photos of the carnival bear when the guide reappears briefly to start a video about the Bolsa de Bielsa. In this case *bolsa* means pocket of resistance, resistance to Franco. It owes its considerable fame to the 43rd division's last stand in 1938. Isolated from the bulk of the Republican army, the division only fled over the pass to France when the situation became impossible, cutting trenches through the snow. (Despite it being June the passes were still not clear.) Not having the time to bury the dead, they doused them in petrol and burned them. Over six thousand civilians and troops, including five hundred with injuries, crossed the frontier. Most of the troops went back to fight again.

After the video is finished the guide comes back again. He doesn't so much *guide* me as *follow* me around.

"That's my mother," he says with evident pride, pointing at a photo of a teenager dressed up as a *madama* in multi-coloured ribbons and lace for carnival. Alone in the dingy rooms, he tells me what the photographs are about, whispering into my ear. It is a most odd experience.

My next stop is the National Park office where the woman behind the counter says that the bridge isn't broken. Outside again in the drizzle, I head for the pharmacy. Stuck to the counter is a strange notice:

> *Recetas húmedas no valen*

I can't really believe that it means "damp prescriptions not valid" so I ask.

"It means what it says," says the pharmacist abruptly, leaving me none the wiser. Either *húmeda* means something like 'out of date' or else it is going to continue to rain for a very long time.

A walk in the Park

It does indeed rain all evening. Sitting in my room, I look at the photos of the dolmen de Tella and the interpretive panel, but the writing is too small to read.

La Ronda de Boltaña

So the dolmen of Tella is still waiting for me when I arrive home. Looking at the photo on my computer I begin to realise that it contains a Pyrenean fairy-tale. The first layer unwraps to reveal a lullaby:

The dolmen of Tella

>Under the dolmen of Tella
>the day sheds its skin like a snake.
>Night approaches, shuffling
>singing a lullaby to make you sleep.
>Close your eyes, little one, and dream,
>see centuries, millennia and eras go by.
>Past and future playing hide and seek,
>that time is made of magic and legends
>under the dolmen, the dolmen of Tella.
>
>Under the dolmen of Tella
>you feel the globe turning and turning,
>exactly like your little crib
>swaying, rocking under the stars.
>Do not think that the earth rotates on its own,
>that without your doing a new dawn will come;
>you too, my child, you will make the dawn;
>if you don't open an eye, day will not arrive
>under the dolmen, the dolmen of Tella.
>
>Under the dolmen of Tella
>your ancestors left their heritage:
>a rich treasure of rocks,

canyons , glaciers, forests and meadows.
Sleep tight, mummy watches over you
keeping the world for when you grow up.
Not one tree or herb will be missing
and the waters will run clear and quiet
beneath the dolmen, the dolmen of Tella.

Under the dolmen of Tella
night has shed its snakeskin.
The light of dawn is approaching,
the gods are sleeping, the men awakening.
The Great Bear of the sky returns to its cavern,
to the gentle lap of the Mother Earth.
Sobrarbe and my child wake up now
that the rooster has sung and another day has begun
beneath the dolmen, the dolmen of Tella.

The poem is credited to the Ronda de Boltaña. Following up the name, I unwrap another layer, a sheet of music, to reveal a tradition which was disappearing, but is being kept alive by the group. *'Dolmen de Tella'* is one of the songs which have sustained the *'ronda'* into the 21st century: the tradition of going from door to door singing, a practice normally rewarded by food and drink. Wassailing, as it would be called in English, but not just at Christmas.

The group was formed twenty years ago in the eponymous village, a Noah's Ark of musicians and instruments: including guitar, lute, bagpipes, clarinet, *trompa* (a kind of oboe), and accordion.

Curiously Manuel Domínguez the lyricist is not local but has, as he says, 'managed to break into the hard disk of a relatively closed society'. So much so that one of his songs *'País Perdido'*, has become the official hymn of the Sobrarbe.

But it's not just a case of sugar-sweet lyrics wrapped up in nostalgia. The *'Habanera Triste'* decries the ongoing scandal of Jánovas, 'one of those phantom reservoirs which for so many years have only collected anger, although they have caused as much misery as if they had collected water'.

A walk in the Park

Habanera Triste (extract)

Every time my mother did the washing
my house turned into a yacht
with sails of white sheets
stretched out in the wind of these mountains

A ship of stone in the valley
anchored for centuries on the banks of the Ara
across from the island of La Velilla
between the shores of Fiscal and Boltaña

How could I imagine, I
who dreamed of the sea
that a cursed reservoir, ayayay
would drown my house.

And although many years have passed
I will never forget that morning
when I discovered that pirates
were not just for fairy tales.

When they boarded the village
and we had to leave home
my childhood suddenly vanished
on seeing my mother's tears.

The saga is a national disgrace. Jánovas, just downriver from Torla, had a population of three hundred. The expulsions started in 1960 with houses being dynamited and olive groves pulled up. Most people had left by 1963 but one old couple stayed on, until they too were finally made homeless in 1984. Still nothing happened, until 2005 when the project was declared economically and ecologically unsound. In 2012 the first rebuilding started. Villagers who left as children are coming back as pensioners.

I had walked through the Sobrarbe without even knowing its name. Enclosed in that photo was a Russian doll: poetry, music, the tradition of the *ronda*, the history of depopulation, the significance of water and, finally the baby, a story of hope.

Bielsa to Pineta

The morning sky is clear but the woods are damp. Half-way up the hillside a photo on a plinth taken in 1938 invites the visitor to make a comparison with the village visible below. The layout hasn't changed much over the last 75 years. But there is one major difference: in the photo the burnt-out houses don't have roofs. Their bare gable ends point accusingly at the sky. The village was dead. Yet the use of stone for the walls ensured that it could rise again.

A little further along, the path levels out completely and starts gurgling. Every so often a hole in the earth reveals a metal grille with fast-flowing water below. The path diverges but at a dam I catch up with the channel again: an umbilical cord feeding the turbines in the valley below.

The Pineta dam is dedicated to the production of electricity. Nothing special there except, as I learned in the museum yesterday, it is much more than just a lump of concrete. Its birth came as a shock to the inhabitants of the Sobrarbe, dynamiting them into the 20th century. When the first engineers arrived in 1918 the locals had no idea of what was about to happen, unlike the residents of Jánovas who knew exactly what was going to happen, even if they were mistaken.

Before 1918 the area lived off stock-raising and the last remnants of the mining industry in quasi-autarchy. The *casa*, like the Basque *etxe*, was both a family residence and an economic unit. Only the *golondrinas* had much experience of life elsewhere, fluttering back from France with implausible tales of luxury glimpsed through the windows of wedding-cake hotels in Cauterets or St-Sauveur.

During construction, 2,000 workers were employed, mostly male labourers, mostly from outside. But there were some jobs for locals: for the dispossessed younger brothers in the Sobrarbe *casas*, there was a once-in-a-lifetime opportunity to earn hard cash, working outside the family circle.

There were several consequences. A new road infrastructure, reorienting external communications: the *golondrinas* – the swallows – young women

A walk in the Park

who migrated seasonally for work, no longer needed to cross the high passes on foot. They could head south instead – if they hadn't already migrated permanently in the arms of some hulk from the building site.

There were other impacts too. Large-scale deforestation, though the damage has now been repaired. Watercourses diverted, blocked by the dams. Lake ecosystems extensively modified: trout could be reintroduced but the eels disappeared.

On top of all that, although the main purpose of the dams was to supply Basque industry, electricity suddenly became a reality in the Sobrarbe.

It was the infancy of a new world. The first glimmer of a changing Pyrenees. And it all happened well before the arrival of significant numbers of tourists. So the dam is more than just a lump of concrete for turning water into fire. It is also the foundation stone of a new era, now a century old.

Walking around the monument my boots sink into the mud, squelching with each step. The woods smell musty but there are no mushrooms to be seen. Instead I find panels noting the presence of greater spotted woodpeckers and treecreepers although I can't see any. But I do catch a glimpse of an animal flashing by, the size of a small cat, with a big tail. It has gone before I can really fix my eyes on it. Then, a minute later I see another panel. The council really has pulled out all the stops; the latest electronic gadgetry ensures visitors have a truly rewarding experience. If the treecreepers are hiding, an ingenious mechanism releases a red squirrel; just in case you don't manage to identify it there is a panel to help.

The path crosses a rural playground, accessible by car, with picnic tables, a Scout camp, and a football pitch. Two miserable policemen eye me up through the closed windows of their air-conditioned 4x4. Difficult to imagine a level of crime here which might justify their presence; they can't know I have just stolen some wild strawberries from the side of the path.

The end of the playground is marked by a wall of black pines, appropriately enough, as Pineta means pine woods. Walking through them takes me to the footbridge, which is broken in two just as the Dutch couple predicted. There was something about the way the woman in the National Park office hesitated when she moved her finger over the map.

The river is ten metres wide and flowing too fast to ford but I don't want to go back. I put one foot on the end of the metal walkway, one hand on each of the handrails and shake hard. Nothing moves. This end, at least, seems to be firmly attached to the bank.

I shuffle along what was once a horizontal deck but which now descends like a gangplank, twisting all the while, with its far end drowned in the river. Then I clamber onto the handrail, over a shipwreck of trunks and branches, up the stones of the central pier and onto the deck of the other half of the bridge. Despite the unusual angle of the central pier, undermined by the current, the second half of the bridge is intact.

Not only has the bridge fallen into the river, but also many sections of the path, and after struggling through the forest for a while I make my way to the road which leads up the valley. A 4x4 comes the other way. The two men are wearing the Sarga uniform.

'*Ordesa ye nazión*' or should it be '*Sarga ye nazión*'?

At the Pineta hostel I am sitting at a table inside when four big blokes enter.

"Eight hours," says one of them, looking at his watch.

"Four large beers," says another, looking at the barman.

"Where have you come from today?" he asks.

"Góriz by the *fajas*."

"What was it like?" I interrupt. "I made a big detour to avoid the *fajas*. Was it difficult?"

"There was a patch of ice. Only one and a half metres across but we had to rope up. After the *collado* there were patches of snow so we kept putting our crampons on and taking them off again... Let's say you need above average experience," replies one of them without a hint of condescension.

They tell me that they are walking a section of the Senda. It has taken them nineteen days; tomorrow they are going back home to Bilbao in the Basque country.

I ask the barman for something light to eat so he brings me a huge mixed salad followed by a large plate of chickpeas. I am more than satisfied and already leaving the table when he comes out of the kitchen with a plate full of pork loin in tomato sauce, followed by a bowl of *natillas* – thick custard with a sprinkling of cinnamon. By the end of the meal I can hardly breathe so I go to sleep it off.

I am just getting out of bed again when a man pokes his nose through the

A walk in the Park

curtain which divides my cubicle from the corridor. He looks as though *he* could do with a big meal.

"I'll move my rubbish," I say.

"No panic," he replies, collapsing on the bunk opposite mine. He is barefoot, carrying a pair of socks in one hand.

"I didn't take my boots off at the river as I was nearly here," he explains.

"I'm Estive,"

"Francisco."

"Where have you come from?"

"Góriz today. And before that the Cabo Higuer."

"Are you with the four Basques?"

"No. I've been following them but we aren't together."

"What were the *fajas* like?"

"*Tenìa mucho miedo* – I was really afraid. Never been so frightened. There was a patch of ice two metres across and I've only got half crampons."

I leave him to unpack.

After the inevitable afternoon downpour, sitting on the bench outside the entrance in the timid sun, the only language to be heard is English. From their accents I would say that the four men are Spanish – they must have just arrived – and the other two people are German. The Germans are one of those couples who dress identically and stick close to each other as if linked by elastic. They are, to use the Spanish expression *'dos mitades de la misma naranja'* – two halves of the same orange. The man comes over to talk to me.

"I hear that you are doing the Senda. We're going to Góriz tomorrow. What's it like?"

"I don't really know. I went round by Bielsa. There's a group of Basques somewhere who'll be able to tell you."

Unable to choose between 'girlfriend' and 'wife', I continue carefully: "Where have you and your friend …"

"She's not my girlfriend. We met after two weeks walking," he jumps in, just a little too hastily.

"… have you come from?"

"The Mediterranean. I left on 21 May."

They don't have crampons and so they have had to diverge from the Senda like me. Looking more closely I recognize that they are not identically dressed.

The Spanish are just doing a week's worth of the GR11, as they do every two years.

East meets west. For the first time this year I feel as though I am walking on a *gran recorrido*.

Sitting here, I'm glad to be back on the primary school benches. The tales brought back from the secondary school *fajas* are just too traumatic. I'm reminded of the vaulting horse in physical education lessons. Every time you succeeded in leaping over it, the teacher raised it a little more. Those who failed crushed their balls. As the teacher wrote in his end-of-term report: 'Tries hard but is a worrier'. I'm glad to be back with the kids.

For the evening meal I am placed on the same table as Francisco. He left the Cabo Higuer three weeks ago and nearly gave up after three days of continuous rain. Tomorrow he is going to Bielsa to resupply.

As for eating, I pace myself.

Pineta to Parzán

When I walk into the washroom next morning a woman is brushing her teeth. She has my rucksack on her back. Then I remember it is in the hallway.

"Hello. That looks like my sack," I say in English, having overheard her American accent yesterday evening.

"But it's not your sack," she replies indignantly.

"I said it *looked* like my sack. I've never seen anybody with one like mine."

We quickly establish that we are both doing the Senda and both heading in the same direction. She goes to finish packing and I go down to eat as much as I am able. Afterwards, rearranging my sack in the hallway I meet Julie again, this time with her husband Walt. They are about to depart but I've still things to do. In any case we are sure to meet again.

"Can I have your email address?" asks Julie.

I'm taken aback.

She continues: "When we did the PCT we lost touch with other walkers and never found out what had happened to them."

I give her my address.

"Can I see how much your rucksacks weigh?" I ask.

A walk in the Park

"Go ahead."

Walt's is about the same as mine but it contains both their pairs of crampons, two ice axes, and a tent. Julie's is much lighter.

"We believe in ultra-light," Julie tells me. I look at their feet. They are wearing shoes. Not heavy boots like me.

"I'm *so* pleased to meet you. We were getting lonely," she gushes.

By the time I have finished packing they are long gone.

I walk up the road to the hermitage chapel – the equivalent of the Bujaruelo chapel but intact – and then up through the humid forest, soon overheating. Stopping for a rest, I realise that I wasn't sufficiently peckish this morning to remember my picnic.

Julie and Walt are crossing the high pastures of the Lalarri when we meet again and continue the conversation started earlier. In the storms they took a yellow day on buses from Auritz to Candanchú, where I started this year. The next day they headed up the Canal Roya like me but they didn't like the look of the snow. So they caught the bus back to Auritz. At that stage they were three days behind me. There's no denying it, they're moving fast. But then they are well-weathered, wiry. They look too ultra-light to be Americans. Ridiculous prejudice. They sound a little Germanic, perhaps second generation immigrants?

"We had a zero day yesterday," says Julie, "because we got soaked the day before going to Bielsa."

"So you didn't go over the *fajas* either?"

"No. We went to the Collado de Añisclo but it was in cloud. We tried to find the path down but it was probably the wrong way and we could see a storm coming. So we went right down the Añisclo canyon instead."

Walt says to me: "You're walking faster than us, so go on ahead"

It's not true but I reply: "See you later."

The sound of rocks tumbling on the slopes above attracts my eyes. A small group of *sarrios* is scrambling up the scree.

I try not to look back so as to maintain the suspense, but keep glimpsing the increasingly spectacular view of the other side of the Pineta valley. Finally I stop to take it all in. The floor of the valley is randomly splashed by the river, rocks, trees, and pasture. Green; hence the valley's other name, the Balle Berde. The cliffs above are remarkably different. Rigorously horizontal lines of exposed rock alternate with strictly straight lines of trees. I count a dozen striations on the slope, like contours precisely etched with the help of a geography teacher. Nature may well abhor them but she hasn't quite forgotten her lines. Higher up Nature has let herself go again in a rollercoaster ride of contorted geology flecked with snow: six mountains side by side, the Three Sisters with the Three Marias hot on their tails.

The Collado de Añisclo is over there too, tucked up in a hollow between the Sisters and the Marias. This is where I would have appeared had I come directly from Góriz; where Julie and Walt turned back in the cloud. I can make out where the Senda bumps its way down over the snowy patches, banging its head every time it tumbles from one of the rocky ledges into the forest, picking itself up again, counting how many more there are to go.

In contrast, on this side of the valley it is summer and the going is easy. The path joins a track up to a pass and then flows down the other side, slipping lazily into the Plana Fonda, a gigantic geological bathtub set into the side of the mountain. With no plughole, when the giants stepped out the waste water, dust, and dirt remained behind, slowly filling up the tub and turning green: cows now enjoy the luxuriant pasture. I am yet again asking myself where the sheep are when I hear some bells. Not the clang of cowbells but a tinkle. The sheep – a dozen or so – are at the Collata las Coronetas, on the rim of the tub where it spills over into the next valley.

But much more surprising than the sheep is a stone lying by the side of the path. Can it really be a Neolithic polisher? What on earth is it doing here? Even more strangely, although it is broken in half, the two ends are together, touching snugly. It looks as though it has been excavated on an archaeological dig, washed, and then placed on the grass by the side of the trench to dry. In a few minutes the finds assistant will come along with a tube of HMG to stick it back together. Only there is no dig. And the stone is completely out of context. I examine it carefully. It is a pebble the size and shape of a spectacle case, with slightly smoothed surfaces and pock marks at one end. It is one of those borderline cases. It might be a linen smoother or it could be a natural pebble.

I weigh up the problem. Definitely not ultra-light. The only solution is to take it with me and ask a local expert. I wrap it in a tee-shirt and put it in my rucksack. The museum in Bielsa wouldn't know what to do with it. I'll have to send it home and continue my researches from there.

A walk in the Park

I pick my way carefully along the rubble-strewn path down into the valley on the other side of the pass. Julie and Walt yomp past and by the time I reach the river they are way ahead.

The track descends slowly to Parzán. Made by miners for their mules, it is easy walking but dull. The miners would have seen a valley lined with pasture, with frequent huts. Now the pasture is being invaded by brambles and trees, and the huts are mostly ruins. I stop at one of the less derelict ones and look inside. The bags of wool stacked in a corner don't even smell of lanolin; they must have been here for years.

After skirting the romantic village of Chisagüés and passing through Parzán, both restored to within an inch of their lives, the Senda arrives at the main road.

Cranes hauling steel beams into position mark the location of a new supermarket. On the other side of the road the ski-hire-antique-shop-restaurant-petrol-station-wine-shop-tobacconist stretched out along the highway looks well organised to cater to every wish of the 400,000 tourists who cross the frontier each year.

Julie and Walt are eating in the restaurant. They have already reached their dessert but invite me to join them.

"The sheep at the pass were the first I've seen this year," I say.

"You're obsessed by sheep, aren't you?" comments Julie.

To change the subject I ask her which State they come from.

"Amsterdam," she replies.

"But you've spent a long time in the US?"

"A fair bit. The PCT took us five months."

"What do you think of Cheryl Strayed's book then?"

"It's good but it's about her, not the PCT. She only did half of the trail anyway. There were places and situations we recognised, of course, like going for six days between resupplies."

"What's it like compared with the Senda?"

"Easier. It's designed for horses so it's never too steep. But you have day after day of pretty much the same thing. You get your big trees in Oregon. Trees on a European scale in Washington. You get your desert areas, or looking over the desert areas with the same vast infinite view going on forever. Unlike the Pyrenees where the views change rapidly. It's like German Tourist says… What is she called? …"

Footprints on the mountains

"Christine," says Walt

"I've read her blog as well," I say. Christine has hiked more than 28,000km since 2004. Her trail name is German Tourist.

"… It's like she says, more up and down, steeper," Julie continues. "You see fewer people here and soon lose sight of each other. The PCT is like a moving hotel."

I can believe that the Senda involves more climbing each day but not that it is easier. 4300km is a long, long way.

Walt adds: "The problem with Cheryl Strayed's book is that all kinds of crazies will come ill-equipped, hoping to 'find themselves'. The Angels are worried that they will cause everybody else lots of problems."

"We met somebody who was back on the PCT after seven years," says Julie. "The last time he walked it with a friend, they were in a blizzard. The friend turned right, he turned left. He met another group of walkers who saved his life. The friend died. They were under-equipped."

"Have you done any other trails?" I ask.

"We've been walking for the last year and a half. We did the Korean Crest Trail. The problem with that was we kept needing to descend from the peaks for water." They tell me more about it before setting off again.

Today they're going to see how far they can get before pitching their tent.

"See you tomorrow," says Julie.

I cross the road to the Hotel Fuen and use the internet to look up what German Tourist actually wrote:

> The Pyrenees have been the most beautiful and spectacular part of my [3,000km] hike. There is no doubt about it. The Pyrenees sometimes even rival the High Sierra in the US in beauty… But did I like the Pyrenees? No, not very much… I felt uncomfortable on the steep stretches over loose scree and the endless boulder fields…

But mostly it was a question of speed:

> Everything took so much longer in the Pyrenees than expected… I very often had to realise that it had taken a whole long hard day to just cover seven or eight kilometres as the crow flies.

A walk in the Park

So, for Christine, do kilometres on the clock really count more than beauty in the eye? As far as I am concerned, it is the kilograms in the rucksack which count so I phone for a taxi to take me back to Bielsa.

I am sitting on the steps of the hotel waiting for the taxi to arrive when a young man comes striding down the road with a rucksack on his back. I offer him a lift.

"What happened?" I ask him pointing to caked blood and lacerations on his arm.

"I fell on the snow at the Puerto de Estós. I've never been so frightened in my life."

In Bielsa I go to the supermarket with my stone. The girl weighs it on the vegetable scales (520g), helps me with the packaging and sells me the stamps. (Months later I return to the area and find a local archaeologist who tells me that the stone is natural.) I fill my rucksack with food and get a taxi back to Parzán.

It's all just too much running around. I'll be glad to get back into my fantasy life where the only thing I need to do is to walk.

The heart of the matter

Parzán to Viadós

Outside it is pitch black but I'm walking along the side of the road anyway so it doesn't matter. It's good to walk in the cool. By the time the sun has risen I am in the Barranco de Urdiceto ravine. The track is a mirror image of yesterday's, up instead of down, cool instead of hot, and built for importing concrete and steel for dams rather than for extracting minerals. Which is why it is paralleled by electricity pylons and stops at a hydroelectric plant.

Just after the end of the track I meet Julie running in my direction.

"I'll be back in a minute," she says as she flies by.

A little further up the track I catch up with Walt who has two rucksacks at his feet.

"She's gone to search for her MP3 player," he says pointing at a hut near to the dam. "We didn't camp in the end."

Julie returns empty-handed: "It must be in my rucksack."

Chatting whilst walking along the path, I hardly notice the climb.

"How do you manage to take so much time off?" I ask.

"I'm an engineering architect," says Walt. "I work on specific projects so I can have extended breaks."

"And I was a head teacher, but I was bored," adds Julie. "So I'm on an extended sabbatical. But I can pick up work when I need to. I went back for four months when Walt had to have an operation."

I look at Walt.

"I injured my shoulder. We were halfway along the PCT but I didn't pay enough attention to it. So when we finished I needed an operation to put it back together."

We reach a junction. Turn left here and we would be very quickly in France, but the Senda turns right. Our boots slither a little on the snow at

The heart of the matter

the head of the valley but not enough to be worth the bother of crampons. Sometimes we prefer to scramble over the rocks. I take off my hat, then my anorak.

At the Collado de Urdiceto, the highest point of the day, I stop for a snack. Julie and Walt continue, bouncing over the spongy moss on their way down, avoiding the narrow runnel inadvertently created by previous walkers, and disappear behind a fold in the cloth. It is still real mountain, way higher than any in Britain, but somehow different: wholesome, like a muesli advert. Vast areas of tufty grass criss-crossed with *veredas*, bedecked with banks of still-dormant rhododendrons and bilberries. Occasional pine trees, cascading streams. Blue gentians in flower. The only jarring note comes from the underlying strata: where the vegetation is cut by streams the purple-red rock shows through like sticky clots of drying blood.

The path becomes a road and a notice announces that I am on the 'Continua Pirineum'. I've never seen the pseudo-Latin name before but I can see where it is coming from.

These cross-frontier paths were the embodiment of the famous *lies and passeries*, medieval agreements between the inhabitants in France and in Spain for whom the Pyrenees were not so much a barrier as a definition of identity. The paths were once so frequented that an inhabitant of Gavarnie, for example, would know the names and faces of many of the inhabitants of Torla.

But the 'long' war (the Spanish Civil War 1936–39, followed by the Second World War 1939–45), an ellipsis in the relationships between many European countries, was a full stop here. Some Spanish sheep still walk to France for the summer pasture but the shepherds don't stay and their huts are invaded by weeds.

Calmette wrote, as early as 1947:

> The idea of the frontier has again taken on its former significance and power. It could be said, without contradiction, that the spirit of Modernity triumphing over the spirit of the Middle Ages is the revenge of geography. A broken logic has been re-established. The chain of mountains that was rubbed out, or almost, has been redrawn on the map with the sharpness of a knife edge. The Pyrenees have been definitively rebuilt.

Seventy years later, the Continua Pirineum is restoring paths and Romanesque churches, aided by the European Union. This is the real irony. A frontier which once didn't really exist is now the object of an initiative called "Europe without frontiers". Something which was born quite naturally from the common interest of the neighbouring mountain communities has become a dossier on the desks of bureaucrats in Brussels.

History repeats itself, the first time as tragedy, the second as tourism.

It isn't the only time that the area has come to the attention of the wider world. In 1985 a Pyrenean fable was written here. It is the story of the Pineta dam rewritten for a modern audience: the roles of men and women have been reversed and sex plays a bigger part. The events took place in Plan, the next village down the valley from here.

It all started on 2 January with the showing of a film on the television in the village bar. '*Caravana de mujeres*' ('Westward the women') recounts the fictional journey of a wagon train of 150 women from Chicago to California in search of husbands. It turned out to be inspirational for the thirteen single men watching it. In their village of 170 inhabitants, they calculated, there were more than forty *tiones* and only one eligible woman. The others had gone south to work in the towns leaving the men stranded in the mountains to look after the animals or work in forestry. They may not have had a New Year's Resolution before, but now they had one: get hitched. Their strategy was to place an advert in the local paper, the *Heraldo de Aragón*:

> Village in the Aragon Pyrenees seeks women between 20 and 40 years old for marriage.

By 10 January this simple advert had turned into a phenomenon. A reporter from *El Mundo* was sent through the snow to investigate. If ten or twenty come to the carnival it will be great, the village carpenter told her. Instead, 10,000 people turned up for the 3-day festival from 7–9 March; not just the three busloads of women from Madrid, Barcelona, and Saragossa, but other hopeful men and women, onlookers, and representatives of the international media.

"It helped to change the mentality of the village which, like most villages, didn't look kindly on people who got together and separated, or on unmarried mothers. In six months we advanced more in this sense than in the previous

The heart of the matter

forty years," remembers the only one of the thirteen men in the bar who didn't find a wife, twenty years later. "I didn't try hard enough," he admits.

But others did try harder. Mariano rang one of the women every day. His future wife, María, remembers living in a hostel for single mothers run by nuns in Madrid. Her children were in boarding school and she only saw them at weekends.

"When I arrived in the village, he was first in line, madly waiting for me."

Mariano explains: "I wanted to get married whatever happened so I asked her formally on the second day. I remember everybody dancing around us crying 'Long live the happy couple',"

They were married on 4 May.

"The best of it was the surge of joy and the lust for life which the village discovered. We were born again," says José María Fantova, another of the thirteen.

The wagon train continued until 1989 and brought together around forty couples, stabilising the population. But the children of those marriages, and indeed many of the couples, have since moved on to new pastures.

The mediatisation of the caravans brought the problem of rural depopulation to the attention of the rest of Spain and beyond without helping to find any long-term solution.

At the Viadós hostel Julie and Walt are just eating their desserts when I arrive, sweating. I sit down next to them.

"Why the Senda?" I ask Julie when she finishes the last mouthful.

"Some friends had a goat farm near Benasque and we went to run it so they could have a holiday. We bought the guide and tried a few short sections, so it has always been in the back of our minds. And now we have the time."

We compare navigation methods. Walt has navigated by the stars – at sea, of course.

"Thirty-three years ago I went to South America," he says. "I told my parents that they would hear from me in a month. Now if our children don't hear from us every day they panic."

Before they walk off to find a campsite further up the valley Julie insists on taking a picture of our three Z-Pack rucksacks side-by-side.

Footprints on the mountains

I finish my lunch, unpack, put my batteries on to charge, then go for a shower. The best moment of the day. When the hot water first hits my naked back I shiver with pleasure. I shut my eyes as all the aches are washed out. But two euros doesn't last very long. Afterwards the Senda takes a siesta.

I am getting into a routine. When I awake I will have a snack, repair my feet, put Voltarene on my knee, plan tomorrow, eat dinner, repack, and be asleep by ten. The routine is a psychological structure as well as an everyday reality. The walking is meaning; the food, shower, and sleep are pleasure. Life is circumscribed. The past doesn't go beyond Candanchú and the future only stretches as far as Benasque, where I hope to be tomorrow evening. The world *below* doesn't count.

The difficulty with my walking routine is that I am out of kilter with everybody else and often somebody arrives just when I am dozing off in the afternoon. In this case he just dumps his sack and leaves me in peace. The second interruption is Francisco, who is equally discreet.

Sitting on one of the logs on the grass in front of the hostel in the early evening, I ask Francisco what time he turned up.

He hesitates, looks at his watch, looks blank: "I can't remember. I'm dead. I'm *so* tired at the end of every day."

"It's the heat... Where did you stay last night?"

"In Bielsa. I went to the Hotel Fuen this morning to see if you were there but it was shut up."

"I left early."

"The track up the valley was really tedious," he continues in quiet desperation. "I'm so tired. I'm only going to Estós tomorrow. I'm thinking of giving up. I've only ever done weekends. Even when I have a day off I don't recover."

"Julie said that it takes four weeks to get into your rhythm." This is not quite true: she actually said that is *supposed* to take four to six weeks but that she never felt she got there.

He digs his mobile phone out of his pocket.

"Look," he says, pointing at the wallpaper image. "That's my wife, or she was then. We're divorced." They are sitting with their arms round each other on the doorstep of this very hostel. "That was before I lost my job, two years ago."

"So you know the area then."

The heart of the matter

"It's where we used to come. But I first came to Estós much earlier, when I was 14, before they rebuilt the hostel."

I look at the path where it continues between the scattered *bordas*, as it climbs up to the Puerto de Estós and the threat of snow. The last time, with a friend, it was classic walking. We circumnavigated Posets on the Three Hostels circuit starting and finishing here, climbing to its summit. "You go first," I said on the way back down the ridge. When we were out of danger she said: "You get vertigo don't you. I'll never forgive you for that, I don't like heights either." From here I can see the summit, pointed, above the black pine forest. A real mountain, well-defined, not lost like Monte Perdido. Defined by the path up the valley to Estós on one side and the return path from Angel Orus on the other. Today, like last time, an irreproachable sky.

I ask some French walkers, barefooted on the lawn, where they have been. There, they say, indicating the same triangle. Snow? Yes. Right to the top? No, the final ridge was clear.

In the evening I am placed at a table with Francisco and the other occupant of my room, a Frenchman. They have no common language so I translate. What is the Frenchman doing? HRP. Has he done other treks? Yes. Where? Nepal, South America. Where is he going tomorrow? France. I try all the habitual pleasantries but he simply isn't interested. He'd rather be sitting on his own. His only voluntary comment is that he 'came down' because he had run out of food. Handsome, fifties. Normally walkers quickly slip into the familiar *tu* but he is decidedly a *vous*. I leave him to eavesdrop on the French group while I talk with Francisco. We talk socks – he has the same as me – and boots – he bought some new ones in Bielsa – and about the path between Candanchú and Sallent – he took a different route to avoid the snow.

Viadós to Benasque

My breakfast is alone on the table in the morning. By the time I have eaten it the Frenchman is standing outside, the only other person showing signs of life. Breakfast? I can't believe that he bothers with such frivolities.

The long gentle fields of snow on the way up to the pass at the Puerto de Estós are easily within my comfort zone. But on the other side a long swathe of white has unravelled from the higher slopes. Two walkers are progressing towards me and the first one reaches me shortly afterwards. We balance on our crampons.

"Where have you come from?" I ask the twenty-something woman in Spanish.

She says something unintelligible. I should have paid more attention to her tee-shirt. It is also unintelligible, but the Ks and Xs are a giveaway. She continues in approximate English and we struggle to communicate until an older man arrives. He has even less English but speaks to me in Spanish. She is his daughter. They have been walking the Three Hostels circuit and this is their last day. She has no difficulty in understanding either of us now, though I notice that her father is careful to address her in Basque.

The snow is steep and the bottom a rocky crash. The guy in the taxi to Bielsa fell here and the snow is well marked by skids but *with crampons* it isn't really dangerous. Even so, I throw myself into the first bed of grass.

I have taken my boots off, wrung out my socks, and nearly finished my lunch when two men appear from the direction of Viadós. Hendaye. 17 June, HRP, GR10, GR11. Alban and Gérard skipped some sections for the usual reasons. They have a support car driven by Alban's wife but she and her husband are going home tomorrow. Gérard is nervous about going on alone. See you later, I say, as they walk off.

The young man and woman I meet later are understandably even more nervous. It is their first day and they have just seen the snow at the head of the valley. They failed to make any sense of Alban and Gérard but they speak English. Crampons? No. Ice axe? No.

"We have just arrived from Israel. We didn't expect snow."

"Where are you heading?"

"Torla."

What do I say? That they are risking their lives? That even walkers who are fully equipped are nervous? They keep repeating how beautiful it all is. They are so happy to be on their long-awaited romantic holiday. They want me to say, don't worry, everything will be fine.

I tell them what I know but they decide to continue, trusting to their walking poles. In the evening, safe in a comfortable hotel, I feel horribly responsible; I should have suggested they go back to Benasque to hire some equipment.

The heart of the matter

The Estós hostel, mid-route, is just as I remember it: a block of a building with the large terrace where we sat watching an ethereal silent film: the full moon rising over the Maladeta massif.

Later I take a diversion into the much more distant past, through the first flowering rhododendrons, along another *vereda*. Veredas are not ostentatiously ancient like a castle or a hillfort but still they owe their origins to hunter-gatherers following the movement of wild herds well before anybody thought of permanent defences. The Senda has picked up tufts of old wool caught in the gorse and spun it together with threads left over from mining, pedlars, forestry, and dams. Millennia of economic activity recycled into something fresh and living, a new story. History written in footprints on the mountains, updated and repackaged for the 21st-century.

I descend tiredly to the Estós reservoir. Just before it, a bridge is being repaired but I don't think anything of it. The reservoir itself, though tranquil, is full to the brim but I don't think anything of that either. It is only later that I recognise the signs.

I have no particular plans for where to stay, but at the end of the valley a well-placed sign decides for me: the Hostal Parque Natural is only five minutes' walk away.

Benasque to the Puente de Coronas

The first hut is only a short walk away but nothing beyond it could be reached before dusk so I will stop there. I intend to sleep in but wake at the usual time.

Waiting for breakfast, strolling on the terrace I peer at the river below. The wide rocky banks, the road ending abruptly, and the big yellow diggers don't make much sense, particularly given how short-sighted I am.

In the meantime, breakfast is served. The *dueña* asks me to translate. Would the young man at the next table be so kind as to have another look for his key? Might he have left it at the chess competition? Yes, he replies. It must be there somewhere. Trevor is playing in the 33rd International Open, one of the 430 competitors.

A taxi takes me to Benasque over scrunching gravel where there should be road. The bits of the jigsaw that remain intact are tens of metres from where they should be, only held together by the tarmac glue. The town itself was saved by a rocky promontory just upstream which took the brunt. Only one building shows any sign of damage but there must have been serious flooding: Doña Sofía, the queen, came to investigate.

Benasque is just like Torla, one of those clean places: mountaineering guides and kayak shops rub gables with discos, pizzerias, and a pub (the Molly Malone). The streets are hung with the flags of many nations. For culture you have the *Galería* Out of Africa.

The graffiti includes 'FUCK YOU SUCKERS'. The work of an Anglophone lout or an educated Spaniard with an extensive grasp of the English vernacular? Or perhaps an innocent catch phrase? '*Mosketeros tasafarinos*' is signed by PóRRi, CRq, JAVI, and XKA: they must be the four musketeers. But what are *tasafarinos*?

When the shops open at ten, I buy as many calories as possible in a bulimic spree in the supermarket. At eleven the taxi takes me back to where I left off.

Just above the Paso Nuevo dam I am overtaken by a man on a mountain bike dripping sweat onto his unfashionably plain tee-shirt. He stops for a rest.

I say: "*¡Hola! ¿A dónde vas?* – where are you going."

"To the waterfall. And you?" he replies, in English.

"*Hasta donde quieren ir mis rodillas* – as far as my knees want to go." It's pretentious and probably grammatically incorrect but always gets a laugh. We continue in English as he gets back on his bike. He pedals slowly, balancing precariously, so I can keep up.

Is he on holiday? Yes, playing chess. Yesterday he was up against the tournament's no. 3 grandmaster. That's the fun of an 'open' tournament. Cycling clears his mind. When he gets back he will eat before the competition starts. I tell him about the actors I met once who were able to learn their lines more easily after a day's walking.

"Where are you from?" I ask.

"Madrid," he replies. I'd expected him to say Bath.

We reach the cascade without noticing the time pass. I splash water over my arms and head as he turns round and goes back for lunch.

A little higher up I'm sitting by the side of the track in the shade of a fir tree when two heavily laden blokes catch up with me. José and Jordi,

The heart of the matter

Catalans, are going to climb the Tuca de Vallibierna tomorrow. They came two months ago but turned back. This time they have crampons. They are going to camp this evening by the lake and need to get a move on.

We talk about the Catalan Costa Brava, where I lived last autumn. José wants to show off his knowledge of English:

"Catalonia is beautiful."

I outbid him. "And Catalonia is not Spain."

This slogan, in English, is to be found spray-painted on signposts everywhere on the Costa Brava, just to make sure tourists are on the right track.

"Like the graffiti…" I trail off, looking at them. I have said the wrong thing.

My rucksack falls apart again, so I have to stop and repair it. They wish me well and speed off.

At the end of the track, the Coronas hut is a pale lime-green box with an emergency radiotelephone in one corner and a layer of dust almost everywhere. I start to work with the broom, brushing the planks of the bunk bed and the long table, pushing the ashes back into the fireplace. A young boy pokes his head through the door, turning to ask his mother if they can sleep here. No, she says, we are going back down on the bus.

I laze the afternoon away on the grass between the hut and the river, looking for faces in the sky, rolling up my anorak to make a pillow. As I drift off, the white noise of the water cascading over the rocks gets louder. I can hear music: a powerful base rhythm with heavy handed drums and a whining mouthorgan. I struggle to identify it. Blues? Howlin' Wolf? I settle into my audible mirage, emptied of all conscious thought, succumbing to the music of this rural discotheque.

At six o'clock the last *Autobus de las nubes* (Cloud bus) brings two men and takes away everyone else. One of the men goes directly into the hut. The other walks a few steps and, taking off his rucksack, looks theatrically at the mountains to the north before also entering. I follow them. We exchange the usual information. Miguel is going to climb Aneto, at 3404m the highest peak in the Pyrenees. Juan's project is even more ambitious: Pico Russell, followed by Aneto, followed by the Diente del Alba, coming back to the hut each night in between.

Thirty minutes later a man opens the door and asks despairingly if he has missed the bus. He and his friends left the hut at dawn but the others are still somewhere on Aneto, dangerously exhausted. He will walk down and try to get a phone signal. At half past seven the sky is beginning to darken when he comes back in a taxi. A quarter of an hour later, three more walkers arrive. At quarter past eight we are beginning to wonder if we will have to use the emergency phone when the remaining eight stagger in. I can't imagine how they do it but, like the soldiers at Bujaruelo, they all squash into the taxi.

Juan and Miguel spend the evening discussing the 212 *tresmiles* (three thousand metre peaks) of the Pyrenees by the light of a candle. Back in big school, mostly I just listen. My only serious contribution is when the talk turns to equipment. Juan has the lightest mattress I have ever held. Miguel an 800g tent. Meanwhile, I empty my rucksack. Catch, I say, throwing it at Juan. It's very light, he says. We are like fashion-obsessed teenagers debating the relative merits of Adidas and Nike, not that any of our equipment is so downmarket.

It is getting late and the conversation is guttering.

"It won't disturb you if I get off at four o'clock, will it?" asks Miguel, rhetorically.

We blow out the candle.

Before I go to sleep I remember Francisco, who ought to be here tonight. I recall the joke he told when we were eating dinner in the Pineta hostel: what happens when a Canadian woman, an American woman, and a Catalan woman go walking together on the Senda? Well, they think they might get lost so the Canadian woman takes a satellite distress signal with her... it was at this point that I understood it wasn't a joke. He wondered if indeed they did get lost because after meeting them a couple of times he never saw them again.

Where is Francisco now? Is he lost? Has he given up? I'm disappointed.

Puente de Coronas to Vielha

Miguel's alarm shatters the blackness, at ten to four. By four o'clock he is outside. By four-twenty Juan has also gone. I leave at five though the sun won't rise for another forty minutes.

The next village is two days away: the first of them in a timeless wilderness without tracks, or dams, or mines, in the heart of the matter, in the shadow of Aneto. Two high passes to cross. Snow in abundance. And at the end of the day a little wooden hut. I'm looking forward to that hut.

In the darkness, my head torch lights up the fir trees. Their pale young shoots swing into view like the candelabras of an enchanted castle and then vanish again. The path climbs up the hillside, carefully placing its feet on the wet soil, slithering about.

I cross a first river on a skew-whiff wooden bridge, thrown into the air by the floods, unintentionally humpbacked. But the second river is impassable and I have to scramble up its bank through scrub to just below the Ibón Bajo de Vallibierna before I can jump over.

The Senda inches around the edge of the lake, along the cliff a few metres above the surface. In a crease in the mountains, the lake itself is completely unruffled, its oily sheen mirroring the grey rocks and cloudless sky. How can it and the stream below be composed of the same element?

There is no room for tents and no Catalans either. It might just be possible to camp near to the second lake but by the time I get there the Catalans will be far away.

I climb up the head of the valley across the snow, great sagging jowls where it has softened, slipped, and refrozen, slavering its way down towards the lake. From the top of the pass, looking down, I peek timidly over the edge where the snow becomes steep. But fear isn't the only emotion hanging in the air. I also feel weary, not physically but mentally. I am pushing my limits. There is a tired inevitability about it all. One day I will overstep. Why do I do this?

When I hiked the Pyrenean Way I asked other people why they were walking. Nobody, not even those who saw the walk as a sporting challenge, nobody admitted to deliberately shooting up adrenalin. At the top of this slope, looking down on the softening snow, I can feel the needle entering the vein.

I could always turn back, tell myself that it is too difficult, that to continue is unreasonable. But I don't want to be like my friend Maurice. Maurice turned back. He turned his back on life.

As far as Maurice was concerned the helicopter flying him to that hospital three years ago was taking him to his grave. And even though the drugs saved him, he died anyway. He had been debonair, gracious and attentive, particularly to younger women. Now he was old and unattractive, or so he thought.

When he started to be ill he didn't go to the doctor until the shaking hands forced him to. And from then on he hid in his house. He didn't want to be seen to be sick. He hadn't planned for old age.

He was afraid of falling. On the rare occasions when he had to go out he would walk bent over, with a stick, laboriously, as if each step were his last. But if he didn't want to talk to someone he could almost break into a run.

Life was folding him up, like yesterday's newspaper. Every day there was less to read.

When I looked into Maurice's eyes I could see my future reflected in his glasses. This is what I really fear: cuddling up to death before that old monkey comes to fetch me, accepting the first tentative touch of that warm embrace. I can't turn back here.

Am I being melodramatic? Real climbers would look at this and laugh, wouldn't they? I am a child again, seeking my mother's hand in the dark.

My mind is racing, incoherent. I recall the Spanish mama in Góriz, accepting her fate. I put one foot out over the edge and my mind goes blank. I tread carefully, planting the ice axe deep in the slush. It is surprisingly soft for the time of day. Once my foot slips from under me but the ice axe holds and I haul myself up again. It is a long ten minutes in the heart of the matter.

Afterwards, the carousel around the Estany de Cap de Llauset and up the hill on the other side takes no time at all. At the second pass I look over the lip. I was sure that there would be less snow here because this pass is lower, but the slope is just as white and steeper. No time for thinking.

Much later I see the Anglios hut in the distance below the snowline, a pathetic garden shed, perched on a hillock between two lakes on a grassy plateau. Looking back, the snow already looks insignificant.

Crossing a wayward stream just before arriving at the hut, I meet a man and a teenager who is probably his daughter. He looks about forty; she can't be more than seventeen. He is too fat; she is too thin. They really ought to do a deal. They've just come up from the valley on their first day on the Senda. They don't have any snow equipment.

"What's it like?" he says.

"Soft snow. Dangerous."

The heart of the matter

View east from the Collada de Vallibierna

"A little dangerous," he revises for the benefit of his daughter.
I won't let him get away with it.
"Dangerous," I repeat.

Close to, the hut is bigger than I'd imagined. Opening the door, the first thing I spot is a blue foam mattress, a mere centimetre thick, but perfect. Too tired to think, too weary to eat, I take off my boots and lie down. My watch says ten-thirty and I have already arrived at my destination.

When I wake up my watch says it is midday. I must eat. Then what? I could study the *222 traps in the king's pawn opening* by Karsten Müller and Rainer Knaak which has been left here. Or perhaps correct the translation of *'Por favor no dejéis basuras en el refugio'*, which is given as 'Take your brushes with you.' But after that what? Even if I do nothing for the rest of the day, I have already achieved more than in a year of sitting in front of a computer. But doing nothing isn't easy. I need to move. I'm in a hurry. Stupid.

The path descends rapidly, past wooden tables and benches, handrails and a snake which slides under the piles of dead leaves before I can identify it. It winds up at a main road. I cross it, one footstep in Aragon, the next in Catalonia. It may not be so easy in the future.

By now my ankles are wobbling and my head is aching from sun and thirst. The Refugio de l'Hospitalet is locked so I beg some water from a group of youngsters. Here again the path has been trashed by the river.

Back at the road again, near the entrance of a tunnel, I take off my rucksack, leaning it against the crash barrier. Veronica and I have a rendezvous here. Iconoclastically, she has booked us into a hotel well away from the Senda, on the other side of the Pyrenees. But I'm a day ahead of schedule so I take off my hat, put on a smile, and look the passing drivers in the eyes, as I used to do forty years ago. It works better now: I have less hair and no competition. So I don't have to wait long. The driver tells me that he and his wife are typical immigrants. Mountain guide in summer, ski instructor in winter, he came from Madrid twenty years ago; his wife is a nurse. They drop me in the centre of Vielha.

Vielha is the capital of the Valle de Arán, politically in Spain but, geographically north of the watershed, logically it should be in France. Or is it in not-quite-independent Catalonia? Or Occitania? The local language is Aranese, a variant of Occitan. But then again 'Arán' means valley, in proto-*Basque*.

I ask a woman the way and she points along the street.

"The hotel's after the big car park."

The Vall Blanca is one of the many new hotels stacked up in the suburbs like packs of playing cards: the town is betting heavily on tourism.

Inside, I have a confusing conversation with the receptionist. Not only have I arrived on the wrong day, but also at the wrong time. The clock behind the desk says seven o'clock but my watch says quarter past five. Where has my life gone? Did I actually sleep for three hours?

In my room, I calculate that I must have arrived at the hut much later than I thought. If I'd known at the time, I would have stayed there. It has been a very long day by any method of measurement.

Under the yoke

Vielha

If you need a new pair of boots, Vielha offers plenty of choice so I ask around and end up at the sole shop that *everybody* recommends. My old pair has developed a hole in one toe and in a few days' time the tread will start to separate from the uppers. Unfortunately the only way to get my feet into the new boots is to remove the padding. I am buying into problems.

Outside again, what surprises me most is the number of Occitan crosses on flags in shop windows, on houses, and in the main square. In my village the yellow cross on a red flag is always present at cultural events. But, although some of the older people still speak Occitan to each other, for most youngsters it is nothing more than a lazy reference to the golden age of troubadours. In the Valle de Arán it is something more, the equivalent of the Spanish bull or the Catalan donkey.

This is the only area in the world where Occitan is an official language, although 150 years ago it was the mother tongue over a wide swathe of southern Europe, from northern Italy almost to the Atlantic. The valley, with a population of 10,000, is its last bastion.

But the Occitan here is not the dialect I hear in my village. The French *le*, translated as *lo* in my Occitan, is *eth* in the Aranese dialect. So the notice under the arches of the town hall is somewhat difficult to interpret. Vielha, it seems to say, is about to celebrate the 700th anniversary of the Era Querimònia, the valley's Magna Carta. The rest of the story is to be found in the museum: the valley had managed to wriggle free from the red claws of feudalism. Long winter months helped keep it safe from its chosen masters in Catalonia. Most of its privileges have since been whittled away but it still has its language.

It also has a hymn: '*Aqueres muntanhes* – those mountains'. When I hear it,

Footprints on the mountains

I recognise the melody of '*Se cantà*', though the words are different. In my village '*Se cantà*' is sung with great reverence.

Se canta, selected verses

Aranese	*English*	*My Occitan*
Aqueres montanhes	Those mountains	*Aquelas montanhas*
Que tant nautes son,	That are so high	*Que tan hautas son,*
M'empèishen de véder	Keep me from seeing	*M'empachan de veire*
Mèns amors an o son.	Where my love has gone.	*Mas amors ont son.*
chorus:	*chorus:*	*chorus:*
Se cantes, perqué cantes?	If you sing, why do you?	*Se canta, que cante,*
Cantes pas per jo,	You're not singing for me,	*Canta pas per ieu,*
Cantes per ma hilha	You're singing for my girl	*Canta per ma mia*
Que non ei près de jo.	Who's not by my side.	*Qu'es al luènh de ieu.*
Nautes, se son nautes,	High, they're so high,	*Baissatz-vos, montanhas,*
Ja s'abaisharàn	But they will lie down,	*Planas, levatz-vos,*
Es mies amoretes	And my dear love	*Per que pòsca veire*
Que s'aproparàn.	Will come closer.	*Mas amors ont son.*

'*Se cantà*' is our heritage from the heyday of Occitania, romantically associated with the greatest Pyrenean of all time, Gaston Fébus, the 14th-century count of Foix, hunter, renowned warrior, man of letters, and lover.

Physically north of 'those mountains', the ambivalent situation of the valley made it the focus of a quixotic attempt to defeat fascism. Hidden history, now being given its rightful place in the books, the attack was the idea of the Spanish Communist Party which thought it could insert a last-minute codicil into the legacy of the Second World War. For them, Franco was just another teetering domino; a few surgical cuts in the *Línea P* would result in a popular uprising. The Allies would rush in to finish the job. Roughly 6,000 volunteers were recruited.

Operación Reconquista de España was launched on 3 October 1944 with a raid on Orreaga, the first of a series of diversionary tactics. The main force crossed into the Valle de Arán on 19 October but failed even to get as far as Vielha. By the end of the month the survivors were back in France. The invasion was doomed before it started: De Gaulle had recognised Franco's regime three days previously. It was yet another failed incursion across the frontier 'fixed' by the 1659 Treaty of the Pyrenees.

And now, in the 21st century, what do the demands for Catalan independence mean for the valley? If its confused past is any guide, its future is unpredictable. The Valle de Aran is a variation in the music of the Pyrenees but still played on a recognisable theme. (The other local eccentric is Andorra. The music there is recognisable, but the theme is not the Pyrenees. When I pass through the country later on the Senda, I am shocked by the dissonance.)

By now Veronica has joined me in the town's museum, coming up the Garonne valley and round the mountain, harassed by traffic lights and missing bits of road. She reminds me that the Valle de Arán means Valley of the valley. When it floods, it floods.

We adore the wall paintings in Romanesque churches and have seen a poster for guided tours so I ask for details, only to be told that the opening has been put back by a week: everybody is out repairing the flood damage. The parish priests must be rolling up their soutanes and getting down to work beside the council road menders.

Vielha to La Restanca

Veronica drives me back to the south end of the tunnel, where I left off, and I head up the *cirque* de Conangles on a well-trodden path. It is easy going, through a small purple patch of columbine, the stairs stealing theatrically up the tiers to the first layer of icing.

I meet a man who asks me for string, pointing to his crocodile-mouth boot by way of explanation. I have a better remedy: Duck tape bought in Vielha. I tell him where to find replacements.

"What's the route like further on?" he asks.

"Lots of snow."

"In my guidebook it doesn't say there will be snow," he complains.

Footprints on the mountains

On my path, the snow gives way to boulders and then to a pleasant mountain ramble. The landscape reminds me of the Bouillouses further east but the Restanca reservoir seen from above is more like a Pacific lagoon. Drifting loose in the middle is a lone raft waiting, impossibly, for some inappropriately dressed top model to clamber aboard.

I step into the beach hut on the shore. Stern instructions forbid taking rucksacks upstairs; baskets are provided. After decanting my life into one of them I announce my arrival. The staff are preparing soup, bopping (as much as is possible while peeling garlic) to the sound of 'Dancing Queen' followed by 'Gimme! Gimme! Gimme (A man after midnight)', released well before they were born.

Sitting on the porch later I get mixed up with a family group: brothers, sisters, a brother-in-law, and someone they have 'adopted', reunited for their annual outing. This year it is the Tour des Encantats. There is much silliness; they are clearly going to have fun.

I point out the clouds. Cheer up you old misery, they say to me, it will be dry by tomorrow.

Another walker comes along the path. Hans has come from Irun *via* Andorra. He skipped a section because of the snow and has now come back to fill it in. He's not in a hurry to go in so we talk about snow. No problem. He casually picks up his ice axe as if to illustrate his method, holding it like an axe and jabbing at the sky.

The promised storm arrives and we all grab our washing and take shelter inside. At dinner time I am placed at a table with Hans, two Catalan men from Barcelona, and the Frenchman who has reappeared. For all the joy that went into making it, the soup is a sad disappointment. I'm the only one to drink two bowlfuls; some of the others don't even finish their first. Nevertheless, I later see the staff peeling more cloves for tomorrow's edition.

Hans tells me of his adventures. Since he retired he has been canoeing in Turkey and dog sledging and skiing across Lapland and Alaska, always solo, but this is the first time he has been on a long-distance walk. Why here, I ask? I saw some nice photos, he replies. On his travels, he takes many photos and writes about his experiences for his family.

"Do you have a blog?" I ask.

He looks at me as though I have made an indecent suggestion: "No!"

Yet later I come across it by chance.

Under the yoke

This is the first time he has appreciated the problem of weight. On a dog sled you don't notice the 45kg.

The Frenchman reveals that he climbed the Aneto *and* the Maladeta in a single day! The Catalans reveal that they have come from the Ernest Mallafré hostel where I am heading. It took them two days; they dawdled.

At the end of the meal Hans says: "That was fine, but I'm losing weight. I eat everything put in front of me but some hostels don't give you enough."

The manager asks if anybody wants breakfast to be left on the table.

"You can have it as early as you like but at six o'clock I will clear everything away and you won't be able to eat later either."

Restanca to Ernest Mallafré

Alone in the canteen, I have finished my breakfast by the appointed time but my walking pole is missing from the lobby; I will have to do without. Then, stepping outside, I nearly trip over it.

The day starts in black and grey. It's only now that I've been walking for a while that the first fringes of colour begin to appear: the turquoise reservoir below, the dark greens of the pines and the only slightly lighter green of the grass. Then the sky bowls in all at once, deliciously rosy.

At the Oelhacrestada pass, instead of dropping into the valley, the Senda continues to climb the flank of the mountain on the other side, now slathered in snow. In my memory the landscape was a glistening virgin white. But when I look at the photos now I can see the pink algae, the grey reflected from the muzzling clouds, the sloppy suds where it has moved and refrozen, and the clumsy needlework where footprints have pricked through the surface. I have been whitewashing out the flaws. But at least the lakes up here are perfect, immaculate even on the photos, still frozen in the centre but painted blue near the shore.

Unexpectedly, I hear voices on the ridge above me, though I have seen nobody since leaving the hostel. We meet up at the Port de Caldes pass and take each other's photos. Afterwards the snow almost disappears and on the way down to Colomers I see something like eighty walkers of all ages.

The staff are just starting their breakfast when I open the door of the Colomers hostel on the edge of the reservoir. I have been warned that the hostels further along are full so I ask the manager if he can radio Ernest Mallafré for me. He fails to get a response.

"The girls must be out emptying the rubbish," I am told, in English. "You can try your mobile phone once you get halfway across the bridge."

"Bridge?" I don't understand, my map doesn't show a bridge here.

"*Presa*," he explains in Spanish. For an engineer it is a dam, for a pedestrian, a bridge.

On the bridge I book a roof. The rain starts and although it doesn't last long it seems to wash all the hardness out of the day. The path wanders its way around boulders, up the valley through the increasingly sparse pines, and along the shores of a rosary of mirror-flat lakes, occasionally dipping its toes into them. The valley is full of water, though the real Aigüestortes, the twisted waters, are further on. I'm filled with an irrepressible childish joy, leaping across the streams.

As far as I can see the only unnatural thing here is the path and that is hardly an eyesore. Not so, says the Prames guide:

> Unfortunately, it is a very artificial park due, above all, to the hydraulic exploitation which since the 1920s has affected the numerous lakes, for which reason it has been excluded from the World Heritage List.
>
> All the lakes [in this sector] are interconnected by underground pipes destined to supply the hydroelectric station at Arties… The eponymous Estany de Sant Maurici has been artificially increased to 2.6hm^3.

Given that almost nowhere in Western Europe below the alpine zone is completely natural, it looks pretty good to me. The landscape could have been much more artificial: the French engineer who mapped it, Colomès de Juillan, was determined to build a trans-Pyrenean railway. It was he who first suggested digging a tunnel through the Cirque de Gavarnie. In the end his legacy is a rather paradoxical one. If his railway had pierced the mountains he might have had a station named after him. Instead he has a mountain: Colomers is a version of Colomès.

For some time now, I have been watching a couple of figures descending from the pass, so it is no surprise when we meet up; except that I didn't expect them to be talking in English. She – she's the talker, the organiser – is in Sitges to write. Her boyfriend – he's wearing a black baseball cap backwards – has joined her from the States and is being shown around. They've lounged on the beach, gone to France to see the cyclists on the Tour de France, gone to Pamplona to see the bulls, and they have now come here for the Chariots of Fire.

"The what?" I ask.

"Chariots of Fire. *Carros de foc* in Catalan."

I shake my head again.

"It's a circular walk. We were going to camp but then we found out that you can't, so the money spent on the tent was wasted." She adds: "We didn't expect so much snow. It wasn't in the guidebook." She tells me where they are going to stay: it sounds pretty much the same as the Tour des Encantats that the French family are doing.

On the other side of the pass the traverse is covered in snow. I am treading gingerly in the horizontal footprints when I hear a dog barking. Slithering down the steep slope after it, a young man shouts: "*Venga* – Come here." He slips on his backside, sliding into the footprints, followed by the collie, and then picks himself up. I look in astonishment at his tee-shirt and shorts.

"I've just been over to the Saboredo hostel to fetch him. He's always following walkers. I'm taking him back to Amitges," he explains as if it was the most natural thing in the world.

Unfortunately he hasn't brought a lead with him; his progress is accompanied by increasingly annoyed whistles and cries of '*venga*' alternating with increasingly mischievous yaps.

By the time I reach the Estany de Sant Maurici, I am hobbling, but at least I am still moving. On the other side of the lake, the remains of two men who preferred hunting *sarrios* to churchgoing will forever remain petrified. This is one of innumerable similar tales in the Pyrenees. Sometimes, as here, the tale hides an underlying pagan layer: Encantats means 'bewitched'.

Four walkers are sitting around a table in the hostel when I arrive and after sorting myself out I join them. We play Pick-up sticks like giddy children as the light fades. Then Carla, the cook, lights the ancient cast iron stove and we hang our washing around it, progressively pulled towards it by the heat. It is a wood cabin, comfortingly organic, reassuringly homely.

When I ask the others what they are doing they repeat the mysterious words *Carros de foc* and pass me a leaflet. I read: 55km, 9200m climbing.

"We're only doing a bit," one of them tells me. "And we're walking."

Footprints on the mountains

It comes in two variants. Sky runners take less than twenty-four hours. I can almost see them breasting the finishing tape to the sound of Vangelis' theme tune at the end of what is a superhuman achievement. Walkers normally take five days. So how can I have walked a third of it today? I compare the leaflet and my map: there's some cheating going on here. It's not 9200m climbing but 4600m climbing and 4600m of descent. It is exactly the same circuit as the family-fun Tour des Encantats but Chariots of Fire just sounds more heroic.

Before eating I have a difficult problem to solve. It comes in the shape of a squat toilet and an aching leg that will no longer bend enough. It is a delicate operation.

The plates have long been cleared away and it is beginning to get dark outside when the door opens abruptly and Hans' face appears in the lamplight. Carla goes to greet him.

The very first thing he says is: "Can I eat?"

"Dinner was at seven o'clock," she replies. I look at my watch. It is now half past eight. He waves at me.

"But can I eat now?"

"I can do you a main course and dessert. Do you also want soup?"

"Yes, soup…"

He slumps down opposite me. Carla opens the stove to put on some more fuel and the smell of wood smoke fills the room.

"I thought you were only going to Colomers," I say.

"I was but I arrived too early, even though I waited for breakfast at the Restanca."

I remind him that he has left his rucksack outside.

"I've been following your spikey tracks," he continues when he returns. "You are very cautious. I could see where you hesitated, turning round and round trying to decide which way to go. I didn't use my crampons at all today."

He is getting hungry and progressively more agitated. He looks around for a price list unsuccessfully, then grabs Carla's arm.

"How much does it cost?"

Carla speaks Catalan, Spanish, and French, but no German and only a little English so I have to translate.

"Sixteen euros for the night, seventeen for dinner, and six for breakfast."

Under the yoke

"OK, if it's a good meal, if it's worth it…"
I reassure him.
"Do you want soup?" asks Carla.
"Yes, I already told you when I arrived that I wanted soup! Why are you asking me again? I already said I wanted soup. Yes I want soup!"

I abridge but it makes no difference. Even though Carla can't quite understand, his tone says it all. I can see her biting her tongue. She goes back into the kitchen and puts some angry rap on the CD player.

Ernest Mallafré to La Guingueta d'Àneu

In the woods, tree trunks delineate the path and balustrades the bridges. A young couple comes up from the direction of Espot; she wafts past but her perfume lingers. I am still bathing in the foreign, heady pleasure when a man lurking by the side of the path disappears into the trees as I approach. He reappears just as suddenly, holding a strimmer like a weapon. I flinch, startled, but then I see his uniform. This is the national park border. I conclude that he is a secret agent disguised as a gardener.

A little further down, a convoy of four 4x4 taxis roaring up the hill crammed with walkers forces me to leap out of the way. Nearby, the graffiti on an electric junction box catches my eye. '*FARLOPA*' is street slang for cocaine; 'H101' is a talented Barcelona street artist, although this scribble is clearly not his work. The hydroelectric power station hums.

But despite the omens Espot is like any other Pyrenean settlement: rough stone walls, cobbled roads, and immaculate vegetable plots. Crossing the bridge, my ears pop and the river cascades in, accompanied by the squeaking of mechanical diggers clearing away the flood debris.

The Senda leaves Espot-Obago, the shady side of the village, on a horizontal gravel track, hurtles into the valley, and then slogs up the other side. I'm drinking all the time but drying out even more rapidly.

A thin girl equipped with boots, long legs, short shorts, a bikini top, and an air of teenage disdain, and what seems likely to be her mother come round the bend. They are both carrying small rucksacks. We say *hola!* but nothing more. Lagging a hundred metres behind them is a man, much more heavily laden in all the senses. He must be the father. British from his accent;

a first. They have come from La Guingueta, starting today and are going to Amitges followed by two weeks on the Senda. Snow? What snow? It must be thirty degrees centigrade here. I turn round to point it out. Where has it gone? I must have been dreaming.

After passing through the hamlet of Estaís the Senda takes me on a horizontal rock-cut track designed for mules, the original 4x4s. The next village, Jou, is an accumulation of insignificant decisions over the centuries. But, viewed from up here La Guingueta, far away in the bottom of the valley, besieged by the main road and electricity pylons, looks like a military camp, except for the holiday-blue swimming pools. I have descended a long way from that thin air and aseptic snow at the Port de Caldes.

In the Hotel Cases in La Guingueta the barman warns me about the impending fiesta and I agree not to complain about the noise. Meanwhile, two Frenchmen standing at the bar are trying to buy a fishing licence on the net using the hotel's computer. They type in the date, the location, and their credit card number but nothing happens. So they try again. And again. They are not interested in my advice. It is only when I go for a walk and watch another fisherman repeatedly casting his line into the reservoir that I understand. The seventeenth time there will be a fish to reel in.

La Guingueta's position on one of the two roads from the Valle de Arán explains the *Línea P nido* chiselled into the cliff. Classically Franco was preparing for the last war. But when the next one came, instead of attacking through the mountains, the forces of democracy invaded by the beaches. And instead of khaki and Kalashnikovs this army came dressed in bikinis and armed with the Beatles.

And they also came here, to the *guingueta*. Think Renoir: '*Le déjeuner des canotiers*'. Despite its youth, the 'riverside bar' has swallowed up the more venerable nearby villages like Jou (administratively speaking).

In the evening, along with half a dozen other lost souls, I go to see the legacy of this conquest. 'The Majony's & Woman' are warming up in the hangar opposite the hotel. It all seems something of a damp squib in this heartless village, particularly now that the rain has started to fall in earnest, so I retreat to the hotel and sleep soundly until a drumroll thunders into my dreams. My watch says 1:22 and the fiesta has just begun. It is still going strong when my alarm goes off.

Under the yoke

La Guingueta d'Àneu to Estaon

I take the lift down to the ground floor. The door opens to reveal a young couple immediately outside, snogging. After mutual apologies I step out into the dark. It is raining lightly on the lugubrious lake under a lilac sky.

The Senda climbs steeply on an old track between juniper bushes, intersecting occasionally with a new tarmac road, so new it isn't on my map. It isn't long before I am drizzling sweat. The road and track converge on Dorve, a hamlet of glorious ruins. Crumbling stone walls for the most part, a few of the houses have been reroofed; one has four jumbo bags of sand and gravel outside. The only building which seems to have endured the village's abandonment intact is the church.

On a board in the main square there is a notice headed POUM. The *Pla d'Ordenació Urbanística Municipal* is a strategic town plan currently the subject of public consultations. Dorve is being specified. Where now sweet-smelling dog roses climb the wall soon there will be name plates. In the past, the postman knew everybody. In the future, street names and house numbers will be needed to identify the anonymous owners of the holiday cottages.

The crystal ball of the POUM has foreseen it all. New roads will irrigate these *ramondes des Pyrenees* and they will bloom again. La Guingueta, on the other hand, will need a bypass.

Sitting on a gate, looking down on La Guingueta yesterday, I had it all wrong. La Guingueta is not the only way forward. Both Jou and Dorve are also part of the future; in their case, a future with a past.

But not everybody is happy:

contra la falsedad	against falsehood
contra la injusticia	against injustice
contra el fórum de la	against the ignorant
incultura urbanita	urbanite consultation

Intriguingly this protest, chalked on a wooden door, is written in Spanish, the language of outsiders, not Catalan. Perhaps this is the work of the village's only inhabitant. He seems to have had problems with the judicial system:

one day he went to his garden and found policemen sprouting between the vegetables and cannabis plants.

I follow a hollow way, treading on the weary stones, on a path which soon breaks out into the open. Here the tumbling terraces and plethora of tracks – thanks to horses – soon lead me astray so I scramble directly up to the pass.

Looking back, the view extends beyond La Guingueta to the ski runs of Espot – landing markers for alien spacecraft – and beyond them up to the snow-spotted heights. In the other direction, the forest continues unbroken. Branches stretch across the path. Fallen trees block it completely. But other walkers must surely have forged their way through before me: it has been warm enough for a Slippery Jack to grow, die, and start to rot.

At the pass, for the first time Andorra's white sails appear on the horizon: the snow starts low. But for the moment it is all downhill again.

I have neither seen nor heard another human being until now. Two German lads. First time in the mountains. Eleven days from Puigcerdà. It took them three hours to circumnavigate a big snowfield on the border. I ask them to say hello to Hans when they meet him.

The descent is painted in purple rhododendrons and golden gorse, circling a hill before an emergency landing in Estaon, affording an aerial view of the roofs, carefully arranged overlapping pancakes of slate. The gardens are full of vegetables, the apple trees laden with fruit.

After the daily domestic and meteorological ritual I walk along glistening cobbled streets freckled with geraniums, begonias, and variegated japonica. The only things which look *really* out of place are the big red boxes, one on every street, or so it seems. Inside each one, curled up like a snake basking in the sun, is a hose. Surely fire can't be a big risk since all the houses are made of stone? A woman is just coming out of her garden, so I ask her. The streets are too narrow for fire engines, she points out, and by the time they arrived it would be too late.

She insists on showing me the family house, built in 1740. She has lived here for 60 years, the last 35 of them all year round. Apart from the couple who run the hostel all the other inhabitants are retired. Six of them rattling around in winter, lost among the forty empty houses.

The fields are steaming, filling the valley below with mist lapping up against the church. It will soon infiltrate the village so I sit on a bench in the last of the sun. Four walkers amble down the street. One of them comes up to me and says *bonjour*, followed by you don't recognise me do you? Gérard. From Estós. Staying down the valley with his friends and going on to Tavascan, like me, tomorrow.

Back at the hostel Maria-Anna is cooking. She tells me that Julie and Walt lunched here three days ago so they must be somewhere in Andorra by now. I last saw them between Viadós and Estós, on the other side of a river, about five minutes ahead of me, but out of earshot. The river was too fast and too deep to ford at the normal point and by the time I had crossed it they were gone. I never did see them again.

Maria-Anna's choice of music is the Blues; her choice of food is gazpacho, couscous with chicken, home-made hamburger and roasted peppers, and perfect melon. At lunch it was pork chops in a *blue cheese sauce*, very 21st-century. Excellent.

In this menu the only thing which stands out as Pyrenean is the pork and even that is not specific to the mountains. It has been a staple of Spanish cuisine for the last 700 years; not so much an ingredient as a passport. If Jews and Muslims wouldn't eat pork then Fernando and Isabel, the *very Catholic* monarchs, most definitely would. Eating pork became an act of faith. Those who didn't were expelled. So the sinfully expensive but exquisite Bellota cured ham is the end product of religious bigotry and centuries of refinement. Maria-Anna knows this from her studies at the School of Tourism at Barcelona University, which must also have something to do with her eclectic cuisine, the new website, and Facebook and LinkedIn pages. She has been working in the area for seven years now and wants to stay, but her friends are all dispersed. Why don't they move into the village, she keeps asking them? She has only just taken over this hostel, though she has worked in Amitges previously.

Thinking about it, most workers in Pyrenean hostels are immigrants, even if they have been living here for the last thirty years. Perhaps you have to come from elsewhere to appreciate the beauty and discount the hardships and isolation. To be able to empathise with visitors. To maintain the illusion of living in the mountains despite running a hostel which keep you indoors most of the day, only reaching those summits of pleasure vicariously.

She asks me to sign the client register. In the last month there have been

32 people staying overnight, mostly Spanish or Catalan, a few Germans and French but only one person from Britain, and he had a Czechoslovakian name. Tonight I am the only guest.

Estaon to Tavascan

Upstream, the Bordes de Nibrós is a ruined hamlet with gaping holes where there should be walls, although some of the roofs are intact and there are signs of maintenance. One of the buildings has a date: 1747. Nibrós looks as though it ought to be the end of the line but the map shows two more deserted hamlets beyond. Attached to villages further down the valley, they were only occupied in summer, but their fate is typical. This kind of unintentional rewilding has had much more impact than any recent outside initiatives.

The Senda turns back on itself and climbs obliquely up the hill, still in the shade. I look back at the houses in the valley and above them at the stunning panorama; but all I can think of is the pain in my leg which has been getting worse for days.

I arrive at the Coll de Jou just as the sun peeks over it. A 'yoke', the name evokes the undulating shape of the ridge. I consume my picnic and start down the opposite side. Another day, another yoke, another valley.

The first walkers are climbing up. A young Catalan on his eleventh day. He begins at seven each morning and keeps going until eight in the evening. Then a runner, wearing only shorts and trainers, accompanied by a collie dog (and the town in his earphones). Followed by a woman of my age, a man who might be her son, and a panting *patou*. Three men with a Chihuahua. And an uncommunicative German.

Stopping for a running repair, by the time I have finished the mother and son come back again. They wait for the dog to catch up. Where are the sheep, I ask? Still in the meadows, she says, pointing to the green and yellow collage opposite. They should have gone up three weeks ago on Midsummer's day and they should come back for San Miguel (29 September), but this year the transhumance will be curtailed. The dog limps up to us and we set off together.

Just before parting, I ask about Tavascan: "There are hotels, aren't there?"

Under the yoke

"It's all hotels," she replies.

The path continues, clinging to the hillside. Sometimes it hacks its way through the rock on a dramatic shelf. Sometimes it narrows to a seam sewn in a meadow dressed in a pink Laura Ashley thistle motif. Cheerful flowers, this valley – the Cardós – is named after them.

Then there are rocky ledges to negotiate. At each drop I look down, feeling strangely uncertain. There's nothing exceptional about the drop but I feel odd. My leg won't bend much so I search for the easiest passage, sometimes turning to face the slope as if it were rock climbing, which it certainly isn't.

The entrance to Tavascan is across a medieval humpbacked bridge. On the other side a statue represents a woman carrying water in pails balanced on a yoke. Just beyond it, a giant rusty snail – a vortex pump – next to the tourist information hut must have come from the hydroelectric power station. But nearby three quern stones from a watermill confusingly share a platform with a giant ant! The theme, I finally appreciate, is work and water, and both are big in Tavascan, much bigger than they appear on the surface.

The only visible element is a small grid of transformers on the edge of the village hooked into the end of the power line which disappears down the valley. The gubbins are hidden at the end of a long tunnel into the core of the mountain. It is the same story as Bielsa but 50 years later. At the height of the construction in 1965 there were 2677 workers. Saturday nights in Tavascan must have been feverish. But today, on a Sunday, everything is quiet.

Gérard and his three friends stroll into the hotel Marxant some time after me. They saw five deer – not *sarrios* he emphasises – at the Coll de Jou. He's no more keen than I am on the idea of snow on the way into Andorra. Unlike me, they are not going to the village of Àreu tomorrow, but directly to the next hostel.

Tavascan to Àreu

At breakfast I ingest a double dose of codeine-paracetamol-ibuprofen.

Outside, a notice describes the Lakes of Exile trail which would take me directly back to France, following in the footsteps of fleeing Republican soldiers. It is tempting. Instead, I cross the river and follow a gurgling pipeline into the woods. Shortly afterwards I stop, put my GPS down on a rock telling myself not to forget it, take off most of my clothing, and walk on. A quarter of an hour later I shine my headlamp on that self-same rock and recover the GPS.

For years a walking pole has been attached to my rucksack, but rarely used. For the last three days it has been in my hand from start to finish. Before the end of the year I will have bought two new poles and started using them on every outing, walking on four pins like a Zimmer frame.

The hillside seems to be stirring from its sleep: a series of mini-avalanches makes me think that the scree is slipping spontaneously until I catch a fleeting glimpse of a *sarrio* – or was it a deer? – bounding away. It isn't just the animals though; the path is also crumbling as walkers pass by. In places the retaining wall has gone and the path with it, leaving me to scramble around the gap. Nothing special, but when I look down I feel inexplicably sick.

By the time the sun has fully risen, my leg has become intolerable. Opening my rucksack, the box of ibuprofen spills out onto the rocks. Picking it up, I read the warning notice: this medicine may cause dizziness. That's the choice then. I put the pills back again.

Below, surrounding the fields, the neglected hedges have grown into trees. In contrast, in the village of Boldís Sobirà not a stone is out of place. Nor a soul to be seen. I read that the population is one-eighth of what it was a century ago. In my lifetime the number of sheep and goats has dropped from 101 to zero. Indeed, the village is cited as an example of 'naturbanisation', a new word to me: town come to country. 'The shrines of nature [such as natural parks] have today become museums where man can contemplate nature and put himself on stage in a much-prized décor.'

Beyond Boldís Sobirà an old drove track, still well-defined, traces its route through birch and fir trees. As it approaches the ridge, it becomes a path and then disappears into the rough grass of a clearing. A warning sign explains the dangers: inside a red triangle the black silhouette of a *patou* is captioned: 'Beware, guard dog at work. Keep a sensible distance away from the sheep'. Nearby a caravan, trailer, white van, and galvanised fencing complete the picture. The only thing missing is the sheep.

Hobbling down towards Àreu, back in the forest, crossing meadows, crossing cattle grids, a curiously macabre scene awaits me. Hung on the trunk of a tree is a plastic bag containing perhaps thirty sachets, labelled in English, each one holding a single disposable contact lens. At the base of the trunk is a crumpled pair of dark blue men's boxer shorts and a matching tee shirt. Crime or accident?

By the time I reach the valley the meadows are being watered with a sprinkler despite the burgeoning clouds. In the village itself the campsite and the outdoor swimming pool are empty. The aparthotel shows no sign of life either, but the Hotel Vall Ferrera is still serving. A group of eighty or so Scouts clambers out of a bus and prepares to troop up the valley. The sound of American country music drifts over from the swimming pool.

After lunch, anaesthetized by beer, I stroll through the streets, struggling to translate the plaques attached to the walls. One displays a fragment from a walking song; another a poem about the Pic d'Estats, the highest mountain in Catalonia, close by. Incongruous smooth white tiles on rough stone walls, the plaques are headed 'L'H' and signed 'Gent de Pau'. An old man is sitting under the shade of an extravagant Virginia creeper. I ask him who is responsible for them.

"They're from L'Hospitalet. Barcelona"

In another street a more rustic inscription commemorates Mossèn Antoni Batlle i Mestre, one of the first Catalan Scout leaders who brought his troops here, also from Barcelona, in the 1930s.

Near the river, a homage to a president of the Club Excursionista Pirenaic reads *'Homes que deixen petja* – men who leave a trace.' That's it: Barcelona can't resist leaving its graffiti.

Most of the houses are ancient. Except, that is, for a new apartment block with its cladding already falling off and an acrow propping up the first-floor balcony, abandoned somewhere between unfinished and decaying.

I hurt too much. I ring for a taxi to take me to the nearest railway station, in Lleida, the next day.

Aftermath

When the taxi arrives, I am embarrassed. The driver is only going to charge me fifty euros. Yesterday he was evasive. It's a long way, he said. But how much will it cost? I don't know, but it will be a good price. Lleida is 160km away so I feared the worst. And now I am embarrassed.

Josep-Maria doesn't hold it against me. He is going to Lleida anyway to pick up two ninety-year-olds and their nieces who are coming from Madrid for six weeks. They are Catalan Catalans, he explains, and have been holidaying in Àreu for the last fifty years. We have hardly travelled fifty metres when we pass a flock of sheep, more than I've seen all this year.

Josep-Maria tells me that he used to be a car mechanic but he became a taxi driver because he likes to talk. And talk he does. About his recent divorce. About starting his business in the mid-1980s; there were few private cars so he paid off his first taxi within a year. About a walker he fetched back from Toulouse. The man had been lost in the mountains and rescued by the French police who took him to hospital. He wanted to collect his car but couldn't remember exactly where he had left it. They searched and eventually found it. A month later he was dead – getting lost was the first sign of a brain tumour.

He points to the reservoir on our left.

"That's new. When I say new I mean it wasn't here when I was a boy. Franco built them."

"What was it like under Franco?"

"We suffered because we were republicans. We *are* republicans."

"And now?"

"We want to be a country. We *are* one. We are the motor of Spain. For every ten euros we put into Spain we only get three back. My father-in-law comes from Granada and so we went there often before we were divorced. The Andalusians don't know how to work. They prefer to live off benefits."

He is a member of CiU (the ruling party in Catalonia) – an activist not a politician, he is quick to point out. He is organising a human chain.

"On 11 September?" I ask. The Catalan government is planning a demonstration in support of independence. 400,000 participants are expected to take part in a line stretching right across Catalonia.

"No, on 25 August, because there will be nobody here on 11 September. We want to have a chain from Àreu to the Pic d'Estats. We've a thousand people signed up already but we need more."

I promise to meet him at the summit. We drive through a remarkably pretty narrow gorge.

"The Congost de Collegats," explains Josep-Maria, "but we call it the Congost de Conygats because there used to be a brothel at the entrance."

I pretend to understand.

Josep-Maria doesn't just like to talk, he also likes to listen, to converse, so I hardly notice the time it takes to drive to Lleida.

Back home my rheumatologist extracts a syringe-full of liquid from my knee.

"Come back in a month and we'll see about the injections, but don't go walking in the meantime."

I'll miss the Pic d'Estats then.

By January I'm just about capable of walking again.

Also in January, my friend Maurice is taken to hospital and seems to be getting better when he dies in his sleep. He is brought home and propped up in bed. I go to see him before the undertaker starts work. The only odd note is the bandage around his head preventing his jaw from dropping open. He looks tired but relaxed ... That's it Maurice. You've got what you wanted.

A week before I'm due to set out the knee still isn't right. My doctor writes out a prescription for anti-inflammatory drugs.

"Normally you are only allowed these if you are recovering from an operation. Don't combine them with anything else," he insists.

I have done almost no preparation.

Return to the heights

False start

There is a better way of getting back to Àreu: staying overnight at L'Escolan, a hostel in Ariège, then crossing the Pyrenean watershed on the Lakes of Exile trail. The winter has been milder than last year and I'm setting off later, so snow shouldn't be a problem. But I take my crampons nevertheless.

I look out of the window of the hostel. The worn-out walking boots which decorate the garden walls are filling up with rain. The low clouds hide the mountains. I ask Jean-Charles and Pauline, the managers, what they think. Not good, they say.

In the morning I don all my waterproofs, soon overtaking a shepherd with his flock. "It's going to rain all day," he informs me dourly. He is the last person I see.

After an easy walk up the Ossèse valley – where the ibex have been released – I reach the first snow, the last remains of an avalanche. The snow has formed a bridge, blocking the path where it crosses a stream. Although it is covered with debris of earth and dead bracken, no reassuring footprints cross it and what I can see of the arch looks thin. Too thin. So instead of crossing it I climb up on one side, grabbing small branches to haul myself up the steeper sections, re-joining the path higher up.

Later, I cross the torrent on the 'Pont des Savoyards' which Jean-Charles, Pauline, and friends have just built, with the help of a donkey to haul the wood. Without it I would have had considerable trouble wading through the white water.

The shepherd was wrong, but although the rain has stopped, the clouds are still blocking the head of the valley. The path peters out in the gloom. Descending below the clouds again I stumble on a credible path which returns into the mist. It butts against an avalanche but I am reassured by a red-and-white waymark. The path is on a narrow horizontal shelf here, but the snow rises out of the ground like an iceberg. The rocks above and below are nearly vertical. It would be difficult to climb up onto the surface of the snow and the extra weight might precipitate the whole mass down over the cliff, tearing its icy fingernails from the ledge.

I might be able to re-join the path a little higher by clambering up the cliff and going round another iceberg but when I do so there is no sign of it. The rocks and the grass are slippery and I narrowly avoid tumbling under the overhang at the edge of the ice and getting stuck, squeezed between the ice and the rock. I can't see more than a few paces. I am shivering. I am tired. I have a foghorn in my head. Go back!

On the way down I slip and sit on one of my new walking poles, breaking it in two.

Back at the hostel, Jean-Charles is serving some tourists sitting in the garden at a table in the sun. When he has finished he asks me, concerned:

"What happened?"

"There was an avalanche blocking the path and I couldn't get round it."

"I thought there wasn't much snow. I didn't think you'd have any difficulty... Even with an ice-axe and crampons?"

I hadn't even thought about using my ice-axe.

"I was in the cloud and I couldn't work out where the path was going... Can I stay here tonight?"

"Of course. We are fully booked but I'll find somewhere for you."

Later, Pauline tells me of one time she and Jean-Charles were rock climbing:

"He was above me when he saw a snake basking near the pitch. He knows that I don't like them so he called back to me and said he would come down. By the time he got to where I was, there was nobody there. I had already climbed back down to the foot of the cliff. There was nothing rational about it but sometimes you know when you have to turn round."

"I should have tried harder... but I didn't like the fog," I reply, feeling small but knowing that I have found friends. (At home, when I study the map carefully I see that was going the wrong way. *Exactly* the wrong way.)

On the way back home I spot a roadside banner proclaiming: '*Grands prédateurs, le désarroi du monde rural* – large predators: countryside in distress'.

In a few days there will be a demonstration in Foix against what farmers are calling an 'administrative dictatorship'. Slovenian bears have been imported: they kill our sheep say the farmers. Vultures have been encouraged by the provision of carcasses: they eat sheep too, say the farmers, although not everybody is convinced. As for the wolves, they have made their own way here from the Alps. The farmers had nearly succeeded in eliminating all three of them definitively.

Inside the hostel it was a different story: a poster argued 'It takes millions of years to create a species and only a few decades to destroy it… or to save it. Together, let's work for biodiversity.'

Jean-Charles told me: "We come from Savoy in the Alps and for us the Pyrenees always meant bears. It was where the bears were. Naturally we were going to use a bear as our logo. But we were told that if we put a bear on a panel on the side of the hostel it would be shot at. So we settled for a *sarrio* instead."

Bears

What is to be done about the Pyrenean bear then? Like all big questions the first difficulty is to formulate it correctly. Because the Pyrenean bear is dead. Definitively. The last female, Cannelle, died in 2004. The last male, Camille, disappeared in 2010. Nothing can save the Pyrenean bear.

Rewind. What is to be done about the bears that live in the Pyrenees? Because about thirty live in the mountains. All have Slovenian genes after the introduction of foreigners in 1996–7 and 2006. The Pyrenean bear is dead. Long live the (Pyrenean) bear.

Although I have been walking in the mountains on both sides of the border for twenty years now, I have never seen a bear. Yet, for something so invisible, they are remarkably present: in the media, at demonstrations, and on 'Unwanted posters'. Like the one I saw when walking the Pyrenean Way near Bagnères-de-Luchon:

> We produce lambs of quality,
> The best on all the markets.
> Sheep are our trade.

Return to the heights

> They are our pride.
> We raise them.
> We love them.
> They are not bait
> And we don't want
> Them to be eaten
> By a badly brought-up bear.

But in the village of Melles later that day the mayor told me: "What you see in the media is a well-orchestrated campaign by a few determined individuals." That was in 2005. But by 2006 things had changed. Those 'few determined individuals' had gained political clout.

1 April: 300 protestors including some mayors in their official regalia converge on the village of Arbas not far from Melles. The council has agreed to the release of a bear in the commune. By the end of the day angry shepherds will have burned a wooden statue of a bear, daubed walls with graffiti, and would have attacked the mayor's house if it hadn't been protected by gendarmes. The town hall will be soaked in blood.

25 April: Nelly Ollin, the environment minister, is coming to Arbas from Paris to be seen welcoming the new arrival. She should have known better: a chorus of clanging pots and pans awaits her. As for the bear, she will be released elsewhere. It was the last time a national politician would so closely associate themselves with the bears and the last time the release site would be announced in advance.

28 April: Another bear, Franska, is released several valleys away.

29 April: I go to see for myself. The protesters are checking vehicles heading up to Superbagnères where the next bear might be released.

"Yesterday we had 200 people here for lunch. But we have decided to split up, with spies along all the access roads," one of the organisers tells me. "We know we can't stop them this time, but if we make enough fuss they'll think twice about trying again."

Three years later and the protests are still continuing. At the annual sheep fair in Tarascon a stout man in black tee-shirt and black trousers thrusts a black-and-yellow leaflet into my hand. He tells me that he wants to protect the *tarasconnais* sheep from bears: "I threw blood at the town hall in Arbas in 2006." He was given a suspended sentence of a month and a half in prison.

A member of the ASPAP[1], he is recruiting for the next demonstration where they will march side-by-side with hunters concerned about possible no-go areas to protect the bears. 7,000 people will turn up.

So why is there so much anger? At first glance the statistics suggest that the damage inflicted by bears is minimal. According to the official report for 2014 the French Pyrenees host 570,000 sheep. The 1290 *estives* cover a surface area of 550,000 hectares.

Bear attacks in France	2006	2010	2015
Animals (mainly sheep) injured or killed by bears	221	167	145
Estimated minimum number of bears	15	19	29

The figure of 145 animals affected seems insignificant when disease, stray dogs, thunderstorms, and other problems kill 10,000–20,000 sheep each year. Certainly the official figures for bear attacks under-report the reality but even so they represent a small percentage of the deaths. On the other hand a large proportion of the attacks were in one small part of Ariège: Couserans. And when a single attack accounts for a score of deaths – typically when sheep panic and run off a cliff – the owner takes it badly.

Nevertheless, owners receive compensation and grants are available for the improvement of shepherds' huts and the training of *patous*.

By way of comparison, wild boar are much more destructive. Of course there are more of them, two million throughout France. But the cost of the damage to crops – 50 million euros annually – is hugely more than the cost of the damage attributed to bears – well under a million euros. And wild boar are involved in some 24,000 traffic accidents, not to mention hunting accidents – with 500,000 wild boar killed each year, collateral damage is to be expected. Despite this, wild boar do not arouse the same focussed wrath.

So, from the point of view of an outsider, the angry rejection aroused by the reintroductions seems exaggerated, both in France and Spain. As do the excesses of passion on the part of some of those who favour the newcomers.

1   *Association de Sauvegarde du Patrimoine d'Ariège-Pyrénées* – Association for the safeguard of the heritage of the Ariège Pyrenees

Return to the heights

Cannelle, in the Toulouse Natural History Museum

The brown bear is not in danger of extinction. And the 'Pyrenean' brown bear is merely a label for bears with progressively less Pyrenees in their blood. The genetic isolate was definitively condemned in 1996. Pyros, born in Slovenia, is the dominant male and the father or grandfather (or both) of the majority of the bears here. A zoo, then.

The reason for the polarisation of viewpoints is, I suspect, that bears have a symbolic value which has little to do with their real nature. Few people have ever seen them in the wild. Even Francis Chevillon, whose sheep share a spring with a bear in Couserans, has never seen *lo Moussu* himself: *despite* living in the *estive* all summer, *despite* seeing the bear's footprints from time to time, and occasionally providing his breakfast.

Since I can't see a real wild bear, I make a special trip to Prats-de-Mollo (the 'meadows' of Mollo, a village I will walk through later this year). There, once a year in February, three bears are released from the castle above the town to rampage as they see fit.

Footprints on the mountains

The bear has seen her. He is only a few paces away and she is petrified, in both senses of the word. In any case she can't run away – she is standing on the edge of a precipice. The bear scuttles towards her, rising to full height on his back legs as he approaches. The girl screams wildly and puts her arms out in front of her. I have the fleeting – absurd – impression that they are going to dance. But the bear tackles her to the ground and they roll over, bumping down the slope at the edge of the precipice, arms and legs entangled. I hear a gunshot. For a second the bear and the girl stop moving. The bear looks around, nose balancing from side to side. Perhaps he has smelt something. Seeing me, he releases his grip and charges.

Half an hour previously I watched from the top of the castle wall as three men were dressed in sheepskins and their arms and faces daubed with cooking oil and soot. A tubular sheepskin hat was rammed onto their heads. When the signal was given, a group of hunters chased these 'bears' one by one out of the castle gate and down the hill towards the town a kilometre away.

If you are attacked by a bear, the experts say, there is no point in running away: a bear can run faster. Don't climb a tree: bears are much better at it. The only thing to do is to talk to it calmly. If sweet nothings fail, try punching it on the nose.

I ignore the advice. I keep running, not looking back, hearing the bear's footsteps as he crashes down the path behind me. I keep running. Ten, fifteen, twenty metres. I don't understand why he hasn't caught up with me, why I can't feel his claws digging into my shoulders. But still, I don't look back until I have caught up with my friends. Then I see that the bear has lost interest in me and has gone for another of our party. I glance back at the girl. She is getting up, a remarkably large tuft of fur in her right hand, covered in dust and with an enormous black oily smudge on her face and clothes, yet apparently intact.

One of the other bears tries to escape but hunters wielding sticks force him in the right direction. The bears, the hunters, and the over-excited crowd which follows them are funnelled through the highest gate in the town's walls. Once inside, there are more attacks and shrieks. Although the bears prefer blondes, many other people end up with black smudges on their faces and clothes. One man finds himself with a wonderfully precise black hand-print on his bald scalp.

Return to the heights

Prats-de-Mollo bear festival

The air reeks of gunpowder and spilt red wine. Young children throw bangers at our feet. Bombards and drums add to the chaos. Sometimes the crowd jumps violently, crushing onlookers already pressed hard back against the houses in the narrow cobbled streets. Every year there are minor injuries. Even today, with frost on the ground, the bears' trajectory is lined with throngs of agitated onlookers half wishing to experience a bear hug, half hoping to avoid the inevitable rough and tumble.

By the end of the day the bears, bruised and exhausted, trailing blood and soot and oil, are corralled into the market place outside the town's east gate. The hunters with their guns and sticks are replaced by barbers with heavy chains, an axe, a basin, and a black pudding. By now the bears are completely black from the soot, in contrast to the barbers, dressed in long white nightshirts and white caps, with arms, legs, and faces flour-whitened. The bears are captured by the barbers. And then shaved with aid of the black puddings and axes. By this stage, much alcohol has been poured down many gullets. To round off the proceedings, the bears, hunters, and barbers make a brave attempt at line dancing before staggering off to the nearest bar.

A few minutes earlier, as the last of the sheepskin 'fur' fell to the ground, this year's bear-in-chief was revealed as a well-known hunk from the Perpignan rugby team. This must partly explain the young women's willingness to be bear-hugged, although this was not always the case. Brigitte Plo, now over 90 years old, looks back: "Symbolically, it was the story of white and black, good and evil. The bear represented evil. He wanted to take a young woman back to his lair to deflower her. She prayed to the Virgin who sent the hunters to rescue her. That's why, when I was young, when the bear caught a girl, the hunters had to fire in the air, so that she didn't 'fall'. That was an important point. At that time they didn't plaster the girls with the oil and soot like now. Girls didn't wear trousers, so we didn't want to be made to fall over. It just wasn't acceptable. That arrived later."

'Aren't the girls afraid of getting hurt?' I ask one of the villagers. 'No,' he says. 'If you watch carefully, when the bear grabs them he always falls on his back so they are cushioned.'

It is then that I realise why the bear never caught me. Being relatively old, male, and wearing glasses saved me.

Another similar festival, in Torla, had disappeared but has recently been reborn. There the bear is captured at the start of the proceedings, paraded, judged, and then condemned to death. He was responsible for all the bad things which happened over the last year. Once he is gone, a fresh new year can begin. Bielsa has its version. The carnival in Ituren possibly belongs to the same genre but there the bear has a bit-part, the limelight having been stolen by the *Joaldunak*. And the plot has been lost, stylised.

As well as renewal, a common theme of the many Pyrenean carnivals is the bear-animal-devil tamed by the human-spirit; sometimes he is resurrected, sometimes killed. Another common theme is the date, 2 February. Traditionally, hibernating animals chose this day to surface from their long sleep. If the sky was clear, winter would continue and they would go back to sleep; if the sky was cloudy they would breakfast in the knowledge that spring was on its way. In the Pyrenees the long-range weather-forecast was the responsibility of the bears. I doubt if anybody actually climbed into a bear's den, but the idea is there, along with the festivities which might accompany it. It is an ancient Europe-wide tradition which was exported to America as Groundhog Day.

In the evening of 2 February, in some villages, the men used to leave the women at home and go out into the dark. Every year they came back saying they had heard the bear fart. Because it 'liberates the souls which have been locked up in him. The souls of those from here who died in their sleep. At first they go underground, where the bear is hibernating. He breathes them in, keeps them and sends them to heaven when he wakes up. During the bear's sleep they live in a kind of purgatory.' A more prosaic explanation is that when a bear hibernates its digestive system slows down resulting in an intestinal plug. Or so they say…

Before Christianity intervened, I imagine that the date varied. But it now coincides with the Presentation of Christ at the temple, a celebration probably destined to eclipse the pagan version. Evidently it didn't totally work. In the past that day must have witnessed many such festivals – one study suggests that at least thirty still survived in the Basque country at the end of the 19th century – but today only a few remain. And a new religion has again messed with the date: the bears must now fart according to the liturgy of holy tourism.

The festivals are part of the Pyrenean identity; even those who wish to eradicate the bears agree. Curiously the festivals only survive in areas where the bears have long disappeared, where they are no longer a threat.

Over the centuries the bear has been clothed with other symbols. The folk tale of *Jean de l'Ours* is ubiquitous and has many versions. Usually the story starts with a young woman being abducted by a bear. From their union a child, Jean, is born. Strong and hirsute like his father, he soon proves powerful enough to push aside the rock which imprisons him and his mother in the bear's cave. Struggling with his duality and unable to fit in with society he is obliged to leave to seek his fortune. After much derring-do he rescues a princess and marries her.

The tale starts with a common bear theme: masculinity version XXX. (According to Gaston Fébus 'when a male bear does his thing with a female, they behave like a man and a woman, lying one on the other'.) Unsurprisingly Christianity had long labelled the bear as wicked; for St Augustine he was the devil incarnate.

Whatever the Church might have to say, in the mountains the bear was king; Gaston Fébus considered him a worthy adversary. Indeed when Gaston died it was reported that he had just returned from a bear hunt. But closer reading of the text suggests that actually he had been chasing deer. It wasn't good copy. A man like Gaston couldn't die in a banal car accident: there had to be something more to it. He had to be associated with a much more emblematic animal.

But it is a mistake to think that the Pyrenean hunters like Gaston Fébus were *solely* responsible for the disappearance of the bears. Before they were pushed back into the Pyrenees, bears were persecuted throughout France. The woods in the mountains were their last refuge and for many centuries they coexisted with the locals. But the massive destruction of the forest in the 19th century to provide fuel for forges, other habitat changes, and the increasing sophistication of guns led to their downfall.

Yet before that happened, and in the same era that saw the deforestation, Couserans lived through a period of cohabitation with the bears that was closer than it had ever been before.

On a wall in the dormitory in the Escolan hostel, an early postcard of nearby Ustou shows two men, each with a bear cub in his arms. Another one depicts a moustachioed *orsalher* with a muzzled bear holding a wooden staff in its paws. Breeding and training bears was a local speciality. In 1839 in Ustou:

> in many houses you would see, peacefully stretched out like faithful hounds either side of the wide hearth, one or several bear cubs, the hope of a dowry for the girls of the house.

By 1890 the *orsalhers* were travelling Europe and North and South America. They could earn 10–17 francs a day at a time when an agricultural labourer was paid 2 francs 25 centimes. When local supplies of bears ran short they were imported from Eastern Europe. Postcards like the ones in the dormitory were widely distributed, especially those illustrating the events in Cominac in March 1906…

A new highly controversial law had been passed in Paris. But the inhabitants of Cominac didn't agree with their church being expropriated. So that when the official arrived at the door he found his way barred by the entire population of 300, four parish priests in their best cassocks, and three fully grown bears held just in check by their *orsalhers*. The official declared his purpose. The parish priest refused to let him enter, replying:

Return to the heights

"Those who built our church were not rich. It was only by walking their bear across the Canadian countryside and under the burning Mexican sun that they had struggled to amass the money the building had cost."

Another priest claimed that they would 'resist to the bitter end because we would prefer to die a bloody death than live in the mud'. The official went away. Although no photographer was present to record the event a reconstruction was staged shortly afterwards. The national press reproduced the photos and Cominac became famous.

Bears were part of the identity of the village, being used *against* authority – a mere century ago, when Ariégeois *loved* bears.

Occasionally a bear becomes too comfortable with the presence of humans. Boutxy was like that. I talk to a shepherd about him: Gérard and his son keep sheep on the Plateau de Beille in summer, bringing them down for lambing.

"We found the lamb's body there," says Gérard, "without its head." He is pointing to a wire fence which surrounds the sheep shed.

"But what happened to the head?"

"He bit it off though the fence."

"How do you know it was a bear?"

"There were prints at the side of the road. He must have come up the lane," he says pointing to the tarmac road from the village of Vebre 200m away. "He attacked a beehive the same day."

"But why didn't the lamb run away?"

"It had just been born and didn't know anything about anything." Gérard is philosophical about the events. Other shepherds are less so.

That was September 2008. By then Boutxy was eleven years old. Son of a Slovenian bear, he spent much of his time around here.

"But I never saw him," says Gérard. "I saw his tracks in the snow. I heard him cry out once making my Mérens (horses) bolt. Another time I saw the hair on my dogs' backs sticking up – I'm sure he was there."

He tells me of the cross-country skier who met Boutxy whilst competing on the Plateau de Beille. The skier was Baptiste Cazaux and the date 14 March 2004. The gendarmes, present in cases of accidents, photographed the scene. Cazaux went on to win the race; Boutxy ambled off.

Footprints on the mountains

Helping with the transhumance

But Boutxy was no Winnie the Pooh, even though 'What about lunch?' was also his favourite question. In 2005, he left fingerprints at over half of the 302 attacks in the Ariège. Then in 2009 he disappeared. One of Gérard's neighbours, Philippe Lacube, appeared on television saying: "Somebody has cleaned the house. I don't want to know who... If there are fewer attacks it is because there are fewer bears... the government doesn't know what happens in the mountains." Boutxy was never seen again.

It isn't only a question of whether the shepherds might eventually adapt to the bears, but also a question of whether the mountains are suitable for them. At the beginning of the 1990s, according to the Fundación Oso Pardo (Spanish Brown Bear Foundation), a recognised American expert came to study the conditions in Cantabria (NW Spain). He was extremely pessimistic: the existing bear population was too small, but above all it lived in an environment which was too humanised. Its possibility of survival was zero. Based on his previous experience, the only relationship possible between bears and humans was apartheid.

In Europe, the advice was ignored and yet almost everywhere the bear population has increased over the last fifty years following reintroductions, natural migration, and conservation measures. According to a paper published in *Science* in 2014, the most dramatic increase was in Finland (150 to 1600–1800). In Cantabria, where there used to be 60 bears, there are now 195–210. The only place in the long list where the number of bears has *not* increased over that time span is here. The Pyrenees aside, the paper claims that *in practice* cohabitation can be seen to work – from the bears' point of view – despite Europe's modern human-dominated landscapes. It doesn't comment on the degree of acceptability or other issues.

So are the Pyrenees an exception? Given that nobody every sees him, what does *Martin* mean in the 21st century for those who support the reintroductions? The bear is an umbrella species, whose protection will help save endangered habitats. More practically, how can France participate in measures to protect species elsewhere if she can't safeguard her own endangered animals? The bear assuages our guilt about lions. The teddy bears of our childhood have no place in the Pyrenean tradition but enable conservationists to tug at our heartstrings without even trying.

On the other hand, for some opponents the bear represents naturbanisation, outside interference. The fight centres around ownership of the mountains. Although the details and the scale are completely different the underlying current is the same as in Janovas: local *versus* global.

And Spain in all this? At any one time perhaps half of the known bears are in Spain. Catalonia has been blowing hot and cold, with its own plan to reintroduce a bear which keeps being postponed. But in February 2016 the Catalans finally announced that they were bringing in another male, to replace the ageing Pyros and increase the genetic pool.

Most of the controversy centres on the Val d'Aran (north of the watershed). Sixteen horses died there in 2014 although the circumstances are not clear. But overall Spain suffers far fewer attacks than France: only 26 in 2014. The bears are mainly present in northern Catalonia, the area stretching from the Val d'Aran in the west through Àreu and the Vall Ferrera to Andorra.

Àreu is my next stop.

Return to Àreu

My second attempt to get to Àreu involves car, high-speed train, bus, and taxi, passing via Narbonne, Barcelona, Lleida, and Llavorsí, where Josep-Maria picks me up. I have been travelling all day. For one of the golden eagles living on the mountain behind my house, in the unlikely event that it decided to fly in a straight line, it would be a mere 120km.

Josep-Maria tells me the human chain from the village to the top of the Pic d'Estats was a success although there were only 500 participants. Catalonia was suitable honoured.

"There haven't been so many since Jordi Pujol came thirty years ago."

Pujol, the first president of Catalonia after the dictatorship, used to come regularly. He was a keen walker and the peak the highest in Catalonia, but there's more to it. The Barcelonan *clubs excursionistas* (walking clubs), as well as leaving their mark in Àreu, had kept the Catalan flame smouldering under the dictatorship. Here, mountains are about identity. In contrast, in Britain in 1932, when the burgeoning urban population besieged Kinder Scout it had been about class.

(The poet Jacint Verdaguer is reputed to have been the first Catalan to reach the summit, in 1883. Verdaguer was an important figure in Catalonia's 'Renaissance'; his epic *Canigó*, about the mountain further east, was an early eruption in the nation-building orogenesis.)

In Àreu two magpies are cawing joyously as the sun goes down. The village, in shadow, is cooling rapidly but the top of Monteixo on the opposite side of the valley is still lit up. If I had arrived a few days earlier I would have been just in time to watch the end of a race to the top. The results have been posted on the village notice board.

The race, the *Milla vertical* (Vertical thousand) was born as poetry; the sweat is a later addition. The author Pep Coll recounts the tradition in *La edad de las piedras*. Once upon a time, he writes, a remarkable man lived in the village. His fabled speed and stamina was to be put to the test on the eve of the village's fiesta. He was to set off from the village square when the setting sun disappeared behind the mountains to the west. Progressively the shadows would climb up the mountain on the opposite side of the valley. His challenge was to reach the summit of the mountain with the sun still shining on his back. If he succeeded, *if he ran faster than the sun*, he would be entitled to choose any dancing partner he wished for the duration of the fiesta.

The summit of Monteixo is 1680m higher than the village. Runners finding themselves in shadow, abandoned by the setting sun, are obliged to abandon the race. Kilian Jornet established the record in 2007 with a time of 59 minutes 41 seconds, the only person to have broken the sixty-minute barrier.

I have another look at the drinking fountain with the memorial plaque I spotted last year. This time I notice the decoration: the soles of hobnailed boots. My first walking boots were like that; they had been my father's and must have been over twenty years old. I would still be using them if I could find any hobnails.

And then there was that other pair of hobnailed boots I found on a dig: side-by-side, as if somebody had stepped out of them and left them to rot. Roman, and nearly two thousand years old. The leather had disappeared but the iron had survived: thirty timeless hobnails. It was a find of absolutely no archaeological value – hobnails are two-a-penny – and as a hardened archaeologist accustomed to handling mementoes of the past it should have been a banal find. But for me it had special value. Unzipping my scientific straight-jacket, I put those shoes back on, stepped across that bustling market square, and walked off down the street.

Àreu to the Refugi de Baiau

At dawn the sky holds just a few whispers of candyfloss. Today I am also racing against the sun, hoping to get as far as possible before my skin burns.

The route starts on tarmac, heading north up the valley. In the half-light I nearly trip over a snake. Looking at it carefully, black with yellow bobbles, pale green underneath, I convince myself it is a grass snake. It hasn't moved for some time.

The road disintegrates into a track which the Senda soon leaves behind to climb along the side of the valley. Walking along this path is a typical Senda experience with pines and firs, silver birch, rowan, broom, a couple of *bordas*, occasional prairies with picnic tables, and interpretive panels. High peaks blocking the way to Andorra. Hidden bears.

But it lacks the fire, the noise, the smoke, and the sparks which gave the valley its name. The Vall Ferrera is remarkable for what it isn't. The industry which bloomed here well into the twentieth century has disappeared. If you want to see iron forges go to nearby Alins on the second weekend of July; the charcoal burners also put in an appearance. If you want to know about the timber industry, go to the sawmill museum. The international market which took place on the Pla de lo Mercat is now only commemorated by the annual *trobada* reinvented in 2013. Only one ancient activity has survived: livestock raising, as witnessed by a straggle of cows and horses at the Pla de Boet.

In places, the path shows traces of revetment and surfacing, relics of the time when carts trundled along it, but apart from that the hobnails have rusted into the landscape. Like the Basques. Àreu is probably a Basque name. In the first millennium AD proto-Basque was spoken here. In other circumstances, Josep-Maria could be arguing for *Basque* independence.

Overhead, the clouds sweep in and I pick up speed on their sails, snatching a hasty lunch before the pending storm. Walking faster now, the just-flowering rhododendrons flash by. But in the forest I am misled by the tangled roots and slow down, repeating my steps, skidding on the lichen.

Finally the woods give way to an exposed landscape of boulders, creamy, pock-marked and green-veined, like Roquefort cheese. Further on the *cirque* is defined by malevolent cliffs, impossible to climb. Worse: snowdrifts block the combes, the only way through to Andorra.

The wind stiffens and although it is only mid-day the light is fading; but in the far distance I can see the hut. With its vertical sides and curved roof sheathed in aluminium, and with a red stripe along the side, it looks like a chocolate wrapped in silver foil. Closer to, it resembles a 19th-century railway carriage. Except that it doesn't have any windows and it is tied down by strong hawsers. It also has a lightning conductor. Set against the size of the mountains it looks pathetic. Above it, the clouds are closing in.

Standing on the platform outside the door, hardly visible under his voluminous clothing, is a young man. I say *"hola"* but he replies in English to tell me that he is deaf and that I must talk to his girlfriend.

Inside, the first thing I notice is the wooden panelling, followed by the emergency radio-telephone connected to what I'd taken to be the lightning conductor: it must be an aerial. Apart from that, the furniture consists of a

Return to the heights

Refugi de Baiau

table and nine bunk beds lining the corridor. A woman sitting on one of the bunks says hello, and the space immediately seems overcrowded. But cosy.

She explains, in English, that they are Bulgarian and have walked from the Cap de Creus on the Mediterranean. She indicates a man who is dozing on a bunk in the far corner. He's been trying to tell them something but he doesn't speak English and they don't speak Spanish. When he stirs I ask him. There's lots of snow to the west, he says. Sometimes he was up to his knees but he managed to get through.

The Bulgarians take us outside and point up at the combe they descended.

"You can avoid the snow by climbing on the rocks but after the pass there are two lakes and you can't avoid it. We were above the water on a steep slope. We didn't like it at all; the snow was soft."

Today was their second attempt to cross from Andorra to Spain. Yesterday, on a different route, they were completely blocked by the snow.

They head off down the valley and we go back into the hut taking off hats, gloves, anoraks, and boots. I sit down on the bench behind the table. Javi goes back to lie down on the tartan mattress. I offer him some chocolate.

"No thanks. I haven't eaten anything since yesterday morning. I've got gut rot and I don't want to risk chocolate. I'll eat something later…"

"I've got some Imodium…"

"I'll be alright. I'm having a day off today to recover. It's my first since Candanchú, three weeks ago." I calculate that I took about the same time.

He is lying on his side with his legs curled up. He has a chubby face, red from the sun, two-day stubble, dark hair, friendly brown eyes. Unfashionably podgy for a mountain man. I show him my shampoo sample bottle talisman and I ask him if he has one, but he hasn't even heard of the idea.

"I haven't come from the Atlantic. I live in Huesca which is why I started at Candanchú. I'm going to the Cap de Creus then over to France and back on the GR10 to Hendaye. Then on the Senda again back home."

That makes at least three month's walking. I must look incredulous because he continues:

"I have already done lots of the Senda. I'm unemployed so I have the time. It's better than sitting at home…"

"Obviously." I don't really know what to say. The scale of the project is so overwhelming. "I took four years to walk the Pyrenean Way," I tell him.

So we talk about the Way and huts.

"Can you look to see if I've got them all?" he asks.

He pulls out a small notebook and opens it in the middle, at a page labelled Banyuls. This is the start of the French part of his walk, on the Mediterranean. He has drawn a line to represent the coast and another heading inland. After a few wiggles the line arrives at a triangle labelled 'Pic de Sailfort'. By the edge of the double page it has reached the Col d'Ouillat. I put on my head torch and shine it on the notebook. I notice the quality of the paper and the finesse of his lines. This is an artist's sketch pad.

"There is a shelter at the Pic de Sailfort. It's just a crevasse in the rocks with a glass roof. You must stay there. Then there's the Refuge Tanyareda. Have you got a map?"

"Yes, but it won't help. It covers the whole of the Pyrenees."

"A GPS?" I ask.

"No. I don't think they are much use. I have a friend who has one but by the time he has turned it on I've already worked out where we are. I don't have a compass either," he insists. "I get lost quite a lot but I always work out which way to go."

"An altimeter?"

"No."

He does have a camera, however. In fact he has two: a 35mm and a 60mm. And a bag full of rolls of film, at least thirty of them.

"Black and white. I develop them myself," he says in response to my question. "Photos should be printed and seen. *That's* photography. Not just archived on a computer and forgotten."

In a conversation which lasts all afternoon and all evening and will recommence tomorrow, we chat about English and Spanish history, Chinese capitalism, Podemos – a new kind of democracy, not just a Spanish political party, he insists – George Orwell, Marguerite Yourcenar, writing – for him it must be on paper – drawing, and alcohol. Beer, he says, is for drinking, wine is much more: a cultural object. Surprisingly, we say little about walking.

It is like being on an intensive language course but by dinnertime my Spanish is scrabbled. Sometimes all the letters are there. Sometimes one or two are missing or there are one or two extra. I use what I have available, cheating outrageously.

I get up to fill my water bottle in the stream and Javi says he will come too. He manoeuvres down the slope like a gecko but I get stuck on a ledge, and have to make an embarrassingly clumsy leap. On the way back he waits to give me a hand.

Eating supper in the hut he tells me he's thirty-five and wants to change his life. That's why he is walking the Pyrenees. We agree that we will set off together tomorrow.

Finally the rain arrives, pitter-pattering on the roof.

A whole country for shopping

Refugi de Baiau to Arans

Javi thinks that I am a liability.

When we left the hut it was icy cold. To avoid the snow in the combe, we scramble up the gawky young rocks. Lacking the polished grace of the boulders in the valley, their sharp edges and random angles slow me down. Javi outdistances me quickly then waits for me to catch up. After half an hour of stop-start walking, I am sure that we are not going the right way. But we are both sure that this is the direction the Bulgarians pointed out.

"It doesn't make sense," says Javi.

"No," I admit. "But the Senda goes over the Portella de Baiau." We should be heading south not east, but Javi doesn't want to believe me. "I'll do whatever you want. You have more experience than me," I mumble.

"No," he snorts angrily. "We'll agree on what's best and do that."

Still, I have difficulty in persuading him that we are heading east when we should be heading south. He goes to investigate.

"It is too steep," he says when he returns. "I don't have any crampons."

While he was away I have had time to study the map.

"There's a path after some lakes. If we go to the pass just ahead we should be able to see them."

Javi forges ahead, at first hopping from rock to rock across the shattered landscape, but when the combe levels out he steps onto the snow. I follow him. The weather is good and we have plenty of time even if we go astray. I step in his footprints, unconcerned, until suddenly the snow gives way and my right leg disappears completely into a hole. My left leg collapses with a sharp crack. I feel a lightning pain in my knee. But the pain disappears; apparently I'm not injured.

A whole country for shopping

On the other hand I am stuck, kneeling on one knee, with the other leg dangling, unable to pull myself out of the hole. I swear and call for help.

"You shouldn't tread on the edge of the snow near the rocks. The sun heats the stone and undermines the snow," says Javi when he arrives.

I can see now that he had side-stepped to avoid the problem. He removes my rucksack and bends over on his hands and knees beside me.

"Put your arm round my back and I'll lift you out."

It doesn't work but eventually I manage to get sufficient purchase on the rock to extract myself. We continue together after that. At the pass we look down onto the first lake and the snowy slopes funnelling into it.

"I think you should put your crampons on," Javi instructs.

He makes a big detour to stick to the rocks but I cross the snow directly.

"Stick your heels in first," he shouts.

Yes, he's right.

"It's too steep there to go down forwards," he tells me. "Turn round to face the slope and use the pick end of your ice axe. Dig the front of your crampons into the slope."

This is where I realise I am a liability. Listening to Javi's confident instructions, I understand that I have barely scratched the surface of mountain walking. I descend to where he is standing at the edge of the rocks.

"You go first," says Javi.

Now, the spikes of my crampons hardly penetrate the surface of the snow but somebody has already left a track. Sometime later we reach more rocks. One of them has been painted.

"Look," I say, "a waymark."

"Stupendous," says Javi enthusiastically, and shakes my hand warmly.

Beyond the next lake, the next pass reveals a long curving valley below with a town way, way down at the end of it. Standing just above the pass is a hut, the size of a garden shed, metallic, all rust and texture. By the time I arrive, Javi has unpacked his light meter and is taking measurements. Graffiti and weather have revealed different strata of paint: red, black, green, and yellow, it looks like a work of art.

"Would you mind standing there? ... Just there..." says Javi pointing to the door which is falling off its hinges.

When he has finished we race each other down the valley. I canter down the snow. Javi sticks to the rocks, leapfrogging over the rusty fissured surface.

Then all the grit crumbles out of the day in the first pastures. The hut here, the Refugi Pla de l'Estany, must be the one the Bulgarians confused with Coma Pedrosa. They were lost without knowing it. Approaching the town of Arinsal, Javi points out a stone wall running across the valley.

"Elmurodeadriano," he says.

I don't understand so he repeats, more slowly: "El muro de Adriano". Hadrian's Wall.

It could almost be a dam, except that the top isn't level and it is pierced by a road tunnel. In the tunnel Javi asks me: "Do you always wear those boots when you are walking?"

They are big, protecting my ankles. I look at his footwear, more shoes than boots. I need my heavy boots for the crampons; he can do without.

"Why?" I ask.

"Nothing."

In the town we walk a long way, past empty hotels and deserted ski lifts, before we find an open café. We are sitting outside when another walker comes along, takes one look at us, and sits down too. I notice that he has an umbrella attached to his rucksack. José has come from the Mediterranean. Two weeks. The only thing that worried him was the Salt de la Núvia, a week ago. In Arans just over the hill, he tells us, you can stay in an aparthotel. Marie-José is delightful. And you can eat in the French restaurant opposite.

I ask in the café about Hadrian's Wall and am told that it is a snow dam. In 1996 an avalanche destroyed several blocks of flats.

Walking through the rest of the village, having left Javi to finish his breakfast, I pass 'The Bull', the 'Derby Irish Pub' and many signs in English. The rest are in Catalan. The buildings are modern, high-rise; the cranes are constructing more. If this is Andorra I hate it.

Once in the forest I forge up the hill. But still I am overtaken by Javi well before the Coll de Jou (another one) and overtaken by the rain before the village of Arans.

The aparthotel seems empty but Marie-Jose has great difficulty with the recently installed internet check-in. Working out a price is even more troublesome until I remind her what José had paid. Finally she shows me to room number 11, opening the door to the smell of polish, and telling me that if I have any problems she is just next door.

A whole country for shopping

In the evening I cross the road to the restaurant, la Font d'Arans. The door is open and the smell of cooking wafting out but no one is to be seen. Hearing faint noises coming from behind a curtain at the back, I advance between the tables calling: *"¿Hay alguien? Y-a quelqu'un?"* until a woman parts the curtain, chewing, fork in hand.

"I'll come back when you've finished eating," I apologise but she invites me to sit down.

Nicole soon tells me that she would like to retire but no one wants to take over. Her husband has been cooking the duck recipes which have made their reputation for the last 26 years. The highlight is *canard à l'orange*.

When she learns that I am walking alone, she decides to set me right, telling tales of solo walkers who died after a minor accident. Then, getting into her stride, she accelerates onto cars: like the driver *on his own* who wandered off the road into a deep ravine and wasn't found for three whole days.

When it comes to settling up I find that the décor and the cooking are not the only things dating to the twentieth century. I've rarely seen prices like this, even in Spain, since the euro went into circulation. The bill is disconcertingly small.

Arans to Encamp

In the morning the Senda takes me to the other side of the river and through La Cortinada. Every single house has been renovated recently: flattened, realigned, and re-windowed. They are all made of stone and have been standing for centuries but they look as though they have just been created on a 3D printer. Stone moves and ages, the skin flakes, bits fall off. But here it is like wallpaper: flat and lifeless. Dishonest architecture.

In the middle of it all a strange field looks as though it has just been planted out. Each plant has four or five oval leaves sprouting from the ground. There's nobody around to ask what they are.

I climb the hill past the golf course, spotting purple heath spotted orchids. The path seems to have been improvised, cutting a swathe through the forest with no zigzags, no concessions to calf muscles. Eventually the climbing stops hurting and the Senda levels out to glide along the contours of the hill.

Footprints on the mountains

The newly varnished bench by the side of the path has undoubtedly been provided by the local council so that walkers can enjoy the view and listen to the sounds of nature. The mountains, mostly covered in forest, are unspectacular though pleasingly green, but it is the valley which attracts attention. The small town of Ordino is stretching its tentacles along the roads which radiate from it, attaching its suckers to the hedgerows and ripping up the few remaining fields to satisfy its consuming hunger. The numerous cranes signal further aggression. And then there is the noise. Previously muffled by the trees, the dull thud of pile-drivers, the high-pitched squealing of the cranes, and the constant roar of traffic, can now be heard full blast. Crisis, what crisis?

The first drops start to fall.

I have just started off again when Javi overtakes. I thought he was long gone.

"I've been taking photos," he tells me.

"It can't be a traditional path," he complains pointing back along the Senda. "Coming out of Arinsal, then down into Arans and out again, it was too steep. In the forest the path could have been made anywhere. There was no reason for it to be so abrupt."

He's right. In the mountains the ideal path has a one-in-six slope. Any steeper and it's too tiring; any less steep and you never get to the top. If it is flat it is definitely not ideal: you are not in the mountains.

"I'm going to Els Agols this evening, a shortcut…" adds Javi.

"I'm only going to Encamp…"

"…but maybe we'll see each other again at Espavers."

On the way up to the Coll d'Ordino, the thick grey wadding of the sky detaches itself in gobbets, infiltrating my waterproofs, my clothes, and my skin. Just before the pass, in the distance I see a crumpled bright blue mass slumped on the path, moving fitfully. Nearby, a black umbrella lies inert on the ground. As I approach, a face pokes out of the blue, then a hand which brushes back a hood to reveal a woman with dark brown hair pulled back in a ponytail. She must be about thirty. She stands up. The umbrella, I can now see, is protecting an expensive reflex camera. She sees me and jumps involuntarily. For a moment we stand there, two hunchbacks face to face. Then I recognise that she can see no more of me than I could see of her so I push back my hood and ask where she has come from.

A whole country for shopping

Switzerland, she replies, via the Cap de Creus. It has taken her sixteen walking days. We exchange news. She saw Javi but they didn't have a common language so they said little more than hello. I tell her about the aparthotel and Baiau, and she tells me about her journey.

"There's a big snow field at the Portella d'Engorgs. It's very steep and I didn't feel at all safe because there was a cliff just below. There was one above as well so I couldn't go round it. Do you have crampons?"

"Yes."

"Without crampons it would be impossible. Even with them I didn't like it. I thought I could see some people below trying to go on the rocks but it looked even dicier."

José didn't mention this. What did he do? Maybe he took another route altogether.

Later I meet an orange and black blob bizarrely labelled 'Mairie de Paris'. This time it hides a man in his fifties. As we are talking his wife joins us. They too have seen Javi, said hello and passed on. I ask about Engorgs.

"We had a look at it. The path is covered in ice and at the top we would have had to climb up a *corniche* of snow. It's too dangerous. We went round it to the south," the man tells me, going on to describe the detour in detail.

We are all sniffling from the cold: the bushes are not tall enough to protect us.

"I'm delaying you," I apologise.

"We're soaked anyway," he says. "It doesn't matter. We're going to stop in Ordino."

Encamp is not even visible yet. I squelch across a marshy plateau bisected by a meandering yellow stream. A wooden noticeboard indicates that this is the Riu d'Urina. I can well believe it. Then I nearly step on a couple of slugs, in their element today, making messy love yin-yang style. They are hermaphrodite; does this mean they have twice the pleasure? Even the rain doesn't disturb them; I don't often envy slugs.

The way down is as steep as the way up and slippery to boot. My glasses are steamed up. The only sound is the swishing of my waterproof trouser legs. I am walking for pleasure.

Down below in Encamp, half-drowned in the mist, cranes poke up above the roofs, knitting yet another row of hotels. Soon, a nondescript ruin announces the edge of the town and I slither down what appears to be the high street. A locally registered car pulls up and two men get out. Before they have had time to run inside I grab them.

"*¿Dónde está el centro del pueblo?* – Where is the town centre?"

They look puzzled and I am about to reformulate the question when they start to discuss the issue. Although they are from Encamp they are unable to decide the exact location of the centre and can only agree that if I keep on going I'm sure to get there, if only I walk long enough.

I conclude that the centre of the town must be the nearest restaurant. The place in question advertises itself with illuminated pictures of amorphous meat products and I am almost dissuaded when I notice that it is nearly full. Then I catch sight of a sign proposing *habitaciones* which clinches the matter.

The ageing waiter looks at me as I push the door open but continues serving another customer and then goes back into the kitchen. I am about to remove my outer layers when I think better of it and go back outside, shake myself like a dog which has just been swimming, and remove my cape and anorak before returning. When I open the door for the second time all eyes are upon me. I regret not having a song-and-dance routine up my sleeve. I am saved by the coat stand which enables me to fuss about and a chair on which to sit to remove my boots. I rummage through my rucksack looking for some dry socks but don't quite dare to empty it onto the floor so I am obliged to keep the wet ones on. Whilst I have been fiddling, the waiter has approached, so that when I stand up we are practically nose to nose.

Nervously, I ask if I can eat. He shows me to a table, pointing to the menu in Catalan, Spanish, French, English, Portuguese, and Russian. Snails are a speciality.

I opt for the *menú del día*. Biting into the tender lamb – and reviewing the day's events in my head – I make a discovery. More useful than an ice axe, crampons, or an emergency blanket. It is as light as air, costs nothing, and never wears out. Like my eyes and my ears, it is built-in: my voice. Today, the information I have gathered about the Portella d'Engorgs will save me from taking an unnecessary risk. Of course, I have asked about the route previously, but never thought of my voice as a safety device.

The waiter tells me he has lived here for sixty years, since he was eight, when his father started up the restaurant. Later on some locals come in and the waiter – by now I have realised that he must be the owner – greets them effusively. The meal is honest home cooking at an honest price. The Caliu d'en Josep is just right and the name appropriate. *Caliu* means warmth. Like the embers of a fire for cooking jacket potatoes, like an affectionate hug, like a ray of sunshine in the rain.

On the other hand, everything I have read about Andorra suggests that it must be a very confusing place indeed. For a start, the head of state is not elected by the Andorrans but by the French. And then there is a second head of state who is not elected by anybody, but appointed by the Pope, himself head of a third state: the Vatican. The co-princes, as they are called, are the French president and the bishop of the small town of La Seu d'Urgell just over the border in Spain. (The bishop takes his orders from Rome not Madrid, so the Spanish government has no influence here, in theory.)

Also, sixty years ago the population was 6,000 with an economy based on the land: crops in the narrow valleys and livestock in the mountains. But by 2014 the Andorrans had turned their backs on the hills. If the statistics are anything to go by, they have spent the last sixty years in bed. There are now 34,000 native Andorrans. But even this figure is only half the tale: an equal number of foreigner workers now live here.

The fields have been replaced by tarmac; the economy is based on a single road, the one that passes through Encamp. In one direction lies France; in the other Spain. The mountains of cheap tobacco and rivers of alcohol which flow along this arterial road have led to chronic congestion with cholesterol hotels being deposited around the old villages. The situation had become critical. The heart of Encamp has recently had a bypass.

Tourism is rampant, with one hundred visitors annually for every inhabitant. Most of the rest is financial services – until 2009 Andorra was on the OECD's grey list of tax havens. One adept was Jordi Pujol – he who climbed the Pic d'Estats, the first president of Catalonia. It just so happens that at the same time as I was walking through Andorra, Pujol was meeting the Spanish fraud squad to confess.

So what is there to be seen on the streets of Encamp? I open the hotel door and turn right. On the far side of the square stands one of those buildings which can only be described as a 'statement'. Like London's Shard or the Gherkin. The façade is a seven storey high mirror. At first glance it appears to be wafer thin, but the paraphernalia is hidden behind Encamp's 'Flat-screen'. Today the screen is off – black – waiting for the sun to switch it on. Even when it is working I imagine that the weather forecast will be dismal. It houses the local council.

The buildings around it are a random collection: frequent granite façades but not much sign of genuine antiquity. Behind it, the houses encircle a field full of those mysterious plants. A passer-by tells me that they are tobacco. Further on there is an ancient mill, a cobbled street, graffiti, a 16th-century church, and an electric vehicle charging station. Hotels everywhere, built on the model of supermarket shelves.

And a house with an inscription chiselled in stone: IHSM21FEb1690. Jesus and Mary, 21 February 1690. This being Andorra, the building is a fanciful pastiche, to the extent that the inscription seems out of place. According to the couple running the tourist office, the house is the Cal Mals Avinguts – the house of the badly matched couple. In the past divorce wasn't possible, so when there was chalk on the blazer one of the partners could come here until they were reconciled.

At the same time as I am enquiring about the house, I ask about tomorrow's weather. It's only going to spit here, I am told. But, what about the mountains? It always rains in the mountains, they chorus.

Encamp to the Refugi de l'Illa

As I progress ever eastwards, the morning and evening ritual anointment takes on an increasingly religious tone. Keeping the faith – applying the unguent, believing – will lead me to the promised sea. But failing to keep the sacrament will result in punishment. For ever and ever. I have recently converted to Vaseline.

Walking out of town, I tunnel under the bypass, tripping over the surplus stents, somehow losing the official route. But since the general direction and the unrelenting climb correspond to my preconceptions I continue. This morning the path holds true, but by this evening my other preconceptions about Andorra will have been modified. Not yet, however.

At the top of the slope I step out of the forest onto the terrace of a lake-side restaurant. At the entrance to the Dama del Llac stands a wooden statue of the eponymous lady – a curvaceous, matronly figure rather than the beguiling sylph of Burne-Jones's imagination – still waiting for today's

Arthurs to appear on the shore. The glimpses of the lake through the pines are just what is needed to give it an air of mystery.

The lake is a reservoir; an engineers' path goes as far as this evening's destination, the Refugi de l'Illa. Further along it, a man in a kiosk tells me that he has only just started his duties for the summer so he doesn't know how many other walkers are out on the Senda. He saw someone who might be Javi pass through in the rain yesterday afternoon.

At this point the path gains a handrail. It passes through a short tunnel in the rock and stops at a stone shelter being cleaned by two council workers. It is here that things become serious again, climbing over the Coll Jovell and into the next valley.

Down below the path, in the Madriu valley, the walls of the former hamlet of Ràmio are crumbling except for four buildings with new roofs; one even has a chimney. Immediately above the settlement whimsical curves of drystone seem to only just retain the grassy terraces, green avalanches threatening to engulf the houses. They seem improbable, as indeed they are – but it is only later that I understand why.

The path, now roughly paved and with occasional traces of concrete, climbs up the valley, never far from the river. At the Fontverd hut the trees are replaced by a green meadow. I am sitting at the table outside as successive waves of walkers roll in – a young Spanish couple, an older French couple, a great storm of twenty Germans with their two Spanish pilots, and a splattering of others. But the sky begins to threaten again and the flow slackens before starting to ebb. Fontverd is the high water mark, at 1880m above sea level.

Further up the valley I meet a fisherman – *nada* he tells me – and a walker.

"I went round the *corniche*, up a gulley just to the north. It was hands-on," Declan informs me in an Irish accent.

The higher up the valley, the lower the vegetation. Proud stands of skyscraping Scots pines are replaced by anarchic clumps of stunted, tortured mountain pine. Then they too give up the struggle leaving only tufts of grass between the worn rocks. Here and there, a marshy lake. Occasional glacier buttercups. Of all the shrubs battling for space on the forest floor lower down, only the rhododendrons have fought their way this high.

The rock being granite, the end of the valley has not been as deeply scoured out as it might have been. The Illa hut is just under the lip, its concrete walls blending in with the boulders around it although its straight lines make it visible for some distance.

The hut has three doors to choose from and as many dormitories, sixty bunks in all. But there is only one mattress, and although it is damp from the leaky roof, I commandeer it and put it out to dry. A lone rucksack lies slumped against the wall but its owner is nowhere to be seen.

Just above the hut the wall of the dam marks the highest part of the hydroelectric scheme. If it fails, it will wash everything away: the hut must have been the workers' accommodation. But the most noticeable thing, after days in the enclosed valleys, is the wide open sky.

It has been a pleasant day's walking in a nice valley, and I modify my view of Andorra: it isn't just urban sprawl. But the valley is nothing exceptional by Pyrenean standards. So that when I am at home writing, I am astonished to find that it is a World Heritage Site, the only one in Andorra. How can it be possible?

The UNESCO documentation cites terraces, transhumance, communal management, and vulnerability. But terraces are by no means exceptional in the Pyrenees. As for transhumance the sheep no longer come here. (I didn't see a single one of the 2500 official residents in Andorra.) Elsewhere in the Pyrenees over a million sheep take to the *estives* in the summer. On this basis, several areas of neighbouring Ariège would be better candidates for World Heritage status. Communal management is also common.

I am thinking of Gavarnie-Monte Perdido, the other Pyrenean World Heritage Site. It is difficult to bracket Gavarnie and Madriu in the same sentence (if your expectations are based on Gavarnie, Madriu will be a disappointment). Gavarnie is not only hugely more spectacular; its impact on writers, the early years of the science of geology, and the 'invention' of mountains as a cultural object is well documented.

So what is special about the Andorran valleys? As the evaluation highlights:

> The Madriu-Perafita-Claror valley is the last remaining vestige of the Andorran rural way of life. It appears to have survived more by chance than planning through the absence of any access road... Considering the extent of development in the rest of Andorra, this is little short of a miracle.

A whole country for shopping

The word which convinced UNESCO must be 'vulnerable'. The site might not be exceptional, but it is the only thing Andorra will ever be able to propose.

Incidentally, the terraces of Ràmio, so improbably pristine, must surely have been renovated thanks to the listing. On the other hand the former sheep pastures are being displaced by trees. More worryingly, there is 'a desire to turn Illa into a manned hostel'.

Perhaps I'm wrong. Perhaps Andorra could have another World Heritage listing up its sleeve. By the beginning of the next century, when the grim harvest of global warming has made shopping a luxury, which country will be best positioned to apply for World Heritage status on the basis that retail therapy was *the* main cultural activity of the late 20th century? If Benidorm can apply, why not Andorra? Already the tourist office website boasts: 'Andorra, a whole country for shopping'.

But this is all hindsight. For the moment I am standing outside the hostel looking at the scenery, thinking beautiful thoughts, waiting for the other walker to come back to reclaim his rucksack.

I am leaning on the rail of the concrete terrace when I hear a sound behind me. Small, Asian, dressed in black, and wearing a red woolly hat, she is not at all what I was expecting. Mei comes from Taiwan but has been working as a waitress in London for the last year. Walking in Andorra is the reward she has promised herself.

I tell her I have come from Encamp. Wow, she says, even though she has come just as far. Then I say I am hoping to get to the Mediterranean. Wow, she says again.

We agree to fetch wood so we empty our rucksacks and assorted plastic bags. The nearest trees are some distance away but they have already been pillaged. Even a kilometre away all the dead branches have been collected. The only combustible material is the pine cones, still sodden from yesterday's downpour.

Back at the hut, spread out on the floor the cones look an impressive pile, but they don't want to burn. What we need is a blazer like my great-aunt Sarah Hannah's. Hers was made of zinc and had a big handle on the back but she loved her husband and I don't think she can ever have resorted to writing on it. I search around but nothing is big enough to cover the front of the hearth to create an updraft. So my strategy is to dry half a dozen cones at a time over the same number of candles. At first they fizz and then smoulder before burning feebly. Mei's strategy is to gather scraps of paper and twigs, pull the driest cones apart and pour olive oil on them, blowing feverishly on the glowing fragments.

"It's a competition," I say, "to see who can get the fire going first."

"No," she retorts, "we've just got to get it lit. It's starting to get cold."

So we spend a happy time, heads together over the hearth, rearranging the kindling, making suggestions, amused by our ineptness. And we talk. The mountains in Taiwan, Mei explains, are high but hardly ever have snow. On the other hand, it rains. She was in London to learn English. Tomorrow she will walk back to the valley by a different path – we study it on her map – and then go off to the airport. Once home she will start a Master's degree in etymology. I tell her that I've been to the Champollion museum in Figeac. Wow! she says.

Finally I abandon the fire and leave her to it, going over to the table on the other side of the room. I have already rejected the canned food, the spaghetti, and even the two boxes of wine left by previous walkers but I am beginning to get hungry. Perhaps there is something of interest concealed below.

"Ha!" I exclaim. "Look at this."

A box of firelighters, half-hidden under the pile. We scrap all our previous efforts and make a neat pile of the driest items and the firelighters. This time the fire catches.

"Help me with the log, please" says Mei.

One end is heavily singed but if we can get it burning properly it will keep us warm through the night. Moving it is a real challenge. The log is a proper tree trunk, not one of the scraggy examples from nearby. I can't understand how it can have arrived here. I can hardly get my arms around to lift it, and Mei, at the other end, has even more difficulty. We drag it, trying to prop it up on a stone but it rolls off and we fall over onto each other. No damage done.

The fire sorted, we start to prepare our food, sharing niblets. I'm eating cold, but Mei is planning to heat some packet soup when we hear voices outside. The door is pushed violently open and two women crash in. We hardly have time to say hello before they have taken over. It's smoky in here they complain, opening all the windows and letting the cold air blast in. We'll go and get some wood, they announce grabbing the bow saw. I tell them it's wet but they come back with armfuls of green branches they have ravaged from the nearest trees and throw them on the fire – I can understand why all the furniture in the hut is non-combustible. The greenery almost smothers our efforts. When the flames finally pick up again they grab the casserole – the only pot which is in reasonable condition – and throw it directly in the middle of the fire. As soon as the water heats up they put the spaghetti in to boil; by the time it is cooked the handles of the pan have melted. They fall on the boxes of wine with great glee.

Finally Mei is allowed to heat her soup. In the midst of all this turmoil, we manage to extract the information that they are working in Andorra but come from the Czech Republic; otherwise they are not interested in communicating. Mei offers me a tisane but I don't have a mug so I empty another of the offerings on the table – a plastic box of Haribo sweets – and slurp from that.

Outside just before dark, clouds have formed in the valley below. They thicken as I watch, boiling over, about to overwhelm us. But before they do, another group of walkers emerges from the mist.

Once the four men have settled in, sitting around the table by the light of our head torches, they tell us that they have driven up from Barcelona today and set off from Encamp early in the afternoon. Tomorrow they will head north at the start of a five-day circular walk. The Catalans talk to each other, the Czechs talk to each other, but their clamour leaves so little audible space in the hut that I hardly get a chance to say another word to Mei.

Swamped by the linguistic invasion I go to bed and Mei follows suit.

Refugi de l'Illa to Refugi de Malnui

At the intersection, the finger-post waves its three fingers at me. On one of them, for the first time, the Cap de Creus is named. It brings me to a halt: still 233km to go.

Earlier, when I struggled out of bed, the fire was long dead. Breakfast was a digestive biscuit and a swig of water. The buttery taste of yesterday morning's fresh croissants, the heady pleasure of Spanish coffee came back to me. Mei – who said she wanted to leave early – has decided to sleep in. The others are still snoring.

At first light the valley is still boiling but the sky, the reservoir, and the rocks which were a cold grey yesterday evening are now a kissable pink.

The first pass is only ten minutes away. I look at the long descent into the valley below and up the hillside opposite, to the next pass: Engorgs, the one I have been warned about. A horse and her foal block the way then skitter off downhill; the gloop, gloop sound, like water bubbling over rock, turns out to be multiple cow bells. There are no roads in this valley either.

The Espavers hut near the river is a dry-stone igloo – a shepherd's *orry* – half underground. It is empty. No sign of Javi, but by this time he too will be well underway. Although for several more days I ask other walkers for news, and some people have seen him, I never catch up.

Just beyond the hut, isolated in the middle of an extensive pasture, is the finger-post, the one with the finger pointing to the Cap de Creus. The other two fingers indicate the Cami dels Bons Homes, a path commemorating Cathar dissenters forced to flee across the Pyrenees some 900 years ago. (The story of the sack of Béziers, where a few dissenters were being hidden by the citizens, is still pertinent today: "Kill them all, God will recognise his own", the Papal legate allegedly said.)

It seems that I have slipped back into Spain without noticing. The next pass is the fearsome Engorgs but, as instructed, I bypass it. On the way, I just manage to avoid stepping in the remarkable pile of horse dung the French couple also warned me about. Beyond it, in the next valley, below the steep scree, a galaxy of sparkling lakes reflects the first cumulus clouds of the day.

I look back at the Engorgs *corniche*. On the rocky lip just above it I can see three specks: a father and two sons I met on the scree. It gives me the opportunity to assess the size of the problem. A long white arc bars the head of the valley. At its thinnest point it is only the height of a helter-skelter, but it looks near-vertical.

Between here and Malniu I meet many walkers and I practise identifying the *Senderistas*. Marxel is Basque and has just retired. I'm walking home, he explains. He has an ice axe and crampons. Then a lightly equipped Catalan couple charge past me, in too much of a hurry to stop. Daia is German and restarted in Puigcerdà yesterday. I warn her about the *corniche* and tell her the way around it.

A whole country for shopping

"I've got gaiters," she replies.
I can't have expressed myself very well.
Christine is Californian but from an Asian family. She is struggling.
It is near the end of the day; I can chat, ask names.

À la compagne de voyage	To the journey's companion,
Dont les yeux, charmant paysage	Whose eyes, charming landscape
Font paraître court le chemin ;	Make the path seem shorter;
Qu'on est seul peut-être à comprendre,	I am perhaps the only one who understands her,
Et qu'on laisse pourtant descendre	And yet still let her walk off
Sans avoir effleuré la main.	Without ever touching her hand.
Chères images aperçues	Treasured visions, half noticed
Espérances d'un jour déçues	The hopes of a day, disappointed
Vous serez dans l'oubli demain ;	You will be forgotten tomorrow;
Pour peu que le bonheur survienne,	But if happiness comes
Il est rare qu'on se souvienne	It is rare that one remembers
Des épisodes du chemin	The events on the way

Les Passantes, by Antoine Pol,
most famously sung by Georges Brassens

The prairies are golden and pink with dandelions and clover; the forest with broom and rhododendrons. At Malniu, sixty cars are parked outside the hostel, which is doing a roaring trade; all the tables inside and outside are full. It is more of a restaurant than a hostel.

I take a siesta in bunk no. 11. When I wake up and go back into the dining room it is almost empty, but a new arrival is making up for it. He has his back to me, so the most noticeable thing is his huge old-fashioned rucksack. He is jabbering away in French and gesticulating at the hostel manager. Is there drinking water further along the Senda? The manager either doesn't know or doesn't understand. I don't really understand the question either. I say I know the path but the Frenchman doesn't hear me.

He pushes his way into the kitchen where the staff are preparing the evening meal. I expect to hear a sharp rebuke but the manager merely tells him to come back later when they are less busy. The walker insists on saying that he has just climbed Teide. When the manager doesn't take any notice, he repeats himself.

He turns round and faces me. With his long white beard and a branch for a walking stick, he looks as though he might have been the model for the logo on the Vieux Campeur[1] bag he is holding in his hand. I notice that he is still wearing his boots, another *faux pas*. By now he has been in the hostel for five minutes but still has his rucksack on his back, though he is visibly exhausted. We agree to talk later, once he has settled in.

While I was asleep the hostel has changed. The cars have gone and the new arrivals are carrying rucksacks instead of picnic baskets. Mountains have replaced lunch as the main topic of conversation. It is as if the hostel has moved a thousand metres higher.

The showers and toilets are outside across the gravel, another sign that the hostel has moved uphill. When Robert, the Frenchman, goes outside to look for them he heads in the wrong direction. When he asks where he can hang his big orange bath towel and flannel to dry, the manager virtually takes him by the hand. I invite him for a beer and we sit at a table in the sun.

"What's the Espavers hut like?" Robert asks.

"Primitive but dry," I reply

"But what's it like *inside*?"

"There's an earth floor, a wooden sleeping platform, and a few empty bottles but it's reasonably clean."

I'm surprised how concerned he is, given that he has a tent tied to his rucksack.

"Is there water?"

"There's the river. I didn't see a spring, but you should reach Illa where there's a tap," I tell him. "Where are you going afterwards?"

"To the Coma Pedrosa hostel. Up the Pic and down to Baiau. To Mounicou, Mérens..."

He picks up his Vieux Campeur bag and extracts a sheet of paper completely covered with tiny writing: details of hostels, passes, altitudes, directions. It is an ambitious project for the four days he has allowed.

---

1 *The Vieux Campeur* (Old Camper) is a French chain of shops with a large range of mountaineering equipment.

"There's snow if you go down the Portella de Baiau…"

"Ah. In which case I'll go down to the Estanys Forcats." He points to the route I took with Javi.

"There's snow there as well but it's less steep."

"I'll have to replan my route then. I haven't brought my crampons and I don't want to take any risks. Not since I saw a bad accident."

I look at him, but apparently he doesn't want to talk about it.

"With my heavy sack I don't want to take chances. Nothing above twenty degrees, now. Though I have done ninety degrees."

"Ninety degrees?"

"Ice climbing, with two ice axes, of course."

"I'll follow the ridge over the Entravessada," he continues, indicating the jumble of rocks Javi and I rejected as impossible.

"Do you know the area?"

"No. It's the only bit of the Pyrenees I don't know."

"So you've done the GR10, the Senda?"

"*Bof!…*" He hesitates.

Bof is a quintessentially French expression meaning, in this case, I'm not sure I can be bothered to tell you.

"I've done them all," he continues after a bit of encouragement. "But I don't like *grandes randonnées*. There's too much road. Today, coming up from Puigcerdà I was constantly being overtaken by cars."

This doesn't correspond to my memory of the GR10, nor the Senda so far. There were only a few days and only a few kilometres on roads.

He sees my GPS.

"I used to work with those before they were called GPS. I was in telecoms."

"But I don't have the impression you use one?"

He points to his nose, and uses another very French expression.

"*Le pif* – my sniffer – is my GPS. That and my altimeter. And a compass when it is foggy. Once I was in the clouds on a glacier with crevasses and I had to zigzag to avoid them. When I arrived I nearly fell over the hostel manager's sledge, the clouds were that thick. But I had navigated well."

"Wow!"

Robert goes to lie down and I go to look around, at the lake, silver, at the pines, black, at the sky, a meteorologist's headache.

For the evening meal, I have been placed with Robert.

"So where else have you been walking?" I ask.

"*Bof!*... Everywhere..."

"The Alps?"

"*Bof!* I've done half of the four-thousands of Europe."

We lapse into silence.

"I overheard you talking about Teide. What was it like?" I try again.

"I've just come back. I bivouacked at the top. You're not supposed to but there was nobody around. It was 25 degrees at 3718m. Exceptional! In the morning I came all the way down to 500m."

"Wow! I've never done so much."

"Once I did 4500m in a day! The longest day ever was from a hostel – he mentions the name but I fail to note it – to Zermatt. I set off at two in the morning and arrived at ten at night. Twenty hours walking!"

"Wow!"

Suddenly Robert remembers the problem of water.

"How much water do you think I should carry?"

I can't think why he is asking *me* but I say:

"I have one and a half litres. You've got some water purifying tablets haven't you?"

"Yes. I've two half litre bottles but for the tablets you need a bottle, don't you? I will buy one." And indeed, after breakfast the next day I hear him asking the manager for a litre bottle of water, in English this time.

Sometimes he has difficulty in articulating his words, even in French. I don't know what to make of him. He lives in Brittany officially but he spends six months every year walking. So I ask him *the* question, the question I still haven't been able to answer to my own satisfaction:

"Why do you find walking so interesting?"

"Even if it isn't interesting, it's different."

"Because you keep moving?"

He nods.

"I want to walk as much as I can. I don't know when it will be my last time."

Before I go to bed I study my feet; the Vaseline is working!

The remembered past

Malniu to Puigcerdà

Breakfast is as early as you want. We are at the same table as last night.

"You won't have any difficulty on the snow," I say to Robert, "with your experience." I regret having even mentioned it.

"No, I'll stick to the rocks," he replies. He hesitates before telling me the story:

"I don't want to take any risks. Not since I saw that accident in the Alps. There were three blokes walking behind me. I went off to climb a peak but came back to the path later on. I could see three tracks in the snow, then one of them went up instead of continuing down. I followed the two going down."

"They had crampons?"

"Yes. The track was getting steeper. Then there was just one set of crampons and a dent in the snow. When I looked over the ledge I could see a helicopter hovering below. I was above it on some rocks so I had to be careful not to dislodge anything. A little later I came across a leg…"

"A leg?"

"… severed at the thigh. That's why I don't walk on snow slopes without crampons… even though they had them."

He asks me where I live and where I am going and then goes to pick up his rucksack. He tries to lift it onto a table but I have to help him. Once it is there he turns round, bends his legs, slips the straps around his shoulders, and then struggles to stand upright.

"How much does it weigh?" I wonder out loud.

"16.2kg without the water."

He hobbles across the car park with his branch in one hand and a walking pole in the other, his left leg hardly bending. Getting going in the morning is the most difficult thing, he told me last night. He is 73 years old.

Wow!

For me the trek today will be nearly all downhill. At first the Senda canters rough-shod, parallel to a wide and well-maintained path a mere ten metres away, as if rugged *Senderistas* need a rugged path. But then it goes its own way and loses itself in the forest to emerge on a muddy track. There are tyre marks but no cars at present.

The sun is low and the light blinding, so that I continue on the track well beyond the turning and only notice the massive signpost when I go back. This is, some claim, a reason for walking in the other direction: to avoid the early morning sun. But I have the wind and rain behind me. And in the morning you are normally in a valley, in the shadow. So this is what makes today exceptional: I am not in a valley. Shading my eyes what I see is not mountains but a blue-grey plateau: fields and hedgerows, roads and villages. This is Cerdanya, an exception in the Pyrenees: almost flat. When in 1659 it was agreed that the mountains were to be divided between France and Spain on the basis of the watershed, this plateau was the object of diplomatic wrangling, only solved by creating a Spanish enclave, Llivia, in what was to become France.

As well as my destination, Puigcerdà, I can also trace the approximate line of the Pyrenean Way, the French GR10, and familiar villages.

On the French Pyrenean Way most people walk from West to East making it more sociable. But on the Senda people walk in both directions. Would the experience be the same walking the other way? Putting aside the suggestion that the climbs are less steep going E–W. Putting aside the wind, rain, and sun, would it make a difference to be heading towards the sunset? I suspect so. Meaning changes depending on where you are coming from.

For the last half hour I have been tiptoeing between the branches of dead trees. The path has disappeared. The first sign of trouble was a layer of amorphous lumps of wood with ragged breaks, broken not cut. Then came piles of bushes, their twigs tinged black. Followed by a shadow forest, tousled, much blacker where the fire had done its worst. In August 2012 some 290 hectares burnt down. Kids playing with matches by all accounts. Despite the intervening years, the earth still smells acrid.

The remembered past

At the edge of the former forest the waymarks reappear. Here, the Senda follows a watercourse which has been redug recently: the banks have yet to be recolonised. The strange thing is that the channel runs *along* the watershed of the grassy ridge. Presumably this is the engineering work which gave the plateau its odd name: pla de Fontenera (plumber's plateau).

Looking across Cerdanya at the French Pyrenean Way, or perhaps it is just the repetitiveness of walking, reminds me of a graffito I saw recently *'¿Cuándo fue la última vez que hiciste algo por primera vez?* – when was the last time you did something for the first time?' Walking the Senda is certainly a challenge, but is it qualitatively different to the Pyrenean Way? Youth is full of firsts, but now they are rarer and I'm not yet ready for the one that really counts. But when will I next do something *really* new?

In the village of Guils, where the ridge meets the plain, they are also considering doing something for the first time. A poster entitled 'Tell Spain what you think' suggests that the inhabitants should be telling Spain *'Sí + Sí'*. Yes, I want Catalonia to become a state. Yes, I want this state to be independent. When they come to vote a few months later 93% will agree. But then dreams are free.

Unlike nightmares. But for some reason the Basque nightmare hasn't been reproduced in Catalonia. Or so I thought before Puigcerdà.

The path to the town is mainly a road with nothing to recommend it. After the inevitable industrial estate, walkers coming from the west like me arrive at the railway station. Although the line crosses the frontier into France it is a homely building, without the hubris of Canfranc.

Opposite the station, a decaying whitewashed wall is the battleground of a graffiti war. A spray-can *senyera estelada*, the lone-star flag of Catalan independence, has been crossed out. The same hand has drawn a Celtic cross (a circle with a vertical cross extending beyond its circumference), a neo-fascist icon. Nearby, a third hand has written *Viva España !!!* and added a swastika. It is now fairly common to see [swastica].cat on walls here. But the battle is not yet finished. A fourth person has crossed the swastika out.

The station is on the plain, with the town centre up the *puig*, linked by a funicular. There are a few people just getting into it so I race up past the defibrillator near the door, up past the Red Cross building near the top, and win.

The centre of town is through narrow streets flanked by shops: it is a

Footprints on the mountains

View from the bell tower, Puigcerdà

large paved square. At one end a bell tower promises views over the surrounding area. From the top visitors can see Puigmal, mountain of evil reputation; Marxel took a short-cut from Núria by way of the summit. Its rolling foothills are beautifully lit by the rays of sun filtering between the clouds. Nearer to is the plain: arable fields where there should be mountains. The hard sombre lines of the town's roofs make for a dramatic contrast.

But the most intriguing thing is the void at my feet when I look over the parapet, where the rest of St Mary's church should be. The destruction dates to the start of the Civil War, a war which still casts a long shadow over Catalonia.

From 21 July 1936 to 27 April 1937 the town was governed by an anarchist council. It would be charitable to say that they valued ends over means, ideology more than human lives.

The most notorious massacre took place in the night of 9 September 1936 just after the arrival of refugees from the destruction of Irun, reinforcing the power of the ruling *junta*. When French journalists asked what had happened they were told: "Twenty-one true fascists have been executed". One of them was only 15 years old. If the Opel sedan registration number B-40691 drew to a halt outside your door, it was time to start saying your prayers.

The first thing the anarchists had done on usurping power was to burn the church. It was to be a return to year zero, *tabula rasa*. They were eventually deposed – some killed – as part of the power struggle with republicans and communists. The broken arcades hanging lifelessly from the walls of the tower are their monument. The empty square their graveyard.

From the square I walk to the hotel – Veronica has booked us into the Del Prado – down a street graced with *tasteful* Coca-Cola signs. In Puigcerdà the red-and-white plastic rectangles have been replaced by oval ironwork plaques hanging into the street like inn signs, including one on a posh delicatessen selling *foie gras*. Can it really be a substitute for Sauternes?

Veronica arrives late, in a taxi. Our car has broken down in the hills. It will take a week to repair.

Puigcerdà

As predicted by last night's weather forecast, it is raining heavily in the morning. Dripping morosely, the policemen at the roundabout outside the gates of the hotel are just standing there. Three or four cars and twice as many policemen. Just standing there, not even stopping cars. They were there all day yesterday as well. When I ask in the hotel reception I am told that it is because the border with France is just down the road. This seems a particularly poor justification given that border controls have been abolished.

Researching the subject, I don't find an explanation but I do discover Catalan terrorism. Three terrorists, members of Terra Lliure (Free land) were arrested just outside this hotel in 1985. One of them, Jaume Fernàndez, incidentally, had been involved in the protests against the death sentence on Txiki (whose memorial I found at Aritxulegui).

Terra Lliure carried out some two hundred attacks starting in 1979. There were many injuries and one death (not counting the four terrorists who blew themselves up by accident). But the collective sense of horror at the 21 deaths when the Basque ETA attacked a Catalan supermarket in 1987 initiated a reappraisal which led to splits in the organisation. By 1995 Terra Lliure had declared itself intellectually bankrupt and shut up shop.

So why didn't I know about them? Perhaps because they were overshadowed by ETA. Perhaps because it was all a long time ago. Watching a recent video of Jaume Fernàndez my first thought is how ordinary, how peaceful he looks. He sounds like a history lecturer.

The town is full of walking mushrooms and we spend much of the time running from shop to shop trying unsuccessfully to buy one. In Catalonia, unlike the Basque country, they are not an everyday necessity. At one point we go into an empty launderette and I take off as many clothes as I decently can and throw them into the tumble dryer.

When the weather improves we walk to a lake, bizarrely situated not in a valley, but just above the town on a ridge. It is equipped with a boardwalk, kiosks, and specimen trees on its shores. On two sides it is flanked by opulent houses built by the Barcelonan bourgeoisie, the first tourists, early in the 20th-century. But although the lake looks as if it must also date to the *belle époque*, both it and the channel which feeds it go much further back. It is probably the oldest waterworks in the Pyrenees still in use. Just as the inhabitants of Bielsa talked of the Pineta dam bringing them into the 20th century, the Puigcerdanencs must have talked of being transported into the 14th: the channel bore along with it irrigation, water mills, drinking water, a means of putting out fires, fishing, and ice.

In the evening we eat at the Taverna d'en Santa, starting with a half tomato each. A beefsteak tomato: drizzled with olive oil and balsamic vinegar, speckled with sea salt and freshly milled pepper, the four slices cover a dinner plate. There are few pips, no cavities: it is flesh incarnate. It is red, the kind of red tomato which doesn't exist in northern Europe. Red throughout, blood red, not pink in places, not white nor green near the calyx. Not a tomato which has seen the sun through dark glasses, it is as sunburnt as an unwary tourist. But redder. And it tastes of tomato. There is nothing insipid about it; it is acid and sweet at the same time. Savoury. Succulent. It tastes of the Mediterranean. Of home.

The remembered past

Puigcerdà to Planoles

I leave Veronica to sleep in, closing the door quietly. My crampons and ice axe have been abandoned as well. Outside, the policemen are gone, the road empty. In the twilight the first few kilometres pass quickly, though the tarmac is hard on the feet.

'*Benvinguts a Age*' says the sign at the entrance to the village. Next to it a half-size plastic cow smiles at me superciliously. The plaster sheep, donkey, and calf grazing on the lawn of the Del Prado hotel were ludicrous; but at least the hotel had the excuse that it couldn't cope with manure, however symbolic the animals might be of the *prados*. The village of Age has no such excuse: the plastic cow is in the corner of a pasture where real cows could be grazing. What is this ridiculous farce? I have already ruminated on naturbanisation. There's no need to rub my nose in it.

The exit from the village is equally symbolic, though unintentionally so. Here, the cemetery is organised into miniature apartments for the eternal life. Seventeen on each of the three floors under the gabled slate roof. Each with a bay window and a view of the mountains.

The Senda strides past fields of wheat – real agriculture – and flowering poppies. Soon, I am on the flank of the mountain, on the balcony, not the roof, but still the view is striking. Back beyond Puigcerdà the Pyrenees are chugging along with steam-engine clouds flowing in their wake. The plain is wide open, available, unlike the enclosed valleys of Andorra.

I have come back to the French–Spanish border, for the first time since Candanchú. Inexplicably, the border doesn't stick to the watershed heading directly up Puigmal but follows the contour lines. The Senda shadows it, meeting up with frontier stones every few hundred metres, 501(i) to 501(vi), then 502. Exactly a hundred to go before the Mediterranean. A helicopter circles above me unnervingly. Even when I make the N sign it doesn't go away.

At a wire fence, I meet a young French couple and ask them where they are heading.

"We don't know. But we aren't lost," the man insists. "It's fine so we are going to climb a hill," he continues. "Then we'll see."

We are standing at the Coll de la creu de Meians. The original *creu* (cross) in question no longer exists but the Barcelonan *Club excursionista* has replaced it and added a plaque in memory of the skier Jordi Prats i Moli.

The helicopter is still circling around as I delve into another forest but it soon flies off. Who's it looking for? Is it something to do with the police at the roundabout in Puigcerdà?

Along the side of the track, stacks of freshly cut timber ooze sap, scented with pine. I spot a Slippery Jack. I open the top of my rucksack to add it to the magnificent *pedos de lobo* I have already collected; a sweet earthy aroma escapes. Predictably, the chef this evening will reject them all.

Dòrria, the next village, is a huddle of restored stone houses and a Romanesque church clinging to the *solana*, the sunny side of the hill. There is no sign of life, except for the presence of a donkey and a 4x4 with a donkey sticker on the back. Both are *Catalan* donkeys. Symbolic.

The one which is munching grass is a member of a sub-species in danger of extinction. On the other hand, the one on the stickers is going from strength to strength. It was originally drawn to highlight the extinction but then kidnapped by some students in 2004. It was a joke to share with friends: the Spanish have their virile bulls (originally roadside advertisements for Osborne sherry); let's have a donkey! The addition of the Catalan flag turned it into a symbol of identity, now widely seen on cars; but it has done nothing to help the living donkeys, still in danger. At the same time, although the Osborne bulls are thriving in the rest of Spain the Catalan sub-species has been repeatedly vandalised and is now extinct.

The Senda continues down to the village of Planoles. I arrive just in time to eat a late lunch at the Fonda Cal Daldó. Apart from the walking I have been eating, as usual: a third of a baguette with jam and two cups of milky coffee for breakfast. Two Mars bars, a big half-baguette tortilla sandwich, an apple, and a bag of crisps *en route*. Lunch starts with two *œufs en cocotte* on a bed of Bolognese sauce, two roasted chicken legs and a big jacket potato with aioli, and finishes with ice cream. In the evening I will add a tuna salad with *piquillos* and green olives, pasta with tomato sauce, home-made *salchichas* – which are a bit like haggis but with more fat – another jacket potato, and a yoghurt because I really can't manage the tempting chocolate cake. I feel like an over-ripe wolf's fart.

In the afternoon I manage to find the energy for a short stroll. In the centre of the village the grocery shop seems to be thriving, undoubtedly thanks to holidaymakers. That must also be the reason for the online weather station and the concrete which holds the cobbles firmly in their place.

The fig tree nearby must also be on holiday here: although the village is on the *solana*, it is higher than anywhere in England. This is the first fig I have noticed since the Cabo Higuer.

There is another precursor of the Mediterranean in the village: an ancient coin in the middle of the street. There's no chance of missing it, given that it is bigger than my head and on a plinth. One side depicts a horse and a rider carrying a palm frond, the other a male head, a design which would have been familiar throughout the Mediterranean basin in the second century BC. Excavations at the find spot also uncovered iron slag; mining was to be important in this area for the next two thousand years.

Planoles to Núria

I want to have the full Núria tourist experience so I'm going to catch the train. But first I have to walk to the station in Queralbs. Anyway, the official route of the Senda is silly. It climbs a long way up and then drops way, way down into a valley to the station only to climb out again immediately when you are exhausted at the end of the day, on a track that parallels the railway. A shortcut exists, walking across the flank of the Puigmal, but that would be cheating.

The line of the Senda on the map is very strange, an impossibly neat scratch in the hillside, as if someone's pen slipped. In reality, the path out of Planoles zig-zags. Initially it follows a road, crossing it several times before finally giving up the struggle and joining the tarmac for the remaining kilometre to the pass. This road was supposed to continue all the way to Núria but it stops abruptly at the edge of the commune of Queralbs. It's not hard to understand why: Planoles would have benefited but the village of Queralbs would have been completely bypassed.

But for the moment I am on the slope above Planoles looking back in the half-light at the village and neighbouring Planes perched on the only flattish land in the valley, sandwiched between the railway and the road linking Puigcerdà to Barcelona. Both villages have a crowded ancient nucleus and extensive modern suburbs with gardens. The flat land, carefully preserved with a minimum of building over the centuries because it was needed for growing food and the vital winter forage, was exactly right for building holiday homes.

The sky is leaden today. Although I've been climbing steadily it wasn't warm in the forest. But now in the picnic area around the Corral Blanc hostel I can feel the glow of the sun on my face. There are no signs of life at the hostel as yet so I plod on through red pines then black ones up to the pass and the ruins of the miners' barracks.

Further along, a marmotte is sitting on a rock watching her four youngsters play. She doesn't whistle despite my visible-from-a-helicopter red anorak, so I sit down, pulling the hood over my head, watching as the youngsters scurry around. Given the date, this must be on one of their first explorations of the outside world. Their mother has her nose in the air, sitting on her haunches like an obedient dog. She is looking directly at me with her big round brown eyes but she doesn't move. She ought to be taking more care.

I whisper 'wolf' to her. They've come back, or at least one has, spotted on these slopes earlier this year, from Italy probably. Marmottes had been absent for millennia until they were deliberately reintroduced in 1948; wolves, absent for a mere century, reintroduced themselves. Perhaps the lack of wolves is one of the factors in the spectacular growth in the marmotte population in the last sixty years.

Things are due to change in the Pyrenees, if the American experience is typical. In the Yellowstone National Park the deliberate reintroduction of grey wolves reduced the population of elk, allowing willows to grow, thus creating a habitat suitable for beavers and moose. Everything is up for grabs, as George Monbiot would say, if the proportion of apex predators changes. If more wolves and bears take up residence will shepherds be discouraged? Will sheep disappear? Will the magic wand of trophic cascades turn grass into rhododendrons and then trees? Where do the ibex fit in to the scheme? In the wolf's mouth?

Of course, it might be just a false alarm.

In the forest which follows, the waymarks disappear. After struggling through the undergrowth, chasing the cows hiding from the sun, I decide to head for the river, the only feature marked on my map which is sure to be identifiable. As a result, I re-join the Senda at the Font del Home Mort

The remembered past

Marmottes

(Dead Man's spring). The spring is fenced off, for safety; but then again, it is the source of Queralbs' drinking water.

The village itself resembles Planoles. You can't tell that it was completely destroyed in Spain's worst ever recorded earthquake, in 1428.

At the station after a long queue I just have time to buy a ticket before the train arrives, a workaday blue and white box. I manage to grab a seat, with my rucksack on my lap, but other passengers have to hang onto the straps. The carriage shakes as the cog engages the rack and we start to climb up the narrow valley, alternately passing through tunnels and looking over precipices. When we emerge from the last of the tunnels at Núria the view has changed.

A man is rowing a boat across the lake; on the grass beyond it families are eating picnics; children are riding ponies. On the roof of the factory a *senyera* is flapping in the breeze. Bare mountains above, purple-headed, provide the backdrop.

Núria

The tube disgorges its contents and most of us head into one or other of the workshops – church, hotel, restaurant, or boutique according to religion. I've been here before and the one part of the Núria experience that I don't wish to repeat is the Youth Hostel where the sausages are watery and the main carbohydrate on the plate is potato crisps. So I am praying that there is space in the eat-as-much-as-you-can hotel. There is.

The hotel is the latest incarnation of the soup kitchen run by Saint Gil for shepherds around AD 700. It is here that he buried the pot, the bell used to announce mealtimes, the cross, and the small statue of Mary and Jesus which were to be miraculously rediscovered four hundred years later.

I cross the granite flags of the esplanade, walk down the steps, and traverse the freshly mown greensward to Saint Gil's hermitage chapel. Dated by the keystone on the arch to 1644, the chapel is austere. A niche with a small statue of the saint has accumulated hundreds of folded scraps of paper, *ex-votos*. I can't read them but traditionally they are from women asking for children, though it's not clear how Saint Gil became involved. He is the patron saint of shepherds.

Round the back of the hotel complex, carefully hidden from view, children – prayers answered? – are jumping up and down on trampolines, trying out a mini climbing wall, or tobogganing down the hillside on giant rubber tyres. The pizzeria and the café are shut. The overnight camping zone is open but empty.

Why has Núria become so symbolic? Catalonia has many symbols. The flag, obviously. St George, the patron saint, and the dragon, the patron enemy. Pic d'Estats and Canigó, for walkers. The *sardana* and *castellers* for dancers and acrobats respectively. *Cagatiós* (shitting logs) and *caganers* (Nativity scene figurines, also shitting) at Christmas. Barça, for football fans (in Britain we say 'cheese' for photos, in Catalonia they say 'Barça' because it is sure to raise a smile). The *diada* on 11 September, a celebration of a defeat, a bit like Dunkirk. The donkeys we have already met. And Montserrat, another religious site. But why Núria?

The origin of Núria's fame is tucked away up the stairs at the back of the church. There, the wooden statue of Mary and Jesus has a small stream of visitors. (Incidentally, it is dated to the 12th century, not the 8th.) The *Mare de Déu* sits on a chair with her son on one knee. It is a Romanesque piece: naïve, with a pleasing simplicity, painted in warm colours. The most striking thing is Jesus. He is looking disinterestedly into space, not with the wide eyes of a child but with the hard eyes of an adult, the prominent chin of a serious man – but in miniature, the size of a three-year-old. The statue has been given a ghastly neo-baroque-style setting topped by two silver angels holding a crown above Mary's head. Curiously, it works well, complementing the original by emphasising its minimalism.

We are invited to kiss the ribbon which dangles from Mary's feet – the statue itself is behind a transparent screen. The screen is not only a question of protecting her shoes from slobber. Twice in the last century she has been kidnapped. On the first occasion, she was spirited across the border by the parish priest. It was 22 July 1936; the anarchists had just taken over in Puigcerdà. She came back in 1941 when Franco had established a garrison in the valley.

The second occasion was 7 July 1967. Five Catholic Boy Scout leaders stole into the church at night and whisked away the statue intending to stop

Footprints on the mountains

Mare de Déu, *Núria*

the canonical coronation – the addition of the neo-baroque crown – due to take place a week later. They objected to a Spanish bishop who would be officiating. The coronation went ahead anyway, with a plaster copy being substituted, guarded initially by machine guns. The kidnappers also demanded that the former Abbot of Montserrat be allowed to return from exile, that Catalans be allowed to choose their own bishops, and the resignation of the incumbent one. They were disputing a cornerstone of Franco's regime, the amalgam of the Catholic Church and the Spanish state. It was only in 1972 after a Catalan had been named bishop of Barcelona that the statue was returned.

In the 1980s Núria was the most popular girl's name in the area and remains one of the most common names in Catalonia. But by that time the valley was already famous and had been so for eons.

The remembered past

The eleven editions of the *History and miracles of the sacred image of Our Lady of Núria* published between 1666 and 1896 must have had something to do with it. Then the rebuilding of the church, skiing, lots of skiing, the rack railway, and the drafting of the first Catalan constitution.

In 1894 the poet Joan Maragall could still write of the Virgin in her loneliness surrounded in winter only by the snow. No longer. Although Núria is encircled by some of the highest peaks of the Pyrenees it doesn't seem high.

Nevertheless, the evening weather forecast for tomorrow predicts −4 degrees Celsius on the ridge, which translates as −10 degrees taking into account the wind chill factor. I go out to see what the sky is like – clear – and meet a group of young Japanese in the covered walkway, bedding down for the night in sleeping bags.

Núria to Setcases

It is probably Thursday. I have eaten a sandwich sitting on the bed and have drunk an insipid cup of tea made with water from the hot tap. Now, I'm climbing up towards the frontier ridge.

My rucksack is light today because I am wearing most of its contents, including gloves and leggings. As the sky rises slowly from the horizon, the hood of my anorak flaps noisily against my steamed-up glasses.

Looking back at Núria I wonder if I have unwittingly embarked on a pilgrimage. No! For me paradise is simply a blue sky.

I look at the grass fringed with hoar frost and stamp on a puddle just to hear the crackling as the ice shatters. Behind me, the summit of Puigmal, caught by the first rays of the sun, turns an unexpected lemon yellow. I pass a small herd of cattle, lying down, keeping warm together.

The pasture has disappeared into a mess of scree and grit. Multiple paths, none persuasive. And then, right in the middle of one of them, in the middle of this desolation, a flower: a cup of pink petals with purple veins, fat yellow stamens and fleshy grey-green leaves. Then a sudden cliff edge and the realisation that I haven't been paying attention.

Walking over to the Noucreus pass, at 2800m the highest point on the Senda, suddenly the sky dominates. The landscape fills with mountains:

Footprints on the mountains

Noucreus

Sarrio, above Núria

mountains lower than the pass; a few marginally higher. But it is the valleys that count. The Carança with its black and blue lakes and its dramatic gorge; I know it well.

I don't need to pay too much attention today but the *nou creus* are here for a reason. Nine small metal crosses: one for each body brought down into the valley after the *torb* had abated, a disaster dating to the mid-19th century, the details having melted with the snowflakes. Just a little further along the Senda, the buckled aluminium plaque on the Tirapits hut records the fate of two hikers also caught in a *torb*, this time in 1986. In 2010 the same phenomenon struck again: nine experienced walkers died. And there were other occasions. Although I blundered up to a gable end by accident, here the roof of the Pyrenees is mostly rounded. It is like walking on the surface of a potato: simple, as long as you can stick to the top. But in a *torb* with the snow swirling around and high winds it must be easy to become disorientated. The names of the mountains confirm the treacherous ambiguity of the landscape: Pic de la Vaca (Cow Mountain) rubs shoulders with Pic de l'Infern (Hell's Mountain).

There is a tenth cross, but it has a different meaning: carved into a granite slab it has the number 510 below it: I don't seem to have made much progress in the last two days. And I'm not making much progress at present either. I have to lean over on one walking pole, adjusting my balance with every exhausting step, afraid that if the wind drops suddenly I will collapse, a clumsy acrobat. Catching my breath, letting it go, I have to think about using my diaphragm, turning my face away from the force. I can almost see the wind. *C'est un vent à décorner des bœufs* – a wind like this could blow the horns off cattle.

Sailing in from the east with the low sun behind them, a young couple make a romantic picture. Hardly in their twenties, flushed, they are radiant. But as soon as they stop the woman starts to shiver. I have already noticed that her pretty orange pantaloons are diaphanous. The man tells me that they slept in the Tirapits hut last night. Despite the big sleeping bags on their rucksacks, despite huddling together, they were frozen.

From here it is all downhill. I've climbed a mountain this morning and there are two to descend. At the end of the day I will still be well above the plain.

This is an ancient path with a real name – *cami de Núria a Setcases* – used for centuries. Borne on the wind, it traverses the flank of Pic de la Vaca and then descends into the head of a valley to the Tirapits hut.

The shelter is a drystone *orry* with grass on the roof, so that the solar panel and radio telephone also growing out of the roof look incongruous, as does the aluminium plaque. Marc and Ramon were just seventeen when they were trapped by the *torb* three days before Christmas. Their epitaph reads: *En la muntanya es troba una bona raó de ser* – On the mountain there is a good reason for living.

To the left of the text the four stripes etched into the surface are plainly visible but it is some time before I recognise the star and put them together to make a *senyera estrelada*. The reason it takes so long is that the plaque is battered and buckled. At first I put this down to the ravages of the environment but now, looking carefully, it seems that the star has been singled out for attack. I would guess the weapon was the pick end of an ice axe.

The hut and plaque could serve as a metaphor for the changing mountains. Back on the ridge the *nou creus* have no names and no epitaphs. They weren't necessary: the only people likely to see them knew the story and, being working shepherds, may not have been able to read anyway. Marc and Ramon, in contrast, would be unknown here if it weren't for the plaque; the people who see it are literate and on holiday. And the Christian symbolism of the *nou creus* is uncontentious today. Unlike the *senyera estrelada*.

Down in the valley the wind is thinner but the sky is denser. I meet a succession of people, including a woman with her 80-year-old father and uncle.

Then I see a boy walking on a fragile snow bridge over a river and heading for the edge. His father, watching from the safety of the path, seems unconcerned but from my viewpoint I can see how thin the snow is. I shout: "*Non, non. C'est dangereux!*" It's the wrong language but the boy stops anyway. The father looks nonplussed until I point out the void underneath.

The proportion of grass increases and then, at the edge of a bluff, the racetracks of the Vallter ski resort slalom into view. Trees reappear and now, in the spaces, cattle – those prosaically named Pyrenean Brown Cows.

Just below, in the Ulldeter hostel I am looking out of the picture windows when a man enters. He asks me where I have come from and when I say Núria he asks excitedly if I have seen a particular flower. He takes me into the dining room and points to a poster. Have I seen one of those but pink, not white? It's not the one I saw this morning but the poster does have mine: a *Ranunculus parnassifolius*. It is classified as vulnerable: high risk of extinction.

Outside again, Ricardo is filling his water bottle from a spring. I know he's called Ricardo because he introduces himself, asks my name, and shakes my hand. He is heading west. He tells me about a little-known unmanned hostel in La Jonquera. You have to get the key from the police station and the only facility is cold water but it's clean.

A little way below Ulldeter, the ski lift and its accompanying carpark lie empty. They are serviced by a new road; the Senda follows the ancestral version, down near the river, paved with flagstones in places but mostly just a grassy track. I strip off and enjoy the steady descent.

I'm getting tired though and by the time I arrive in Setcases after a stretch on tarmac my eyes are half-closed by fatigue, all the details lost in an archetype: narrow streets lined with flowers, the ancient stone walls soaking up the heat, the brook tripping merrily over miniature cascades. Motorcars have not yet been invented, the little shop sells all you really need, and the benches are populated by families who have lived here for generations.

When I wake up, I still like the village but my inner curmudgeon wishes it were perfect. It could so easily be a ruin. Instead, there are 195 inhabitants, eight hotels, and a ski resort. The 266 holiday houses have mostly been built or renovated with care and modern intrusions are limited. Perhaps you cannot buy bread and most other staples, but you can find honey, cheese, dried sausages, and dried wild mushrooms, even though you have to fight your way through the plastic pigs and wooden spoons to pay for them.

Setcases to Beget

I shivered all evening yesterday. Even in bed I was cold, adding progressively more bedclothes and finally covering my head with a blanket. This morning the mirror in the bathroom diagnoses sunstroke.

Outside, a car pulls up under a streetlight. The driver lets a spaniel out of the back and extracts a wicker basket from the boot. While he is changing his shoes I walk on into the darkness but on the slope he catches up. He is looking for mushrooms to sell in the shop in Setcases.

"Are wolf's farts edible?" I check.

"Yes, but nobody around here believes it."

It can't just be the name; *trompette de la mort* (death's trumpet) is hardly more encouraging and yet they are much-prized in France.

The mushroom man forges ahead, the dog barking for a while, until they disappear into a forest labelled 'Training of hunting dogs'.

I walk along a *vereda* and then across pasture to the top of a dome where the Senda turns abruptly left. Two prominent red-and-white Xs mark the turn but I have already stopped before noticing them. I can hardly breathe, though there is no wind today. I stare at the view, talking off my rucksack mechanically, floating. Just for an instant, every single step is justified.

A barbed wire fence separates me from a dream world: the textured turquoise forest and the smoothly rounded pastures; the floating volcanic islands shading from baby blue to indigo; beyond them, water – the Mediterranean – still a silvery pink, despite the hours which have passed since dawn. The sky, also a silvery pink at the horizon, drifts into an *eau de nil* green. In the distance, over Olot, two red hot air balloons are rising slowly. Nearer to, cows and palomino horses have bells which tinkle as they graze.

Perhaps I can make out the Albères where the Pyrenees cartwheel into the sea. Perhaps Llançà, a port of call on the penultimate day. The clouds above me are breaking up, with bands of light cascading through them, shimmering. I haven't lived 'in the moment' like this since Vallibierna.

Turning round, the mountains to the west are vividly sharp under a clear sky. Too well-defined, they look ordinary in comparison. I am balanced on a fulcrum. One step forwards and there will be no going back. A mere seventy kilometres if I could only continue straight on. But the two big Xs are uncompromising. The Senda turns left.

Breathing out again, anxious to record the moment, I take numerous photos and videos with my camera and then repeat them on my phone. But already this fleeting consecration is melting in the heat of the sun.

After the dark pine forest at the Collada de la Fembra Morta (Dead Woman's Pass) the Senda follows one of the many fingers of pasture descending towards the village of Molló.

I hear a furious barking but at first I can't see the dog through the long grass and bracken. He makes out that he is going to bite my ankles, though he never actually does so, and doesn't stop until his owners shout at him.

The remembered past

They had been lying down a little way off and are now sitting up. He accompanies me back to them, tail now wagging wildly.

They are sitting on a foam mattress, surrounded by a scatter of goods and chattels spread over a wide area like wind-blown rubbish. From Madrid, young, in love, and literally laid-back, they are showing no signs of imminent departure. If anything, it is the dog which wants to get moving. We agree that he is a hero. A Westie, he has been walking for the last two weeks on legs the size of matchsticks. They have come from Cap de Creus and are heading for the Atlantic.

Viewed from above, the most striking thing about the village of Molló is the terracotta roofs. In the mountains the roofs were slate or stone. Here, there are still many rustic buildings but also others with pretentions: wrought iron balconies, rendered walls painted in pastels, window openings outlined in stone. While I am drinking coffee at a table in the Plaça Major, my phone picks up a free public Wi-Fi signal; a waiter is arranging place settings in the restaurant; and when I go to the butchers to buy food for the next two days – dried sausages and hard cheese – I have to stand in a queue.

On the other side of the village a road leads to Prats de Mollo where the bear festival takes place. (*Prats* is Catalan for meadows and although they have been French for the last 350 years some are still used by Spanish breeders for their mares.)

For me there is a path leading down to the river and a monkey-puzzle tree. Beyond it, forest, flowery hay meadows, a high-tension electricity line, and innumerable electric fences. Then holm oak, sweet chestnut, box, coppicing, a derelict telegraph pole and a pleasant shady stroll in an ivy-clad gorge down to the village of Beget. A long slithery brown thing crosses the trail; I don't have time to identify it.

The path disgorges into Beget at a parking lot full of cars; the letterboxes are grouped here as well, 27 in all. Only pedestrians are allowed any further down the cobbles of memory lane. The church is the first door on the left, guarded by gargoyles. Inside, the baroque gold and pink cherubs cry out for attention like difficult children but the most interesting item is a carved wooden figure of Christ, not so much for its size – two metres – or its age – twelfth-century – but for the story of how he was saved when all seemed lost.

Footprints on the mountains

Beget

Forewarned, like the priest in Núria, that the Reds were coming, the villagers dragged the church pews out of the door and set fire to them. When the horsemen of the apocalypse arrived waving the banner of the Federación Anarquista Ibérica they were told that the work had already been done. They went away not knowing that the Christ Majestad had been hidden under the stairs in the boys' school and that the baroque altar back was intact.

The church stands apart from the rest of the village, isolated on an extensive circular platform with steps at the edge, like a stack of pancakes. Its golden stone, rounded apse, and Romanesque frills set it apart from the grey stone and utilitarian rectangles of the centuries-old houses.

The houses may well have been strictly functional in the past, and they still retain their wooden balconies – for drying underwear and taking the air, though no longer for knitting – but a certain aesthetic has been imposed. I'm rather impressed by one house in particular which could be a self-parody: the façade is adorned with agricultural implements – a rake, a two-man log saw, a ladder, a yoke, a cow bell, a smith's bellows, and more.

The remembered past

Beget is nostalgia written in stone, best viewed sitting at a table outside Can Jeroni, looking over the bridge which arches across the gorge. As I watch, a ginger cat jumps down from the parapet onto the flagstones.

At the Hostal El Forn, Enric tells me that the village used to be a thriving community until the road arrived in 1965 and everybody left. More accurately, Barcelona moved in and the village lost its independence, devoured by the much bigger Camprodón.

I ask Enric about the paintings decorating the restaurant wall: a hunting scene, a pig killing, and a man riding a donkey side-saddle.

"A friend of mine did them."

"But they look early 20th century from the clothes… "

"He copied them from old photos, in exchange for meals."

I see another example of the artist's work, possibly a copy of a painting by Toulouse-Lautrec, in the gents' toilet. A man wearing a top hat sits on a chair in a dark room. Standing in front of him are three women. One is wearing a virginal white froufrou dress. The other two – the choice of a blonde or a brunette – are wearing boas around their shoulders and knee-high stockings but nothing else. Jumping a century forwards, some things have changed. The gents' also contains a fully equipped baby-changing table.

Beget to Talaixà

I am still tasting the bacon through my teeth when I leave the hostel mid-morning. The road out of the village crosses fields of hay drying in the sun and another crop I don't recognise – like maize but it isn't quite right. I'm overtaken by a white van with a collie dog running alongside, barking. It stops just ahead so I ask the driver about the crop. "Sorghum, for cattle," he replies, driving off with one hand on the wheel and the other dangling out of the window holding a lead.

Also being exercised – though I don't realise it at first – is a gang of teenage boys gambolling along the road in high spirits. It is only when they have disappeared around a bend and another boy walking along the road tells me he is a wolf cub that I identify them as a flock of sheep. Their fold is a little further along the valley, unmistakeably flagged by the sound of youth music and a makeshift sign pointing to the summer camp of their Barcelonan Scout troop.

The highlight of my day – at least until I reach Talaixà – is to meet somebody coming the other way in the middle of the forest and to stop for a chat. Even from a distance I can see that this is a *Senderista*, absorbed with their rucksack in the middle of the track. I scuff my shoes on the gravel. She turns to look at me, anxious, so I walk up to her slowly and keep my distance. I try Spanish but we soon settle on English; she is Czech.

"When I started out," she says, "I had 35kg in my sack. Five litres of water and a whole load of food from home."

"Where did you stay last night?"

"On the other side of the river, off the path. I don't want to be too obvious, being a girl and on my own… Last night I heard a rustling around my tent but I think it was only a wild boar."

She offers me a biscuit and munches one herself. We swop information.

Laura first came to the Pyrenees ten years ago but this is her first long-distance walk. It is a banal conversation but just talking to someone about the Senda is such a pleasure.

"There is an English man who hangs around the supermarket in Albanyà being helpful," she adds. He doesn't try to pick me up when I get there.

She fixes her ponytail revealing a big circular earring-talisman sparkling in the sun. As she lifts up her rucksack, her knees wrinkle under the weight. She shrugs the rucksack from one brown shoulder to the other. "Sunburn," she says, then *"Buen camino."*

Climbing up through the forest, I stumble across a derelict farmstead and a pair of discarded walking boots. Good quality, worn but not unusable, they have been carefully placed on top of fence posts like totems.

I have been told that there is no water at Talaixà so I am walking slowly to keep cool. When I cross the romantically named Palanca del Samsó (Samson's fulcrum), the bridge that Laura talked about, I consider trying the water; but it has passed through Beget and I'm suspicious of the verb. Above, the Font del Vaquer, next to the ruined farm of the same name, has a stone basin but it is completely dry. But, against all expectations, in Talaixà there *is* a water tap although a sign warns that it is 'not tested' and it comes from the grass-covered roof of the hostel, where birds are nesting.

I had anticipated more ruins but only a few stub walls poke through the brambles; the only buildings with roofs are the hostel and the church. Most of the hostel is firmly secured with metal shutters, but one door swings open when I push it. There's a tiled floor to trip over, a shelf with a bottle of olive oil and a can of coffee, a bunk bed, two narrow wooden benches, and an armchair. No table. No chimney. On one wall a set of instructions pleads: 'Silence is precious. Respect resting walkers', 'Don't cut the fruit trees down for firewood' and the uncompromising 'Please piss and shit well away from the house'.

I eat off my lap and then slump down on that tatty but wonderfully comfortable olive-green leather armchair. So comfortable that I fall asleep only to be roused by the squeak of the door opening.

"I'm sorry," says the man. "I didn't know there was anyone there."

"No problem," I say, introducing myself.

"It's odd. Sitting there in the shadow you could be Rodri. It was his armchair, you know."

"The man on the dedication?" A plaque above the door honours him. "Did you know him?"

He explains some more, but then searches around and drags a sheaf of paper out from under one of the benches. When he has gone, I read it.

Rodri lived here for nearly twenty years. Sometimes he said he had been a miner, sometimes a policeman, sometimes a mason – maybe he had been all of them – but what he wanted to do in Talaixà was to run a bar. He might have made something of it if he had been younger but he was already retired when he bought the house. The local hunters made his life difficult, but he was stubborn. It is thanks to him that the hostel exists.

At first he had a friend to keep him company but the friend left when things got tough. Rodri stayed on, growing vegetables and planting fruit trees but still with his dream of a bar for walkers. Then in 1988 a company bought the whole valley and put up wire fences. 'El Racionero' and his hunting cronies wanted to turn the hillside into a private estate and they nearly succeeded; beware Rodri, a hunting accident can always be arranged.

But Rodri fought on. They wanted him out, and they didn't want walkers either. That was their big mistake; the walkers were organised, and Rodri saw the opportunity. In exchange for food every second Saturday he would lease them somewhere to use as a hostel. And since walkers and tourists were the only hope for an economic revival the local council backed them up and classified the paths. It would no longer be possible to keep strangers out. It was a big fight, like Jánovas.

The privatisation of the Pyrenees still continues, nevertheless, in France as well as in Spain. In 2012 Groupama Insurance came up with the wheeze of selling exclusive hunting permits at 3750 euros each. It banned walkers from the Pic du Madres. Faced with the power of the internet and a single protest march (to the summit) the capitalists retreated.

But it was more difficult back in those days, in Talaixà. The capitalists left eventually, but Rodri was getting on. He was helicoptered out one winter when the snow became too much, and then another time when a tick bite got infected. Finally old age defeated him. Now virtually nothing remains here except the hostel and a hopeful hand-painted sign asserting that the village has not been abandoned.

But Rodri has left *something* because the walkers finished the restoration and created the free hut in which I am sitting. Perhaps it is the first shoot of spring, but not much has yet changed since the 1960s when the last of the villagers left. Poor people, living off a few sheep and making charcoal, they were driven out by the arrival of bottled gas down in the valley. The charcoal they produced was no longer needed for cooking. They left rapidly, abandoning a community centuries old.

The cold frames now overflowing with mint and the drip-feed watering system must have been Rodri's work. The plum tree, the apple, the cherry, the pear, the fig, the vine too. For me, Rodri is one of those quiet heroes who have planted the grapes of hope in some of the most unpromising areas of the Pyrenees which were in terminal decline. They were not burdened by ancestral certainty that their community was doomed or by the vision of an easier life on the plain. For the locals they were 'hippies' – although those who *really* were hippies left when the first winter arrived. Those who stayed worked hard, creating their own *Walden*.

I could cite many of them, but I'm thinking in particular of Jeannette and Bernard Gaschard who started a goat farm on an abandoned hillside in the Corbières in 1965. I'm thinking of their struggle against the power of money, with Paco Rabanne, the couturier, in the role of capitalist. '*La terre appartient à celui qui la travaille* – land belongs to those who work it' was their rallying cry. Their children still live on the farm and now supply cheese to a three-star Michelin restaurant.

The remembered past

The 'hippies' are part of Pyrenean folklore and have contributed more than many people would like to admit. They brought life with them (Rodri was unusually old). A different generation, a human renovation as well as a physical one.

Talaixà is Beget's impoverished little sister. In Beget the newcomers have money and bring the city with them; their renovations include satellite dishes. They buy a second house just as the first begins to empty; but there will be no fledglings in this new nest. Talaixà, on the other hand, has no road, no electricity, no water, no hope. God bless the child.

During the afternoon and evening various people come up the various paths, nibble something and then go back down again. A couple of Spanish men walking the Senda in the other direction consider stopping but they don't have enough water. They met somebody who had come from Candanchú and corresponds to Javi's description earlier today.

In the evening, sitting on the bench outside the door to catch the last of the sunlight, I read the guest book. The Westie was called Raspa. He thanks the walking club for sharing this special place, signing with a paw print. More enigmatically one unsigned entry reads 'NO HAY PEOR MUERTE QUE SER COMIDO POR LOS CERDOS – there's no death worse than being eaten by pigs'. How about 'If the Spanish war begins on 9 November [the date of the unofficial Catalan independence referendum], come here for a rest' or 'Chaos and destruction in the suburbs, peace and tranquillity in the mountains'?

In the evening I sit on the bench outside the door, looking out at the world. How big it is; how far it goes; how disconnected I am. The sky is charged with crimson which flits from place to place. The birds, oblivious, are tweeting short sentences.

Talaixà to Albanya

Salt de la Núvia, Salt del Vicari, Salt del Capellà (the Bride's Leap, the Vicar's Leap, the Chaplin's Leap). When I noticed these names on the map yesterday evening, I suddenly remembered José's warning for the first time since Arinsal. And today I can see why: the path is cut into the cliff.

If I'm anxious, it's not because I fear slipping on wet rock, the collapse of the path, or catching my shoelaces in a branch, though I do. It's the word 'leap' I don't like. On the edge of a precipice – not always but often, and only if I am on my own – it isn't that my head spins, it's just that the longer I stay the stronger the pull of gravity. It's not vertigo. It's not the void. I'm not *afraid* of the void. It is like a force building up in me. It starts somewhere in my chest, a burning feeling, spreading, taking over. Now? It has nothing to do with my state of mind. It is more like a prediction.

I have to sit down. For it to be really tempting, the precipice has to be unforgivingly vertical and regrettably high. I must be able to step back ten paces, shut my eyes and run until I feel nothing under my feet but keep running anyway. I've practised. Now? Gravity is becoming stronger. Better than years vegetating with cancer? Now? Is this it? Now?

No, not now. I have a purpose, even though it is absurd: the Mediterranean.

I laugh it off, making up a story for this all-purpose Lover's Leap: the story of the vicar officiating at a marriage ceremony, smitten by the bride, fluffing his lines, and accidentally marrying himself to her. He leaps, she leaps and then the chaplain follows suit. It has great dramatic potential: already I can see the cliff-hangers.

By the time I have filled in the details I have reached the other end of the vertiginous section. There were a few shuffling steps from time to time, some big drops to fear, each twinned with a breath-taking view of the gorge crushed between the tense, bulging muscles of the cliffs, but it was nothing special. Not this time.

Once again in the comfort of the forest, a clapping sound filters through the trees. Unmistakeably, the clapping of human hands, like applause. For me? I listen carefully. It can't be anything else: a single pair of hands clapping, alone in the forest. A few seconds later a flash of lime-green and black cries: "It's cold," clapping its hands again as I leap out of its way. Soon afterwards another jogger appears: "Have you seen...?" "Yes," I reply and he is gone.

The Font de Sant Aniol d'Aguja welcomes me with a gurgling sound before I can even see it. I am slurping at the water, letting it dribble over my face and down my tee-shirt, when a man comes up behind me.

Bernard started at the Cap de Creus but he has run out of maps, so I give him the sheets I no longer need. Would I like some muesli in exchange? It seemed like a good idea in Nantes but after six days it has begun to

The remembered past

pale. He says that he camped near the hostel last night, pointing to a stone structure.

The word 'hostel' is optimistic. The structure has been a hostel in the past and the scaffolding suggests that it will be one in the future, but for the present it doesn't even have a roof. A notice explains that today the walking clubs are helicoptering in more materials, asking for volunteers.

Next to the ruin is a rudimentary chapel. Its crypt apparently conserves holy water which cures the effects of the evil eye, but the remedy is kept behind a locked door, out of sight. Not that the door helped in the turmoil of 1938. Only the foundations date to AD 859; the civil war also shot through here. The chapel didn't leap; it was pushed.

As I walk across a swaying bridge and along the path through the undergrowth, I am greeted by the croak of a toad and a succession of walkers with bits of wood and bags of cement poking out of their rucksacks. I ask one of them:

"When does the helicopter arrive?"

"We are the helicopter," he says. When I don't understand he whirls his arms around.

Amongst the helicopter pilots is a young woman in a sparkly outfit who didn't have time to change after the night club; jewellery rattling, her only concession to the mountains is a pair of flip-flops. Flip-flops... The *walker* abhors relatively sensible things like cotton tee-shirts and wooden walking sticks. For him, even round shoe laces are infra-dig. But flip-flops are so way out they don't even count. The *walker* wears an anorak and a bobble hat in Paris; shorts, white socks, and sandals in a three-star restaurant. He spotted the GPS as the next must-have fashion accessory around 2001 and is still wondering why some people haven't yet picked up the signal. The *walker* has recently downloaded a clinometer for his mobile phone. The *walker* is a fashion victim on a steep downhill slope. It has taken me some time to realise this. It is true that I sometimes look goofy off-mountain, but I don't care. As Thoreau wrote:

> Beware of all enterprises [activities] that require new clothes, and not rather a new wearer of clothes. If there is not a new man, how can the new clothes be made to fit? If you have any enterprise before you, try it in your old clothes... Our moulting season, like that of the fowls, must be a crisis in our lives.

That sparkly woman knew what she was doing.

Where the path meets the road, a sign points to Albanyà but the stickers attached to it go much further. One, with the hashtag of #albiolades, accuses the mayor of a Barcelona suburb of being a fascist, right-wing, Spanish-loving xenophobe. The hashtag of the other sticker is a clenched fist. The writing, in Cyrillic, intrigues me. The Zenit St Petersburg Ultras, football hooligans known for their overt racism, have also been here. Strange fruit in this pastoral scene.

It is a long hot walk to Albanyà, meeting eight lycra-clad French cyclists and two German *Senderistas*. The cicadas are chirping lazily; laughter splashes over from the river. I hurry past the Bassegoda Park campsite which is leaking sewage into a roadside ditch, and hobble back much more slowly when I discover that Albanyà is shut. I am allocated a chalet.

The storm arrives and the mini-golfers retire to the club house for early aperitifs; the swimmers are also afraid of getting wet. In the evening the restaurant is crowded but most of the youngsters are not there for the food. They are gathered in front of a giant screen showing the World Cup final, Germany against Argentina. The teams line up and the band plays the German national anthem. The audience suddenly stops talking, stands up and sings respectfully. When the Argentinean anthem starts normal conversation resumes.

A footnote to my day: when I take off my socks and the various plasters, the state of affairs becomes evident. After two weeks' walking, Vaseline and Compeed no longer quite contain the damage.

Albanyà to La Vajol

I am saved by the bell. I can't answer the question anyway and I'm going to fail, so it doesn't matter that the invigilator has taken away the green *cazuela* pot. I don't even know why I am bothering to take the exam for a second time. I won't get better marks. Outside, the alarm goes.

Outside for real, in the humid dawn, a woman is making her way across the deserted campsite. Julia is French: yet another lone female walking the Senda towards the Atlantic. There have been more women than men on their own this year, in an inversion of the usual ratio. Also more non-Europeans.

The remembered past

The night porter lets me out of the gate and, after traversing Albanyà again, I stubbornly follow a track which exists on the map but not on the ground, up into the woods until it becomes impenetrable trees. Back in the village on a plausible track, having literally lost an hour, I ask a man in a 4x4 if he knows where the path is.

"Here," he says, "you are on it. There used to be a sign but they broke it."

"They? Who?"

"I don't know."

I don't want to meet 'them'. The countryside is less friendly here than on the most dangerous slopes above. Since the *nou creus*, I've been descending; with remissions, it is true, but descending nevertheless. I am now less than ten percent of what I was at the top. Now, I am fenced in – or out depending on your viewpoint – by barbed wire and guard dogs. The summits were on a higher moral level.

More positively, since Setcases the spray from the Mediterranean has become more frequent: terracotta tiles and rendered walls painted in pastels at first, then cicadas, fig trees, and prickly pears; and now rosemary bushes and Aleppo pines. Dishevelled holm oaks squat the understory. A cork oak, stripped of her bark up to the shoulders, exposes her beautifully tanned torso to the sun. Over the years, a few bottles of wine must have been drunk in her honour.

I am also encouraged by a home-made notice at the side of the track advertising accommodation. Although La Vajol is a day and a half walking away and I am already late, it is doable.

The base rock changes from a dusty gold to a dusty vermilion – a tadpole nursery pond is lined with pink sentiments – then to gold again, as the geology shifts. I walk at the side of the track, my feet kneading the pine needles, savouring the perfumed mattress.

The waymarks are missing and other walkers too. Several times I follow the dusty track past a turning and need to return. The best indication that I am on course is a scrap of paper by the side of the path: from an English guide to the Senda.

Finally I meet another *Senderista*: Tony, from Murcia, dressed in a yellow tee-shirt and black shorts, buzzing along. Then, within a few minutes, a French couple, and a German on his own. Although the German man doesn't stop, I later read his blog. The Senda took him 37 days (it will take me 50). He went on to complete the Pyrenean Way in 30 days, half the time I took! He is followed by a German couple, she sporty looking, he perhaps ten years older, looking worse for wear. They have all set off from Maçanet de Cabrenys this morning.

The village is surrounded by fortifications, but I hardly give them a glance. Arriving in the main square, I slump onto a red plastic chair emblazoned with an Estrella Damm logo and pick up the menu from the red plastic table. When I take my sunglasses off to wipe the sweat from my face the intense light hurts. Instant headache. When I put my glasses back on again I look around, vaguely taking in the stone walls, the classy façade of the café, and the family with two young children that has just arrived, until my eyes spot a strange pole in the middle of the square. The slender pole rises perhaps four metres out of a plinth, terminating in a vertical loop. I examine it lazily from my seat. One of the children is more adventurous: he clambers onto the plinth – four stone chairs arranged back to back – and tries to climb it.

"¡Baixa!" shouts his anxious father, half-belying his (post-box-red) tee-shirt which sports a very British-looking crown and the words: "Keep calm and speak Catalan."

"What does it mean?" I ask after we have introduced ourselves.

"The Spanish government wants to make Catalan non-compulsory in schools, so this is our way of resisting."

The slogan, despite all appearances, is a child of its time, born on Twitter one day in December 2012. The next day there was a website and by the end of the week it was being exhibited in the Spanish parliament. *It is in English.*

The father also tells me about the pole.

"It's been here for hundreds of years," he explains. "All the kids try to climb up it and touch the ring. I did it for the first time when I was sixteen, to impress a girl." A rite of passage then. Without thinking, I glance at the woman but he shakes his head.

"But what is it?" I ask.

"Who knows? I had to learn a poem at school: Roland – you know, Charlemagne's nephew – threw it here from Céret [in France]."

It's called *la barra d'en Rotllan* (Roland's bar).

Service is slow and nobody has come out of the bar – the other one – so I go in followed by the father. The kids come as well and immediately decide to race each other up the rival spiral staircases. Having reached the balcony they look timidly over the wrought iron balustrade. A wagging finger calms them. The balcony gives the bar the air of a dance hall, although the furniture would get in the way. The table football is the next thing to attract the kids' attention.

On the wall a photograph shows the bar as it was in 1908. Very little has changed except that a hundred years ago the chairs were occupied exclusively by men, many with extravagant moustaches and still wearing their flat caps though they were indoors.

Outside again, beer in hand, I pay more attention to the façade. The walls of the ground floor are stone. The first floor, rendered and painted pale orange, is enlivened by seven Mozarabic windows. The second floor, delimited by a row of green ceramic tiles, is faced with pink bricks. No, it's not a hodgepodge: it really is unusually stylish.

The key to the building is not in the door but in the carving above it:

Sociedad de socorros mutous = la Union maçanetense = Protector de los pobres
Mutual help society = the Maçanet Union = Protector of the poor

At one end a shield depicts Roland's bar and what is probably a cork oak; at the other end a second shield bears the name B. Molar and the date 1906.

The Union was a friendly society (discussing politics or religion was banned). Baltazar Molar was the promoter of the project, the idea being to add the profits from the bar to workers' subscriptions to the Union. If a worker was unable to wield a cork-stripping axe he would receive a payment – cork being the biggest industry at the time; iron working was another. If he was seriously ill members would take turns to stay by his bed or fetch medicines from a pharmacy. The Union had its own supply of bandages and syringes – who needs doctors? As a last resort the Union would pay the funeral expenses. The only thing it wouldn't pay for was diseases caught 'voluntarily', such as those caused by 'incontinence with women'. It isn't clear if incontinence with alcohol came under this category. *¡Salut!* Your health!

It's not just a bar then; it is also a monument to workers' solidarity.

I could stay here overnight but the Mediterranean is pulling, so I walk down the Carrer Llarg, a *very* long straight street flanked with houses. It is followed by an equally long avenue of plane trees. Finally the Senda becomes a path and starts to climb up to La Vajol. Then I lose track, find it, and lose it again before opting for the road. This is the old route of the Senda; the waymarks have been obliterated with grey paint.

In La Vajol itself, a modest red plaque proclaims that this hamlet of 94 inhabitants was once the capital of Spain. It sounds like an exaggeration but a tour of the village provides the details. It transpires that the village once had an art gallery with an international reputation. The deposits in the local bank came to around 500 million dollars. There were several thousand inhabitants. The date was 1 February 1939.

For the Republicans, defeat had become inevitable. By the time the government arrived here there was nothing left to govern. Barcelona had fallen on 26 January. By 5 February, the President of the Republic Azaña, the Prime Minister Negrín, and the presidents of Catalonia and the Basque country had all passed through La Vajol on their way to exile.

But one of the events off-stage presaged a new consciousness. Like Hendaye railway station, like Zugarramurdi, La Vajol is one of those few places in the Pyrenees which has a claim to have influenced world history. And all because the gallery which had moved here brought with it Velazquez' 'Meninas', Titian's 'Venus with an Organist and Cupid' and Goya's 'Third of May 1808' as well as numerous other works of art. The gallery, of course, was Madrid's Prado.

Azaña told Negrín: "The Prado museum is more important for Spain than the Republic and the monarchy together". The most significant works from Madrid had been moved via Valencia to La Vajol, mostly being housed in a former talc mine, the Mina Canta. (This was where the Republic's gold was banked as well.) Starting on 4 February the treasures were packed off in 71 lorries, first to Perpignan and then to the League of Nations in Geneva. Moving the artwork was a risky business but damage was limited: Goya's 'Third of May 1808' was torn but its war wounds soon healed up.

The transfer had only been finalised in the course of the previous evening. It was financed by an unprecedented international consortium: the National Portrait Gallery, the Tate Gallery, the Wallace Collection, the Louvre, the Museum of Art and History of Geneva, the Rijkmuseum of Amsterdam, the Metropolitan Museum of New York, the Royal Museum of Fine Art of Brussels, and the French National Museums. La Vajol was there when *World Heritage* was being defined.

The remembered past

Franco accused Negrín and company of robbery. He claimed that the cellars of the Prado or the vaults of the Bank of Spain would have been sufficiently safe – they would have been too damp – and he demanded that the works be restored to Spain. The League of Nations caved in and started returning them on 9 May with the final consignment arriving in Madrid on 7 September 1939, on a night train travelling without lights to avoid attack. The second act of Second World War had begun just one week earlier, but the works were safe; saved not only from the Fascist bombs but also from the *pinturas negras* world of the anarchists.

La Vajol is extensively labelled, as if it were a museum, but one of the commemorative statues stands out. Cast in bronze, a young girl walking with a crutch under one armpit is clinging to the hand of her father. Where her left leg should be, there is nothing. The statue is based on a photograph – *the* defining photograph of the Retirada, seen everywhere – and is a remarkable work of art but, compared to the two-dimensional photograph, it lacks depth. Although the statue is true to life, in this village where people come for holidays and to have fun, it is difficult to believe.

In contrast, in the original photograph Alícia and her father are framed by other refugees. One of them is Alícia's younger brother, the five-year-old Amadeo, also hobbling: he has a wooden leg. He is being helped by an older man, Thomas Coll from Prats de Mollo. The stump of *his* wooden leg, lost in the First World War, can just be made out. On the other side of Amadeo his brother Antonio is walking normally. He was the only child to escape uninjured (his mother had sent him back to fetch her thimble when the bomb dropped; she didn't survive).

None of the family appears to have baggage but next to them a well-dressed young man in a long coat has placed his suitcase and a demijohn in a wicker basket on the road and is turning round to look at a companion who is carrying a large bundle. Rich or poor, they are all trudging across the hills on a desperate path somewhere between Mollo and Prats de Mollo. The photographer has captured the whole story and given it a sense of motion.

The other thing to see in La Vajol is the Mediterranean. It is still far away but it is taking on substance. It is almost palpable. I can almost smell it. I can see the end of the world.

I stay in Ca la Conxita's apartment and eat in their restaurant, surrounded by photos and books on the Retirada.

Into the fire

La Vajol to Requesens

The horizon is burning when I leave the apartment. Today I will reach La Jonquera. I have a list of things to do there, but first there is a long walk downhill.

On the edge of La Vajol another plaque remembers:

> The hundreds of thousands of Spanish republicans
> who preferred living in exile to submitting to fascism.
>
> Juan Negrín Foundation, 1 February 2010

No cars, no petrol: the refugees walked out of *necessity*. In the West, nobody does that anymore. *Except refugees.*

I have been reading Rebecca Solnit's *Wanderlust*. As she points out, it is only relatively recently that walking has been liberated by mechanical transport, just as painting was freed by photography.

Of course, walking as a 'leisure' activity already existed in the form of pilgrimage. And Rousseau and Wordsworth had promoted its virtues to the reading classes in the 18th and early 19th centuries. But the construction of the first passenger railway in 1825 set travelling on a new track. By the beginning of the 21st century, in the West, we only walk for pleasure.

There are now few places that people wish to visit which are more than a couple of hours walk away. Thankfully, those places which *are* only accessible by walking are not just located in remote corners of Borneo, but in many parts of the developed world.

Now, we arrive without travelling. Paradoxically, the *further* we go the less we travel. What is sitting in a metal tube looking out at the Atlantic for six

Into the fire

hours when compared with walking anywhere for the same length of time? And the *faster* we go, the less we travel: compare the experience of going from London to Madrid by plane, or car, or bike for example. Any means of displacement includes departure and arrival but that isn't travel. Only when walking – and to a lesser extent when riding a horse or a bicycle, or rowing a boat – are we sufficiently close and sufficiently attentive to the environment around us for movement to count as travel.

Walking has come a long way from its origins, filling its rucksack with new ideas: protest marches evoking military marches as displays of power, notably Gandhi's Salt March in 1930 and Martin Luther King's 1965 walk to Montgomery; charity walks; and long distance walking, ostensibly for *pleasure*.

I say ostensibly because I have just caught up with another walker in the forest. He looks like Ernest Hemingway towards the end of his life except that he is bent over and shuffling along. And French.

"Where have you come from?" I ask.

"Encamp."

"I've come from Àreu this year and Hondarribia two years ago. And you?"

"Encamp."

"I'm astonished I haven't seen you before now. When did you start?"

"22 June."

Twelve days before I passed through the town.

"You must have had lots of rain, like me," he complains.

"Not really. I try to arrive by four o'clock."

"Tea-time," he insists. As far as native French are concerned, the English all take tea at four o'clock. He has hardly raised his eyes from the ground.

"Come and walk with me," I say hopefully.

"I'm going much slower than you. Don't wait. Goodbye," he says shaking his heavy head.

I leave him in his oyster. Perhaps he's afraid I will try to open the shell.

The next person I meet is dressed in black, as is his bike.

"The gears are broken," is the first thing he tells me. "I couldn't get it repaired in La Jonquera so I'm pushing it to Maçanet. There's a cycling club there so I hope someone will be able to repair it." He is smiling. We have a long conversation in which he reveals that he is heading for the Atlantic having already completed the Senda on foot.

Footprints on the mountains

Walking along, my boots kick up fragments of charcoal. The trunks of the trees are black, with silly clumps of green leaves sprouting from them like tufts of mistletoe. It is two years now since the conflagration. It started somewhere near here, raced down the hillside driven by fierce winds, hurdled the motorway, and climbed up the other side. The fingers of fire selectively thinned the forest, plucking out the pines but leaving the oak and olive trees to regenerate.

Fire here, water and ice in the valleys, wind on the summits: modelling the landscape.

In the valley, I weave under the high-speed railway, over the motorway and across the main drag to the edge of La Jonquera, frontier town *par excellence*. The Escudero café-restaurant-hypermarket is doing a desultory early morning trade with a handful of truckers and tourists. Sitting down at a melamine table, I peer out of the windows at the slow-moving stream of traffic – 20,000 people a day stop here – at the dust, the grease, and the grime.

Behind the gaudy façade hides a quite different town of small shops, cafés, and traditional restaurants on what used to be the main street. My first objectives are the post office where I send my cold weather gear home – it is already hot and the sun has hardly yet woken up – and a corner shop where I load up with food.

Further down the street, an oversized rectangular steel and glass block, looking like a refugee from the shopping centre, houses the Museum of Exile, opened in 2007. I go inside and relive one of the events which has shaped the way I think about the Pyrenees.

Even before passing through La Vajol, I already knew the story because Joseph, one of my neighbours, was one of those frightened children who crossed the frontier at the end of January or the beginning of February 1939. The road from La Jonquera up to the pass at Le Perthus was taken by perhaps half of the 500,000 refugees who left Spain at the end of the civil war. A human avalanche cascaded down the opposite side into France, only stopping when it reached the *camps de concentration*.

At that time the words didn't have the negative connotations they have today. But that didn't make things much better in the makeshift camps set up in the snow on the beach at Argelès. Initially the only shelter was the hollows in the sand which the refugees dug themselves. Driftwood was collected for fires. The principal structure was the barbed wire fence. The principal organisation was the soldiers with guns to keep them there.

One small item in the museum catches my eye: a *Souvenir album of the Spanish exodus*, eighteen detachable postcards, treating the episode as if it were some kind of folklore carnival parade, with photos taken at the beginning before the full extent of the human disaster became known.

Suppressed for decades under Franco, in the last twenty years the story of the Retirada has become a *visible* part of the history of the Pyrenees, materialised by numerous museums, monuments, and heritage trails. As the last eyewitnesses die of old age, Spain is belatedly attempting to recover its repressed childhood memories.

Coming out of the bleak museum I don't have the heart to visit the fleshpots. I had thought it could be an interesting diversion. When was the last time you did something for the first time? But I have seen enough of the dark side of humanity already today. Anyway I'm too hot… or not hot enough. To judge by the graffiti *farlopa* must also be available. I'll just have another breakfast.

By the time I finally make up my mind to leave town the temperature has risen to thirty degrees. On the way out I walk between two trees wearing rainbow leggings: yarn bombing has reached the Pyrenees. The multi-coloured trunks look particularly poignant when I recall the joyless black ones seen earlier. The knitters say they want to create *'un poble bonic, curós i presumit* – a beautiful town, careful of its appearance and proud'. The women of La Jonquera have been sitting down together with their needles in a home-knitted initiative to counter the town's reputation for booze, fags, and tarts.

From the hill, looking back at the parallel roads and railway emphasises just how linear La Jonquera is. It isn't somewhere to stop, just a place of transit. Being a sidewalk is the town's joy and pain.

Although some zones are unscathed on this side of the motorway, where the fire has torched the forest the damage is much worse than before, with the trees reduced to blackened broomsticks vainly sweeping the sky.

At the recently restored Santa Llúcia hermitage, picnickers are welcomed with stone tables and garden seats but the barbecue hearths have been imprisoned behind bars (even though they weren't guilty this time). The yarn bombers have struck again. I fill up at the spring.

Footprints on the mountains

A boulder in one of the terrace walls has been daubed with white paint: "*Dolça Catalunya pàtria del meu cor*". The words come from a well-known song which has long been emblematic for Catalans.

L'Emigrant	*The Emigrant*
Dolça Catalunya	Sweet Catalonia
pàtria del meu cor,	homeland of my heart,
quan de tu s'allunya	when I am away from you
d'enyorança es mor.	nostalgia is death
Hermosa vall, bressol de ma infantesa,	Beautiful valley, cradle of my childhood,
blanc Pirineu,	white Pyrenees
marges i rius, ermita al cel suspesa,	wastes and rivers, chapel suspended in
per sempre adéu!	the sky,
Arpes del bosc, pinsans i caderneres,	forever goodbye!
cantau, cantau,	Harps of the forest, finches and gold-
jo dic plorant a boscos i riberes:	finches,
adéu-siau!	sing, sing,
…	I say crying to forests and shores:
	farewell!

Jacint Verdaguer, *c* 1874

This is the Verdaguer of *Canigó*; I can just make out the eponymous mountain through the woods, over in France.

The path continues to climb and then starts to descend slowly on a dirt track hugging the flanks of the mountain. Burning under the sun, I am not paying much attention when a sudden gust of wind blows in from nowhere and then stops just as abruptly. From somewhere nearby comes the sound of a bell tolling, an implausible clang in the middle of the forest. Then another gust arrives and it repeats, as if the bell is swinging in the wind: a dull thud accompanied by a mechanical squeaking, it must be cracked. I walk along looking into the trees, trying to identify the source. Then I see it, just a few paces from the path: the tail section of an aircraft sticking out of the steep hillside. The rudder is flapping uselessly from side to side, knocking

Into the fire

on its hinges. Although the wreckage is held in place by spindly holm oaks and must have been here for some time the red, blue and white paint is still visible.

I scramble up past more scraps of fuselage to see if there is a better view of it from the ridge. Only 30m higher and the aircraft would have made it. On the way back down I find the engine: intermeshing cogs, rusty exhaust pipes, and the shafts of three propeller blades. Nearby a plaque explains, in French

Here
Jean-Pierre Davenet
Roland Denard
Jack Le Bel
Jacques Ogier
died
on board their aircraft
fighting the fire
19 July 1986
Passer-by, remember

I'm not likely to forget. The skin of the aircraft and its entrails are imprinted in my mind. The broken bodies of the victims have just been extracted and the crash investigators have just finished their job but the pungent smell of the fire is still present in everybody's nostrils. The last officials due on the scene, the scrap merchant undertakers coming for the dead machinery, will arrive at any moment.

But when they came they didn't finish the job, and now 30 years later this part of the forest has narrowly escaped another fire. It seems indecent: I have intruded on the funeral of a stranger.

But not everybody feels the same way. Some of the passers-by have etched their names into the tail fin. Not just a few but hundreds of them, some adding the date of their ephemeral visit. To the extent that the entire horizontal stabiliser is covered in names; dense multi-layered graffiti. And not just names. For some it was an opportunity to declare their passion. M+M enclosed their love in a heart in 94, Manolo and Laura were here together, O♥T. On a grave!

Footprints on the mountains

Back on the Senda a second plaque also records the event for the benefit of Catalan speakers, adding that the fire razed a total of 30,000ha. This time 'only' 15,000ha (150km^2) was burnt.

Requesens is a few kilometres further along the track. With its tile kiln, lime kiln, brick kiln, ice well, saw mill, snack bar, farm-house, charcoal burners, and fantasy castle it could be a low-key Pyrenean theme park: an artifice of the tourist industry evoking the time when there were other industries here. But, apart from the romantically renovated castle, these are genuine relics, left to crumble where they were built. Even the castle is genuine, from the ankles down. It accounts for the rest of the inventory.

In the snack bar-restaurant the lugubrious manageress is just damping down her barbecue but finds time to sell me nibbles to eat under the sweet chestnut tree. She shuts up shop and heads for home and I head for the hut through what was once the fantasy castle's arboretum. The trees are still there: cypresses, limes, firs, cedars, and stands of tall maritime pines. Last year's needles and cones are dry. Lighting a fire would be no problem, but I've nothing to cook and no need for heat.

The hut has a bunk bed with white ceramic tiles for a mattress, and a steel table and benches which fold down from the wall – nothing more. So I spend the evening outside in the mottled shade of the cork oaks, relieved that the dour Frenchman doesn't turn up, repairing an indecent rip in my trousers: with Duck tape it doesn't take long.

The tiles are hard to start with but seem to get softer in the night.

Requesens to Espolla

The day opens with a squeak as I pull on the door. My toes are a mess of torn flesh and spilt blood where once were blisters. I dreamt last night that I was being interviewed. I can only remember one question:

"Why?"

I replied: "After a certain point it becomes an obligation."

I'm still not sure I'm going to make it. The last time, on the French side, I got to within two days of the end but had to give up.

At the edge of the track a stack of cork bark awaits collection. By the look of the moss covering it, the curled-up shells must have been here for some time and will wait somewhat longer. Meanwhile the trees nearby have regrown their skin: their evolutionary response to forest fire.

A woodpecker machine-guns a tree. A nearby harrumph and a scrabbling noise leave me baffled until I look at the ground and recognise the prints of a wild boar. Somewhere in the distance bells are tinkling although I can't see the sheep either.

On Laura's recommendation I am taking a short cut, slicing off a big loop in the Senda and staying in Espolla today. There is nothing at Vilamaniscle, the recommended overnight stop, she said. It will mean a much longer day tomorrow, but I don't regret it. Espolla turns out to be worth the visit.

The going is good on the track. My rucksack squeaks rhythmically as the weight passes from one shoulder to the other: 'ret-là-Mar-sow | ret-là-Mar-sow'. My boots on the gravel provide the base line: clump-clump | clump-clump. For counterpoint I have the metal ends of my walking poles click-clicking on the stones, occasionally missing a beat. The cicadas take the place of the snare drum.

A long while before I arrive, I can see Espolla down on the plain, notable for the domed church tower projecting high above it, encircled by the greens and greys of the vineyards and olive groves. Near the edge of the village, a telegraph pole hosts three direction signs indicating health walks. Below them is a pictogram labelled "safe zone" with a rifle crossed out.

The seven men basking in the sun on the bench at the crossroads in the centre of Espolla must have been waiting for me. When I hesitate, one of them jumps up and asks if he can help and then guides me to a door saying that this is the best place to stay in the village. But when he rings the bell of the Mas Can Salas no one answers, so he takes me to the Bar Fraternal. I cool down under the slowly-whirring ceiling fan. The waitress tries the phone a second time and a few minutes later a man rushes through the door. Narcís introduces himself and invites me to follow him back to his castle. The outside, as I have already seen, doesn't look particularly old, but when he opens the door and my eyes have accustomed themselves to the dim lighting, I understand.

"My family has always lived here," he says leading me into a stone-walled cellar. I shiver. "I was born here and have never left."

Walking across the cobbles, he points out a raised floor, like a bed.

"That was the base of a bread oven."

The bricks used for the vaulted ceiling must have been part of it, given the signs of burning. My nose twitches: the room smells of soap.

"Made from our olive oil," he tells me.

He leads me upstairs, literally turning on the light – it is one of those retro switches which turns – and offers me a drink on the terrace.

I ask Narcís about the wild boars, the one I heard in the clearing and the ones I saw listed in the Bar Fraternal hunters' log.

"Do you go hunting?" Most men of his age and background in the Pyrenees are very keen.

"No. I don't like it. It's not a sport, it's a plague. Now that they have interbred with domestic pigs, instead of having litters of two or three, they have eight or nine. And they eat our grapes."

"They must know they are safe there."

"Maybe I can't shoot them, but I've another idea. I'm going to experiment with a radio."

It sounds a bit like playing classical music to keep bored youngsters from defacing urban bus shelters.

Somewhere in the luxuriant garden opposite there must be a peacock. I can't see it, but it keeps crying out for a mate.

Narcís confirms that the Fraternal is like the Union in Maçanet, an important part of village life, as it has been for well over a century.

"If you want to eat lunch there I'll book you in."

"Please."

I have a lie down – after tasting a sample of Garnatxa d'Espolla from the carafe by the bed – and fall asleep, briefly. I am roused by the piping of a flute and the jingle-jangle of a tambourine man outside my window. A troupe of young people is being led round the corner by the musicians, laughing, spinning, and swinging as they go. Grabbing my flip-flops I rush downstairs through the cellar only to hesitate when I see someone lying in the bread oven in the semi-darkness. I say hello and she replies, after which I can't think of anything appropriate to say except goodbye.

I follow the notes of the piper, catching up with the twenty-somethings outside the Fraternal. The waitress comes out and whispers to one woman who breaks into song. A man replies, continuing in the same vein. At which point they all merge into the Fraternal's ballroom, singing in chorus; it is quite enchanting.

Into the fire

When I enter the café the leaflets on the tables explain that this is the 12th Annual Espolla Reunion of Improvised Singers. The high point will be a verbal jousting competition, the Catalan musical variant of the Basque *bertsolari* contests. Here well-known tunes are used to provide the rhythm. It was a dying art in the 1980s but its requiem has been rewritten as a nursery rhyme, complete with hash tag:

Perquè els folkis 2.0	Because the folkies 2.0
no quedin en entredit	will certainly never be beat
provoco el noi del Pandero	provoking the tambourine man
i inauguro el #garrotweet	they started the #garrotweet

*free translation; *garrotín* is one of the many Catalan words for improvised singing

The men from the bench have followed me in. Two of them order coffees as they sit down. After a while four of them move to another table and start playing cards. All goes well initially but then voices are raised and the game finishes abruptly.

In the meantime I am still waiting to be served lunch. Although I've managed to wrangle a drink I haven't even managed to see what is on the menu, except for one possibility: above the bar a metallic plaque in the shape of a snail is captioned:

Si cargols vols menjar	If it's snails you want to eat,
en Josep te'ls fara	Josep will do them for you

But not today, it's too dry, I'm told. Actually I have the impression that if Narcís hadn't booked me in I would have had to starve. The restaurant is bustling. I watch two lads playing table football – the toy teams still wear knee-length shorts – glance at the television, and then mooch around the room, looking at the notices. On one wall two glass cases house the holy relics of the *Societat de Socors Mutus*. One is a banner with a vignette showing St Sebastien pierced by arrows, dating to 1873. The second, from 1927, shows the town's shield: a castle tower with a hen on top. Quite by chance, I have just heard the explanation.

"Once upon a time," Narcís told me, "the townsfolk noticed a bird perched on the castle battlements so they sent a boy up for the eggs. 'There aren't any,' he shouted down. '¿És un pollo o una polla? – is it a cock or a hen?' 'És polla.' That's where the town's name comes from."

Many of the shields around here include a castle or a chess-piece rook but as far as I know it is the only one which incorporates a joke. (Historians say that the name derives from the Latin for hill, or possibly for cave…)

Also in the glass case are two references to what must be a long choral tradition: the bottom of the banner is embroidered "*Amics del Cant* – Friends of singing"; and a handwritten sheaf of paper reproduces the lyrics of *l'Emigrant*.

In the early evening, I explore the cemetery: Narcís has sent me here for asking too many questions. It is further than I thought. Most of the cemetery is prim and proper, but behind one wall is a desolate area with a single grave. 'Quique' and 'Celes' died on 26 August 1949. The police who killed them said they were bandits and had them buried in an unmarked grave. Fifty years later, the Fraternal organised a series of events in their honour but until that moment, such was the efficacy of Franco's censorship, some villagers didn't know the whole story.

'Quique' and 'Celes' were the *noms de guerre* of two young anarchists from Barcelona. They were returning from an operation – sabotage and robbing jewellery shops – when they and their three companions of the Facerías *maquis* were ambushed a few minutes' walk from the frontier. The others escaped.

Whilst walking the Pyrenees, I have encountered occasional references to the *maquis* – a power station blown up near Bielsa in 1949, for example. But it is only now that I discover the several *thousand* attacks in the first few years after the abortive invasion of the Valle de Arán. The last *maquis* was killed as late as 1965. By hiding the motivations of these men and labelling them as common criminals, the censors had efficiently erased them from the historical record.

With the help of a push from the Historical Memory Law the pendulum of time has swung back. Perhaps too far; the post-war guerrillas have been resurrected as heroes, though I do wonder just how much the last few were simply stuck in the past, unable to accept that the world had moved on.

The village holds another surprise, hidden away behind a herb garden:

tortoises. They live in a small enclosure, being bred to supplement the numbers in the hills. With their shells of black rectangles framed by yellow borders they look just like the one my sister loved in the 1960s. The youngsters, the size of oysters, are hiding in the shade.

"Why have they died out?" I ask their keeper.

"They were collected for selling as pets."

They are Hermann's tortoises. Although they thrive in captivity they are endangered in their natural habitat. It is now illegal to capture them in the wild.

"Nobody kills their predators anymore," says the keeper. "When there were lambs in the mountains to protect, and rabbits and partridges were hunted it was different. The predators were kept under control: foxes, badgers, genets, wild boar… But now there are hardly any sheep here to safeguard. And wild boars roam everywhere."

"I thought the shells protected them."

"Not the shells of their eggs, and not until they are 3–4 years old when the shells start to harden."

So fewer sheep and less hunting mean more wildlife but fewer tortoises. As does fire.

Later I take a *paseo* round the village on my way back to the Fraternal. As the sun drops, hundreds of house martins come out after their siesta, zipping up and down the streets until the wide open beaks of their fledglings call them back to their mud huts under the eaves. I spend a convivial evening in the bar, again with the improvising singers in the next room, but this time also in the company of a French couple, one half of whom I have already met in the bread oven.

An open-air dance is programmed for this evening but by the time I retire to bed the musicians are only just warming up. I'm sleepy and afraid the tambourine man will keep me awake; I put plugs in my ears.

Espolla to Port de la Selva

I dream I am going to miss a plane. It is one of those recurrent dreams you get when you need to get up early and are afraid you won't wake up. Then the plane crashes into the hillside in the smoke.

Footprints on the mountains

As promised Narcís has made breakfast. A tray and a thermos would have done, but Narcís insisted that farmers rise early. So here I am sitting at the kitchen table, supping my coffee. Would I like more orange juice? Another home-made madeleine? Some cake, he asks, offering me plates decorated with paper doilies. Would I like to take a bit of dried sausage for lunch? In front of me, lined up like soldiers, I have the choice of six varieties. In short, I eat like a king. And then Narcís gives me five euros back, saying that his wife has overcharged, and accompanies me to the outskirts of the village to make sure I get on the right track. He shakes my hand, saying:

"I like walkers. They are so clean and so organised."

He hasn't been looking too carefully then.

The white line on the horizon shades into blue grey above and then black. Venus is there again, the moon sulky. I am wearing shorts and a tee-shirt.

A box for used shotgun cartridges marks the edge of the vines and olives and the start of the rough scrub *matorral* but soon afterwards the vines appear again and the track takes me to the edge of Rabós. I meet a woman in her seventies dressed in a gingham-checked nylon housecoat – the blue, not the pink version – which she still hasn't managed to wear out. She is limping along with a stick behind a sprightly Pekinese. But apart from her I see nobody. After that a long stretch of tarmac takes me through Vilamaniscle and beyond. The only remarkable feature is the number of cattle grids.

Then the Senda finds a more agreeable dirt track and wanders along the hillside above the river Valleta. On the opposite side of the valley stone embankments define long, long terraces, strips of earth curving around the sides of the hills. One above another, the work of generations of farmers, the walls cannot be more than a couple of paces apart: a cartographer couldn't describe the slope better. But their rocky lines are now being smudged by the self-seeded trees, successors to the olive trees killed off – along with the last generation of farmers – in 1956. This time fire had an alibi. It was winter: water – ice – was quickly found guilty.

At this scale and viewed from the other side of the valley the walls are delicate brushstrokes; but further along an open cast quarry has scoured the landscape.

Down below, Llançà is paddling its feet in the sea. I could go down to

Into the fire

the shore and legitimately claim that I have walked from the Atlantic to the Mediterranean. I could stop. I could stay overnight: I have already walked a respectable distance, my skin is burning and my feet hurt. But it is only mid-morning so I cross the edge of the town and start to climb again.

In my practice walks I would have dusted this section off in an hour, but it takes me three to reach the Monastery of Saint Pere de Rodes. Three hours in the heat of the day, overtaken by a cheerful Spaniard walking as if the hill didn't exist, despite having stayed up drinking until 3 am. Three hours with no shade, burnished with sweat.

Just before the monastery I am overtaken by the Roses Express. Disguised in a Belle Époque outfit, complete with chimney, the steam engine would look quite convincing if it weren't for the huge tractor tyres and the rate at which it is tackling the slope. Some children wave at me as they pass and I make an effort to wave back.

At the monastery, I pay the entrance fee, look at the plan and then head directly for the restaurant. The very polite waiter places me in a discreet corner. The tables have cloth covers. I eat morosely, because I need to, looking at the view down to Port de la Selva, hardly able to conceive walking there.

Outside again, the only thing I look at is my feet. My mind is blank. The monastery has been here for 1200 years but I'm not interested. Much later, in the village of La Selva de Mar, I think I have arrived at my destination, believing it to be part of El Port de la Selva. I hear some English voices and follow them down a street overflowing with bougainvillea to the Stop, where I am told I have to continue. Monica, who owns the bar, also tells me: "I used to live in Whitstable."

The name means something to me but I can't think what. Then I remember: "My sister lives there."

"Really? Whereabouts?" she asks me.

I can't bring the address to mind. I start to panic but just say: "Near the sea," lamely before going out into the heat again.

There was woefully little *selva* – forest – above the village and even less below.

Port de la Selva is a little cooler but the beach is still full of sunbathers. I have been walking all day but I have hardly *seen* anything.

The 'hostel' is a restaurant near the shore coupled with an apartment block up on the hill. Sitting on the bed in my room I remove my sweat-soaked socks, undertake some surgery, slather on some antiseptic, and hang my feet out to dry over the end of the bed.

In the evening, putting on my flip-flops to go down to the restaurant I try to walk without using my feet. My walking poles, left in the room, would have been useful; instead I cling onto any available bits of street furniture. Disappointingly, in the restaurant as in the apartment block, there are no other walkers with whom to share my experiences, so I pick on the poor waitress; I don't suppose that she will be interested in how far I have walked so I invite her to lift my nearly empty rucksack and see how light it is. She does so reluctantly and smiles feebly. I knew she wouldn't be interested: she is very pregnant and has something weightier on her mind.

Walking back up the hill in flip-flops is even more difficult than walking down: my bare feet keep slipping out and crunching in the grit. And after half an hour in the dark I realise that I don't recognise any of the buildings. I can see that I am in a town and know that I shouldn't be afraid but I don't know how I got here or where I am going. I have only drunk one glass of beer. I sit down on the pavement and look around. How can I possibly be lost? What can I do about it? There's nobody to ask. Anyway I can't remember the name of the place where I am staying. I hardly even know who I am. The only solution is to retrace my steps until I recognise something. The first place I recall is the restaurant: I went wrong almost immediately.

Port de la Selva to Cap de Creus

The port must have slept badly last night. Yesterday evening, viewed from the balcony before going out, it looked ready to party; this morning it looks sullen.

In the *garrigue* an animal the size of a dog crosses the path ahead of me. A flash of ginger, it vanishes quickly, finishing with the end of its tail, white. A fox. I grin, *so* pleased to see it. I'm rather less comfortable with the sudden

Into the fire

humming of a large number of bees circulating around one particular cork oak but they ignore me.

The crumbling terraces here once held regimented vineyards, then olive groves, and then tourists. The grape vines were killed by a plague of phylloxera from France; the olive groves were killed by the freeze of 1956. The tourists were merely evicted. They had also come from France, in their thousands, to a Club Med, part of the uncontrolled development of the Spanish coastline. With the difference that here the Catalan government bought and demolished the holiday houses and organised the removal of the other invaders. Mostly. The Hottentot figs, the Barbary figs, and the *agave americana*, representatives of two different continents, were carefully removed from the former Club Med gardens but some had already fled into the wild. Some of the rubbish also seems to have escaped notice: I find myself crunching over broken shards of glass, broken plates, broken bottles, bits of shoes, plastic, and asbestos tiling.

Now human influence is being eradicated and natural vegetation returning. Or it would be if it weren't for the fury of the elements. The *tramontane* blows strongly, scooping up the dust and hurling it into the waves, stoking the forest fires: the flames which killed the airmen on the other side of Requesens reached as far as here. And when the *tramontane* stops the *marin* takes over, sprinkling the rocks with sea salt.

In the middle of all this tumult the Sant Baldiri de Taballera hermitage and the hamlet which surrounded it stood firm for over a thousand years, but it too has been in ruins for the last century.

A thin young man comes along the path, bright and happy on his first day but as I approach the final square *my* feet are dragging. Unlike that other young man I met at the Cap Higuer, I cannot envisage continuing. The seventeen days of walking this year have worn me down. The fifty days have worn my boots out. Twice.

Just before the end, a home-made signpost topped by the whitened skull of a cow stands forlorn at the side of the path. At the top, painted in gold, a stick man wearing a beret strides along with a large stick in one hand. The words 'Palo de Roma – the stick of Rome', might be a clue but the distances listed suggest a variety of other destinations: Santiago de Compostelle 1100km, Paris 1369km (way too much), Rome 2132km, about twice the real distance. The *Marxa de la resistencia* ultra-trail also gets a mention.

Footprints on the mountains

Cap Higuer is 910km away with 41km of climbing.

The Senda is rapidly dissolving in a geological stewing pot in which the half-melted ingredients are still just identifiable: a bizarre recipe of honeycomb, white chocolate, kidneys, cauliflower florets, curtain pleats, and bark, folded-in but not yet combined.

[It] is and should continue to be pure geology forever, without anything that can cause damage to it; I do state it. It is a mythological place made for the gods more than for men and it should continue as is.

Salvador Dalí

He was writing in 1961, a year before the arrival of Club Med, 32 years after he painted the 'Face of the Great Masturbator' partly inspired by one of the rock formations.

The lighthouse at the edge of the world has been visible for some time but I ignore both it and the visitor centre and steer for the bar-restaurant, sit down under the camouflage netting on the terrace and order a beer, then another. With my back against the wall of the building, I stare vacantly at the bay below, half-smiling, half-crying until the woman who is sitting directly opposite me pointedly picks up her drink and her book and moves to another table.

There are crowds here but nobody to celebrate with and I don't try the waitress, although I later learn that she would have given me a free pint courtesy of the English manager.

When Veronica rolls up, the next move takes us to the lighthouse and beyond. I struggle to stand up. I blunder two steps forward then stumble sideways repeatedly down to the shore. Despite the crowd thronging around the lighthouse few other people are trying to descend to the Mediterranean.

It hurts. Everything hurts. Even with my poles I find it difficult to remain upright; I can't even keep up with Veronica. She comes to a halt at the top of a steep slope.

"I'm not going to bother going down to the water," I say.

"You can't stop here," she protests, annoyed at my weakness.

So I leave my rucksack with her and scramble to the water while she fits the telephoto lens onto her camera for a photo of me pouring out a final libation into the waves.

I have arrived, but the only thing that matters is that I won't have to walk anymore. No fun, no feasting. No sense of triumph. It is the journey that counts, not the destination. I'm too tired to celebrate.

When Veronica asks me what the difference is between the Pyrenean Way and the Senda, I summarise:

"The Pyrenean Way starts and ends on a lazy beach. On the Senda you have to struggle over rocks."

In the wake

I have been here for two days now, with my feet weeping real tears, hanging over the end of the bed. Propped up, I have plenty of time to think. In the beginning, I wondered what the Pyrenees would be like on the other side of the looking glass, but as I slid along its surface it wasn't so much the distorted reflections that surprised me but how easy it has been to pass through the mirror. Hannibal; pilgrims on the Way of St James; Cathars; pedlars; pigeons and *golondrinas*; sheep and cattle; Napoleon's armies; smugglers; Ramond, Russell and company; phylloxera; Spanish religious statues, political refugees, paintings, and gold; Jews and pilots; *maquis*; economic migrants; terrorists; tourists; skiers. All crossed the Pyrenees.

Although, *for outsiders* the mountains were always a barrier, for the inhabitants, they defined their community. A Pyrenean republic with common traditions – bear festivals, 'witches' – and a shared economy – based on pastoralism, forestry, and mining. Not French, not Spanish. A community which has now been eroded not so much by the emergence of nation-states as by the building of cities. A community which has been torn apart to such an extent in the last century that Brussels has seen fit to allocate money to stitch it back together again.

Let's not exaggerate the connections; despite the links, for the last 150 years the mountains have been more of a fence than a gate. Imagine for a moment that Euskadi and Catalonia are independent. Stretch that idea to include the unlikely demolition of the local equivalent of the Berlin Wall – the Pyrenees – and the inclusion of the historic Basque and Catalan areas in France in the new states. Like East Germany, the zones to the north of the Wall would have a heck of a lot of catching up to do.

Why did I do the walk, then? When I reached the end of the Pyrenean Way in France I asked myself the same question: for the scenery, for the exercise, to get away from the computer? The main reason, I concluded, was that it was good to do something instinctive, something programmed into my DNA. I was reconnecting with nature. If I get up early in the morning, any morning, and go for a walk, any walk, anywhere, I feel that I have lived; my day needs no other justification. So long-distance walking must be living multiplied by days.

But it was never a totally satisfactory explanation. Why didn't I walk along the Canal du Midi, for example? Why mountains? There must be more to it.

If walking – here, now – were a *natural* activity then it would be universally valued. But it isn't natural. It is merely a cultural phenomenon born a century and a half ago, like sunbathing, to value or not. My kind of walking is a legacy of the Kinder Scout movement, transmitted by my parents brought up in the mill towns near Leeds and who 'walked out', as they used to say, in the Pennines. I'm happy with that.

By the time the third day dawns I realise that I must go to see my doctor.

"I wondered why you were wearing flip-flops," he says as I show him my feet and tell him about my trek.

He cleans my wounds and prods my lymph nodes. Afterwards, not content with just looking at the obvious symptoms, he gives me a thorough check-up. Firstly blood pressure, circulation, and lungs. Normal. Then vertigo. He takes my head in his hands and twists it to one side and then the other. Then makes me lie down quickly.

"Do you feel dizzy?" he asks.

"No." I'm not afraid of heights then.

"You have pushed the machine a bit too far this time," he concludes. As I get dressed again he tidies the books on his desk and starts writing the prescription. I sit down opposite him and wait for him to finish, vaguely scanning the pile of books. The one which has made its way to the top is a manufacturer's guide to Viagra.

"Anything else?" he asks.

Into the fire

"No." It's not that either. But I can hardly complain that Vaseline is not the elixir of youth I'd believed it to be.

In any case the prescription is for antiseptic cream, anti-inflammatory drugs, and bandages coated with silver that the pharmacy has to order specially.

The blisters heal, leaving the base of my foot enveloped in three years' worth of dead skin. Over the next two months I rub at it, picking it at the edges with delicious pleasure, eliminating the footprint of the Senda.

Once the red has changed to white and I can walk comfortably again I go back to the Mediterranean, but not to the Cap de Creus, to Narbonne instead. And not to walk but to sail. As a child, my dreams were full of *Swallows and Amazons* but I somehow missed out on the reality.

At Narbonne harbour I borrow a Dart 16, a sports catamaran for a crew of two, from the sailing club. The autumn is unusually calm. At first the flaccid windsock on the quay is reassuring, but the lack of wind becomes frustrating once I have learnt the ropes. It is only on the last day of the season, in November, that the windsock fills up and the catamaran really starts to whizz along. Henri at the tiller pulls in the mainsail and I follow suit with the jib. The tell-tales are horizontal; we accelerate, bouncing over the foam. When we are going fast enough Henri pushes the tiller to come about. On the next tack, the wind increases and the catamaran speeds up even more. The hull flies, skipping over the waves. I hook myself onto the trapeze cable and push out with my legs, standing on the hull leaning out almost horizontally, hiking my weight to reduce the heel. All goes well for some time but the wind is increasingly blustery. I have to bend my knees and transfer my weight from one foot to the other to stay balanced. I am exploding with anxiety but held together by the exhilaration of the moment. The adrenalin comes in a rush. I know what is going to happen but dismiss it; maybe it won't come to that. Then bigger waves come crashing in and I scamper along the hull and back again trying to keep balance. But I go too far, lose my footing, and fall into the blue. Henri doesn't ease the sheet quickly enough and, without my weight to counterbalance the wind, the catamaran capsizes.

On the way back home in the car, singing, I find myself accelerating into the corners and leaning as I go round them as if I were riding a motorbike.

Footprints on the mountains

When I describe my day to Veronica she says: "The bit you enjoyed most was falling in, wasn't it?"

When did you last do something new for the first time? Today.

Caminante, son tus huellas	Walker, your footprints are
el camino y nada más;	the path, and nothing more.
Caminante, no hay camino,	Walker, there is no path,
se hace camino al andar.	the path is made by walking.
Al andar se hace el camino,	Walking makes the path
y al volver la vista atrás	and looking back at it
se ve la senda que nunca	you see the track that never
se ha de volver a pisar.	will be walked again.
Caminante no hay camino	Walker, there is no path
sino estelas en la mar.	only wakes in the sea.

extract from *Caminante no hay camino* by Antonio Machado

Acknowledgements

I am indebted to Claude Premillieu who helped identify the plants, to Marie Broll who painted the cover artwork, and to the Ronda de Boltaña for permission to reproduce their lyrics. Jordi Estèbe kindly took me in search of ibex and has allowed me to use his photos. As usual, Veronica has painstakingly corrected the text and made many suggestions for improvement. Many other people have helped me write this book and I would like to thank them all, particularly the walkers – whose names I have changed.

Annotated bibliography

Although it was published many decades ago Pierre Minvielle's (1980) *Les Pyrénées des quarante vallées*, Paris: Denoël, is still a wonderful introduction to the mountains. Another excellent overview is: A. Lévy (ed.) (2000) *Le dictionnaire des Pyrénées* (2nd edn), Toulouse: Privat.

As for guides to the Senda I recommend the Prames (2012) *GR 11 Senda Pirenaica de mar a mar* (7 ed.) for the 1:40,000 maps and the background information. Brian Johnson has recently updated the Cicerone guide, *The GR11 trail – la Senda* (2014) which now also has detailed maps.

The references below are listed in order of appearance.

- Hermandad de Pescadores: hermandadpescadores.com/.
- Irun Alarde: alardepublico.org/es/visita-guiada.php.
- Video of the *Gudari Eguna*: dailymotion.com/video/x319wc_gudari-eguna-06-aritxulegi_news.
- The events in Zugarramurdi are extensively discussed in Gustav Henningsen (2010) *El abogado de las brujas*. Alianza Editoria.
- Orson Welles can be seen on youtube.com/watch?v=gopqGyRgKD8.
- *Gigantes* in the main square of Elizondo: youtube.com/watch?v=mu0SveY1kEE.
- Ituren carnival: Mikel Oxkoidi Pérez and Karlos Irujo Asurmendi (2009) *Carnavales de Lanz – Ituren – Zubieta*. Panoramo, 40.
- *Video of Ituren's carnival in 2011:* youtube.com/watch?v=E3F-S6oYvvM.
- Pays Quint: Gérard Caubet (2011) *Étonnantes Pyrénées*. Rando-Éditions/La Balaguère (pp. 215–17). In 1936 both Franco and the republicans claimed sovereignty. To avoid any problems France paid twice. It made no difference. The residents, all French citizens, were interned for the duration of the civil war.

Annotated bibliography

- Way of St James : Bernard Gicquel (2003) *La Légende de Compostelle*. Tallandier.
  Pablo Arribas (2009) *Coquins, gueux, catins… sur le Chemin de Saint-Jacques*. Pau: Éditions Cairn.
  Statistics: chemin-compostelle.info/informations-pratiques-pelerinage-compostelle/statistiques-sur-compostelle.html.
  UNESCO World Heritage listing: whc.unesco.org/en/list/669
- *Veredas* in France: Graham Robb (2008) *The discovery of France*. Picador (pp 143–5).
- Isaba: youtube.com/watch?v=nJDC9t2LiCI.
- Neré, the bear near Isaba: http://www.diariodenavarra.es/noticias/navarra/zona_norte_oriental/2013/01/12/la_presencia_del_oso_aumenta_navarra_deja_ataques_2012_103704_1010.html
- Jen, adventurer of the year 2012: adventure.nationalgeographic.com/adventure/adventurers-of-the-year/2012/jennifer-pharr-davis/.
- Canfranc: ladepeche.fr/article/2008/02/24/436894-canfranc-ce-titanic-refait-surface.html.
- Statistics on Sallent de Gállego and Formigal: bonansa.aragob.es:81/iaest/fic_mun/pdf/22204.pdf.
- Frontiers, depopulation, and the projected railway between Gavarnie and Ordesa: Annie Brives (2012) *Pyrénées sans frontières*. Pau: Éditions Cairn (p 50).
- Regimiento de Cazadores de Montaña 'América' 66: ejercito.mde.es/unidades/Navarra/rczm/Noticias/2013/005.html.
- Ibex: Kees Woutersen (2012) *El bucardo de los Pirineos*. Huesca: Kees Woutersen Publicaciones (p 152).
  Parc Naturel Régional des Pyrénées Ariégeioses (2012) *Réintroduction du bouquetin ibérique (*Capra Pyrenaica*) dans les Pyrénées françaises. Faisabilité dans le Parc Naturel Régional des Pyrénées Ariégeioses*. Version 2 8 novembre 2012. On cloning see: news.nationalgeographic.com/news/2009/02/090210-bucardo-clone.html#sthash.cpUQm2L1.dpuf.
- Lucien Briet: Claire Dalzin (2007) *À travers le Haut-Aragon dans les pas de Lucien Briet, 1902–1911*. Pau: Éditions Cairn (p 40).
- Ronda de Boltaña: rondadors.com.
- Janovas: alacarta.aragontelevision.es/programas/unidad-movil/pueblos-recuperados-28092012-2132.

- German Tourist on the Senda: christine-on-big-trip.blogspot.fr/2012/08/hiking-pyrenees-conclusion-and-tips.html.
- Continua Pirineum: continuapirineum.com.
- The *caravana de mujeres* is extensively documented in the archives of *El Mundo*, elmundo.es.
- Maria Jose Prados Velasco (2008) *Naturbanization: new identities and processes for rural-natural areas*. CRC Press.
- Wild boar: oncfs.gouv.fr/IMG/file/mammiferes/ongules/tableau/tableaux_chasse_nationaux.xls. Curiously, in France hunters are considered responsible for the boars' damage to crops, with their associations coughing up the compensation.
- The Ariège *Archives départementales* have published a superb book on the relationship between humans and wild animals. Although it centres on the historical aspects, it is an indispensable guide for understanding the contemporary bear controversy: Claudine Pailhès (ed) (2013) *L'homme et l'animal sauvage dans les Pyrénées ariégeoises*. Foix: Conseil Général de l'Ariège.
- Bears in the French Pyrenees: Farid Benhammou *et al* (2005) *L'ours des Pyrénées: les quatre vérités*. Toulouse: Privat.
  David Chétrit (2012) *La réintroduction de l'ours : l'histoire d'une manipulation*. Toulouse : Privat.
- Bears in the Spanish Pyrenees: Eugeni Casanova (2002) *Crónica de un extermino: el oso de los Pirineos*. Lleida: Editorial Milenio. fundacionosopardo.org/
- UNESCO evaluation of the Madriu valley: whc.unesco.org/archive/advisory_body_evaluation/1160.pdf
- Rewilding: George Monbiot (2013) *Feral: searching for enchantment on the frontiers of rewilding*. Penguin.
- The treasures of the Prado and La Vajol: elpais.com/diario/2010/01/23/cultura/1264201201_850215.html
- On walking and what it means: Rebecca Solnit (2014) *Wanderlust*. Cambridge: Granta.

Printed in Great Britain
by Amazon